Mobility, Meaning
and the
Transformations of Things

edited by

Hans Peter Hahn and Hadas Weiss

Oxbow Books
Oxford and Oakville

Published by
Oxbow Books, Oxford, UK

© Oxbow Books and the individual authors, 2013

ISBN 978-1-84217-525-5

This book is available direct from

Oxbow Books, Oxford, UK
(Phone: 01865-241249; Fax: 01865-794449)

and

The David Brown Book Company
PO Box 511, Oakville, CT 06779, USA
(Phone: 860-945-9329; Fax: 860-945-9468)

or from our website
www.oxbowbooks.com

A CIP record is available for this book from the British Library

Library of Congress Cataloging-in-Publication Data

Mobility, meaning and the transformations of things : shifting contexts of material culture through
    time and space / edited by Hans Peter Hahn and Hadas Weiss.
        pages cm
    "The contributions to this book are based on presentations and discussions at a conference, held in
October 2011, entitled 'Itineraries of the Material: Shifting Contexts of Value and Things in Time and
Space' at the Goethe University in Frankfurt."
    Includes bibliographical references.
    ISBN 978-1-84217-525-5
    1. Material culture--Case studies. 2. Material culture--Congresses. I. Hahn, Hans Peter, author,
editor of compilation. II. Weiss, Hadas, author, editor of compilation. III. Title.
    GN406.I75 2013
    306--dc23

                    2012044311

This book is an outcome of the academic work of the Research Training Group 'Value and
Equivalence' (http://www.value-and-equivalence.de/) (GRK 1576). the printing of the book
has been sponsored by the German Research Foundation (DFG)

Printed in Great Britain by
Short Run Press, Exeter

Contents

Preface

Movements of things mark the relevance of material culture in shaping identities and negotiating cultural relations. Things move close to people, they recede or they create connections between people. With every shift, they change their role and meaning. People expend a great deal of energy and resources to bring things closer to them, but also to get rid of them. In some contexts, the value of an object is determined by the journey it has made before coming within one's reach. This book addresses a wide range of movements of things and the corresponding shifts in their valuation. It intends thereby to overcome the perception of objects as static and unchanging. It focuses on how the objects change through movements in time, space or social spheres.

Combining approaches from archaeology and social anthropology, this book amasses evidence of the variability of things in relation to their mobility. Avoiding the pitfalls of overemphasizing the agency of things, the different contributions reflect on the adequate metaphor to capture the transformations of things though their mobility, as well as the transformation of people through the acquisition and appropriation of things. All of the contributions share the assumption that a closer examination of the shifts of meanings, time and materiality, grants a deeper understanding of objects themselves.

The contributions to this book are based on presentations and discussions at a conference, held in October 2011, entitled 'Itineraries of the Material: Shifting Contexts of Value and Things in Time and Space' at the Goethe University in Frankfurt. The event was part of the scientific program of the Research Training Group 'Value and Equivalence' (GRK 1576). The publication of this book and the conference proceedings were supported by the German Research Foundation (DFG). We would like to express our gratitude to Robert Parkin and Björn Schipper for helping with the editing process. We also want to thank the anonymous referees whose close readings and trenchant advice have contributed substantially to the quality of the texts in this volume. Finally, we extend our sincere gratitude to all of the contributors to this publication.

The conference and this book bring together some accomplished and experienced researchers in the field of material culture and object biographies with the doctoral students of the Research Training Group that organized the event. We are pleased to have found common ground for a fruitful discussion, and to have established a high standard for communicating the range of studies and perspectives. The book presents the most compelling insights achieved through the conference, and we expect it to be an important contribution to the study of material culture.

Hans Peter Hahn
Hadas Weiss

Chapter 1

Introduction: Biographies, travels and itineraries of things

Hans Peter Hahn and Hadas Weiss

> *"We want to convey the sense that a 'world' – an often fragmented and fragile set of material and non-material assumptions and resources – can itself be made mobile, seemingly translated from one […] location to another, even as it is transformed in the process"*
>
> (Basu and Coleman 2008, 313, our italics).

In his well-known essay, 'Resonance and wonder', Stephen Greenblatt (1990) starts with an anecdote about a priest's hat, displayed in an exhibition about the history of Christ Church College in Oxford. There is more to this red hat than meets the eye. Beyond being the hat of Cardinal Wolsey, the founder of the college, it had been a Christ Church College archived item since the mid-nineteenth century, after an itinerant history that included several owners. As Greenberg notes, it is this particular tale of the object's shifts and moves, including occasional threats to its material existence, which evokes the visitors' interest and curiosity. Cultural artefacts never stand still, are never inert. Their existence is always embedded in a multitude of contexts, with tensions surrounding their roles, usages and meanings. Objects are meaningful only in relation to conflicts, negotiations and appropriations. Things shift in a wide range of modes, and very often it is through these particular alterations that they assume a specific meaning. The specific advantage of this focus on mobility is to "shed light on hidden as well as conspicuous movements of peoples, objects, images" (Greenblatt 2009, 250). The objective of this volume is to raise awareness of mobile things and their various kinds of shifts, and subsequently, of their changing roles and meanings.

The contributions to this volume deal with the mobility of things from the point of view of different disciplines. Within the framework of material culture, questions about mobility and the focus on shifts of location and meaning have been addressed predominantly through two concepts, *biographies of things* and *travelling objects*. Both concepts refer to shifts in space and time, as well as to the transformation of things through different contextualizations. When preparing for the conference that provided the opportunity to present the chapters assembled in this volume, we had the impression that, although each of these concepts is useful, they also have some serious limitations.

In the following pages we shall present our perceptions of the achievements and shortcomings of these concepts before trying to present a synthesis. We deal with these concepts by understanding them as metaphors. *Object biographies* and *travelling objects* work through metaphorical associations, drawing their meaning from quite different domains of the social. This contributes to their success, as they have come to be two of the most frequently used metaphors for dealing with material culture. And yet, some of the associated images are misleading or at least problematic. The aim of this volume is therefore to overcome the unnecessary reduction in how we perceive the mobility of things, which is arguably an unintentional by-product of these metaphors.

We shall underline our objective by suggesting another metaphor, which appears to be much better suited to capturing the mobility of things, and particularly the mobility of those objects featured in the chapters of this volume. We propose the term *itineraries*. The idea of an itinerary combines the pathways, stations and transitions of modern-day travellers, as prescribed, for example, in a flight schedule, with the much older idea of a particular path such as a pilgrimage, leading to the transformation of the traveller by successfully passing through discrete stages.

Biographies of objects

Since the appearance of Igor Kopytoff's seminal article 'The cultural biography of things' (Kopytoff 1986), first published in the edited volume 'The social life of things' (Appadurai 1986), the biographical perspective has been salient.[1] Looking at the biography of an object as a means of approaching its *social life* is a widely adopted strategy. The passages of an object from its *birth* to its *death* or destruction – that is, to when it becomes rubbish – occur through different stations, and each moment in the object's lifespan seems to have a distinct role (Hahn 2005, 40–45). For example, a new car evokes a quite different context compared to a used one, and once a car has achieved the status of a classic car, it is again quite differently perceived. Changes not only happen at the level of perception and contextualization, but also in usage: what is new warrants greater care and caution, whereas a car of a certain age may be expected to resist more enduring practices. Again, if the car is quite old, and if it has become a rare item, special caution is called for to preserve what is then considered something unique and therefore of specific value.

Kopytoff's particular achievement is to connect the passage through different contexts to different valuations. It is not always use value, but in some moments of an object's life also a mnemonic value or a personal value, which is attached to the object. Whereas the *new object* may appear on someone's horizon as a commodity with a fixed or negotiable price, in later stages of the biography there may be moments when the very same object becomes an unalienable personal object (Weiner 1992; 1994). More generally, Kopytoff points to two opposing tendencies, which can be identified in almost all biographies of things. He labels these tendencies 'commoditization' and 'singularization' (Kopytoff 1986, 65). It is never simply an individual owners' desire to sell an object at a given moment, but a topic of social and cultural negotiations, which gives more or less legitimacy to each of these tendencies, and sometimes even intentionally excludes one of them when dealing with an object. For example, once they reach a certain age objects of art are no longer allowed to be sold on the art markets of many European countries.

Particular moments in the life history of an object may be more revealing for its social embedding; a closer look at these instances can show how significantly the role of an object has changed. The ways in which histories of objects and people inform each other can be described through a closer examination of the moments of transformation of objects and also of people themselves (Gosden and Marshall 1999). This is not only a question of socially acknowledged meanings like stigma or prestige, but also a practical question of the knowledge required for dealing appropriately with the object in question. Furthermore, the stories associated with an object and evoked by its presence require special care (Svensson 2008). This applies to old things that may have special relevance as memory objects, reminding the owners about specific events in their lives. The close relationship between durable objects and tradition has already been highlighted by historians (Assmann 1992; 1995). Objects of tradition can be regarded as actors of evocation (Seremetakis 1994). They can be relevant for individuals, but also for collective events, which significantly change the course of many people's lives (Kuntz 1990).

In his book 'Tradition', Edward Shils (1981) devotes an entire chapter to sometimes astonishing effects of the shifting meanings of objects with a particular longevity. At first glance this text consists of little more than a list of the kinds of objects that exist for a long time and therefore play an important part in the memory of earlier historical eras. The sometimes varied and dramatic histories of monuments, archaeologically identified treasures etc. are good examples of object biographies. These things appear, then they disappear or are forgotten – sometimes for centuries – and then, in new horizons of time, or in different environments, they reappear to play an entirely new and different role. There is no doubt about the continuity of the material objects as such, but sometimes this continuity is simply the basis for a completely new definition of them. A poignant example in this volume is how the beehive huts among the Mao of Ethiopia have lost their erstwhile practical functions to become phantom dwellings, which, as Alfredo González-Ruibal explains, was necessary to produce an idealization of the Mao as an independent forest people that was no longer tenable. Currently, studies of memory and material culture have stressed this point: even materially unchanged objects and memorized topics might assume quite different roles. The stories associated with things are also relevant for new objects, that is, innovations. In cases in which people have little experience in practical matters, they are more sensitive to cautionary tales reporting harmful consequences. These warnings are especially frequent in the context of technological innovations, but new kinds of food are also typical. People are inclined to believe stories about the malfunctioning or harmful consequences of the consumption of new foodstuffs, and it may take some time for individual experiences to become sufficiently widespread for such fears to be overcome.

All these implications can be related to the concept of biographies, and they show how much an object's perception can change during its lifespan. More recently Janet Hoskins (1998) has shown convincingly that objects can be charged with meaning within quite brief moments if they are present in specific contexts of an individual's or a family's life. Objects that were present during a marriage, or in the instance of an accident, are subjectively much more important than other, materially identical objects that have not been present at the event in question. Biographies of things, Hoskins says, are entangled with people's histories. They jointly create a network of relevancies. The immanence of an object cannot explain why it is meaningful at a later moment.

This brings us back to our initial scepticism about the metaphorical meaning of the term *biography*. A biography covers a lifespan, representing a basic linearity of ageing that unfolds a multiplicity of attached stories, meanings and so on. Hoskins extends this notion by referring to the image of a network. The network has knots which are constituted crossings between things and people. Instead of the suggested linearity of a biography, the network of lines, that is, the many biographies, and the nodes, or crossings of the lines, better represents the mutual transformations caused by the interaction between people and things (Küchler 2001).

Against this background it is unsurprising that a fair amount of recent research on object biographies deals with the assumed *end* of things. More than any other moment of an object's *life*, describing the *end* of an object reveals the problems with the metaphor of a *biography*. The *end* of an object is a vexing perspective.[2] Even the observation of decay can be accompanied by disgust as well as with empathy and the specific revaluation of the object in question (Buchli and Lucas 2001; DeSilvey 2006). The change of the surface of an object is a feature that can engender positive emotions as well as its dismissal. An object can fall into pieces and be re-established (Gregson *et al.* 2009). The idea of a definite disappearance or final step, similar to the death of a person, that is inspired by the term *biography* hardly captures all of the changes that can be observed in the context of an object.[3] As Anamaria Depner suggests in chapter six with respect to a single discarded earring, new meanings can emerge for an object that ended its use during its first *life-span* – considering the after-live as a second life. This invites us to imagine those things that become waste. We find many cases in which they just cause more trouble in the status of waste, or produce new meanings and permit new usages after being discarded. Archaeological evidence show that objects may gain new functions once they have been designated as *rubbish* by their original owners (Rathje and Murphy 1992). Radical changes in the valuation of materials and objects may also lead to the re-use of waste. What had been classified as worthless becomes at a later moment an object of valuation and desire (Stam 1999).

And how does one classify items in tombs that are dedicated to accommodating the dead in their afterlife? Two contributors to this volume provoke such a reflection. Joseph Maran treats amber objects found in Early Mycenaean burials as challenging their assumed usage as jewellery alone, while Gordana Ciric examines Roman coins in medieval cemeteries in terms of their transformed functions. Are these things *dead*, or is it more appropriate to speak about a *second life*, as they are rediscovered by archaeologists, or worse, by a robber? Objects might become valuables merely by virtue of their having been excluded from everyday life at an earlier stage of their existence. These reflections about the afterlife or second life of things do not sit well with the metaphor of biography. This lack of fit should be perceived as a problem in the concept as such. We should look for a different understanding, a more differentiated concept, taking into account the aforementioned aspects of networks as the mode of production of meaning, as well as the surprising relevance of resurrections of things.

Travelling objects

This perspective on the mobility of things is closely related to the idea that things follow specific pathways, which may be routes and destinations that have little in common with those of people, institutions or traditions. An important example of this is the diffusion of cultivated plants, which were adopted in many places worldwide, even though the farmers growing these plants might have had no idea about the origin of these plants (Hancock 1992). The global distribution of plants like maize and coconuts indicates how things may travel and thereby change peoples' ways of life wherever they arrive.

For the objective of this edited volume, it is of some relevance to inquire about the specific features of things as material objects when they travel. Since the important essay of James Clifford (1992), 'Traveling cultures', the mobility of cultures in a larger framework has loomed large in cultural anthropology. The same applies to archaeology, as shown in the works of Mary Helms (1988). However, the interest of the contributions in this volume is more specific. It is not about the travelling of cultures as such, but more distinctively about the mobility of the objects, which sometimes differs from cultures. Stepping beyond Clifford's seminal paper, we need to conceptualize the specific modes and transformations that occur when things move.

In many cases, things that are perceived as originating elsewhere play a specific role. They may be assigned a superior value on account of their *coming from elsewhere* (Orlove 1997; Hooper 2000). One possible reason for this is the idea that *traces from the origin* have been inscribed in the actual object (Benfoughal and Boulay 2006, 16). Another possible reason is an imagined distance between origin and actual place of usage. Travelling over a great distance without damage lends these things an aura of particularity.[4] Archaeology has many examples of things of outstanding value and renown that were transferred over long distances. This holds true for Mediterranean imports to the Celtic cultures of Southern Germany. These valuable objects represented the particular social rank of their owners and helped distinguish the class of noblemen from the rest of the society (Biel 1985). A good example in this volume is provided by Annelou van Gijn and Karsten Wentink, who show how, in the Middle Neolithic, Michelsberg tools imported to the wetlands lost their original function and acquired a special status that helped define the identities of the importing societies. Similar phenomena have been observed for modern societies, for example, in the case of *Western Goods* in many previously colonies (Belk *et al.* 1997). The particular appreciation of things that had been travelling is usually explained by the general acknowledgement of a social or cultural hierarchy. In the context of modern colonialism, Richard Wilk (1996) speaks about 'emulation', articulated by such preferences for things from abroad. Through the acquisition of goods from the metropolises, consumers in the former colonies may overcome the subjectively perceived desynchronisation. The sense of being backward can thereby be eliminated.

We should not forget the more general fact that the European history of consumption has always included a preference for exotic commodities. Examples of this are tea, coffee, silk and Indian cloth (Wills 1993), but also porcelain and many other goods. More recent examples are the products of Italian cuisine or non-European artwork. Their imagined distance and uniqueness, or at least exclusivity, rendered these travelling goods constitutive elements of conspicuous consumption (Veblen 1899). Writers of novels were well aware of this, and the outstanding role of things that travelled across continents, or at least from one country to another, became a recurrent theme in belletrist literature. In novels, such travelling things have particular value, either because of their uniqueness, or because of their association with specific events (Niehaus 2009; Schmidt-Linsenhoff and Coskun 2010).

There has been a paradigm shift in the recognition of travelling objects. In archaeology as much as in cultural anthropology, objects of a definite form have long been associated with a specific culture. In both disciplines, the assignment of territories and time horizons has contributed to the qualification of things of a specific form as indicators of continuity and cultural coherence at the locality under investigation. Things found at one place that obviously came from elsewhere figured as less relevant in describing the local culture. The unity of production, distribution and consumption was considered an essential condition for the local reproduction of culture (Hahn 2008): craftspeople produced a particular form because the tradition required these procedures. In households, these items were in use because the usage of any others appeared to be against the cultural order of that community.

Globalization attributed quite a different role to travelling things: objects are relevant, not because they are associated with a place, but because of their mobility. Culture is constituted by the local transmission of traditions, inherited knowledge or regional specificities that, through exchanges and transnational relations, were often constituted by commodities traded over long distances. In this framework cultures as such do travel, but more relevant is the mobility of things. Global flows of goods were one of the core domains of exchange and mobility, as described by Arjun Appadurai (1990, 296) in his term 'ethnoscapes'. Globally travelling goods and their particular appreciation were an important argument for the cultural dimension of globalization; they were crucial for the popular metaphor of *flows* of people and goods. Particular items that fit well with this metaphor are media devices (TV sets), fashion and communication technologies, such as mobile phones.

We refer to the relevance of travelling goods in the early, predominantly affirmative phase of globalization, in order to highlight the limits of this approach. The power of the *flows* and images of global *circulation* was convincing only for a brief historical moment. Very quickly critical voices reminded the globalization theorists that social and cultural differences have not disappeared. On the contrary, their endurance has led to new forms of violence worldwide (Appadurai 2006). Borders and spatial limits did not become irrelevant, and the differences between rich and poor had not been dissolved (Garhammer 2003; Nyamnjoh 2004).

It is more appropriate, therefore, to speak of the reconfiguration of space and new practices of emplacement (Englund 2002). Globalization brought about the emergence of new borders that blocked the mobility of particular goods, like weapons, medicine and drugs. Peter Oakley demonstrates in chapter five how the movement of substances like gold or silver have, through the hallmarking process, been restricted to territorial borders. Things like media, on the contrary, easily cross those borders. It is more appropriate to state that the metaphor of travelling things applies to just some goods at specific historical moments. The same holds true for the image of *flows* that was able to gain some resonance only at a particular moment and in the wealthy societies of the West.

Considering the perspective of those countries that are removed from these flows, or that participate in them only to a very limited degree, Gülitz Ger and Russell W. Belk coined the term 'consumptionscapes' (Ger and Belk 1996). By referring to landscapes of consumption, Ger and Belk underline the fact that the commodities in question circulate easily in some areas, but are not available to people living in other regions of the globe. The condition of particular societies and their specific integration into global markets is more important than the circulation, flows or travels of goods. Economics and governmental regulations, among other forces, work for or against their mobility.

Our criticism of the metaphor of travelling goods is related to these deficits in explaining unequal access to things. After all, it is not things as such that travel, but people and their economic and social status that place these commodities in or out of their reach. As Mario Schmidt argues with respect to wampum beads in chapter ten, objects could even be perceived as accessible status objects while actually operating to preserve existing hierarchies. It may be misleading to suggest that things travel. It is more appropriate to speak of social, economic and cultural differences that push things from one place to another, or even obstruct their movement. The mobility of things is not an autonomous experience, but the consequence of particular practices and cultural differences.

Itineraries of things

So far we have dealt with two approaches to the mobility of things, and pointed out their respective strengths and shortcomings. There is no reason to doubt the important contribution of the two concepts for progress in material culture studies, in particular in the effort to deconstruct the image of things as static or unchangeable. However, we have pointed to these concepts as being only a partial reflection of the actual range of objects and their roles. The shortcomings of the *object biographies* metaphor are evident: moments like *birth* are difficult to pinpoint, and similar problems emerge with respect to the object's *death*. Archaeological and ethnographic investigations more often attest to the transformations of things. New objects emerge through the remodelling of other objects, and objects that have been buried receive much more attention upon rediscovery. We have also pointed to the increased interest in waste and garbage, which can be interpreted as an afterlife of things.

The metaphor of *travelling* things also appears problematic to us. The assumption of mobility as a universal property that is somehow inherent in all things is implausible. The image of a journey or of travel undertaken by the object is somewhat biased in having prioritized a specific group of objects: mobile items provoke more attention than those that, for various reasons, cannot travel.

The objective of this volume is to examine the possibilities of conceptualizing the transformation of things through shifts in time and space without falling prey to the problematic implications of the terms *biography* or *travel*. We understand the transformation of things to be an important aspect of material culture. We seek to approach it without taking the *birth* or *death* of things as necessary benchmarks. Nor do we find it useful to refer solely to a model that suggests things that travel.

We argue that the mobility of things has a larger and more comprehensive meaning, which manifests itself in many social economic and cultural processes. The empirical case studies featured in this volume pose an additional limitation on biographies or travel as guiding metaphors. Many of the objects they discuss pass through long periods of stasis before becoming engaged in actual transformations. It is possible that the objects themselves initiate these transformations. But it is also possible that a more general shift in the social order causes a revaluation or even redefinition of the objects, a different usage or a new context, which makes the objects shift. This is what happened, for example, after the neoliberal restructuring of Cameroonian society restored the political relevance of kings, as Jean-Pierre Warnier explains in this volume: offerings became re-signified as containers of ancestral authority. It is important to understand extended periods of stasis not as death and resurrection, but as continuity, and as having a specific potential to transition from an inert state to a state of mobility.

For the complex and sometimes entangled forms of mobility, we suggest the term *itinerary*. More than any other concept, the notion of an itinerary highlights the non-linear character of an object's mobility and the subsequent changes in its contexts and roles. Carl Knappett's discussion of imprints in chapter three is a fitting example of the possible anachronicity of objects that collapses together past and present. An itinerary further suggests moments of inertness as well as moments of rapid transformation. Itineraries describe pathways that do not lead directly to a given goal, but take an irregular and convoluted course with a multitude of meanderings. A clear and concise definition can be found in Webster's Dictionary: "Itinerary, a. [L. itinerarius: cf. F. itinéraire. See Itinerant.] Itinerant; traveling; passing from place to place; done on a journey" (Merriam-Webster 1913, 793).

An itinerary is associated with the itinerant, which, in the metaphorical usage, refers to the thing itself. Whereas the traveller does engage in travel intentionally, with a destination in mind, the term *itinerant* emphasises a mobile form of existence. Whoever is itinerant cannot stand still. The itinerant moves without the explicit intention of travelling. He does so because being itinerant is part of his existence. To itinerate is also a verbal expression: when things (or people) itinerate, they travel along a previously set course, including stopovers. Provided it is made clear that there are external powers that drive a thing to move or stand still, this metaphor fits quite well the objective promoted by this volume. The external driving forces are, of course, the people acquiring things, dealing with them, or trying to get rid of them.

There is a secondary meaning, referring to a priest's itinerary, the prescribed path he has to follow. Although the mobility of things does not always follow a planned route, this also fits our understanding because there is always a cultural definition of those changes in an object's existence that increase its value and those that do not. Objects may gain considerable value through specific transformations, but they can also fail to do so and end up as rubbish. As Selma Abdelhamid shows in chapter seven with respect to Roman amphorae, the choice to discard or reuse them itself entails a social investment in the value attributed to them. Understanding the mobility of a thing requires taking into account that any shift in context or place changes its value.

Itineraries have the particular advantage of moving the spotlight away from the identity or individuality of an object. Questions about the uniqueness of an object can only be addressed by taking into account the perspectives of the men and women who are dealing with it. Whether an object is an individual item (i.e., it is not divisible) is a problematic question, which needs to be answered differently at any moment of its existence. It is quite possible that material objects become fragmented and reunited later on, or that a fragment of an object is considered to have the same meaning, value (and use) as the object itself (Chapman and Gajdarska 2007). Things have the capacity to be present in different contexts, to appear differently in each of these moments, and finally – due to their sometimes astonishing changeability – to absorb meanings in particular modes. In this volume, Roberta Gilchrist demonstrates how the meaning of medieval heirlooms emerges out of the intersection of two distinct contexts – namely a family life-course and church sacraments – to produce their sacralisation. This kind of capacity is underscored by the metaphor of the itinerary, which gives us new insights into the ways in which values are generated, maintained, rejected or even destroyed.

Things are itinerant without themselves actively engaging in travel. Along their way – which may very well include extended periods of inertness and stasis in the sense of *not being used* or *being buried* – things may appear on the horizon of perception, and they may recede. Wherever they do so they may be perceived as new, but they may also be attributed to a different world. This extraordinary changeability, which is not intended by the objects but inheres in them, should be regarded as a constitutive element of material culture.

The contributions in this volume demonstrate, through distinct perspectives and with reference to a wide array of things and motilities, the sensitivities promoted by the metaphor of itineraries. If attention to non-linearity is among the foremost of these, it already looms large in chapter two, where Alfredo González-Ruibal discusses the case of beehive huts among the Mao of Ethiopia. Generations of contact with expanding groups and increasing external threats is turning the once autonomous Mao into a marginalized underclass. This historical trajectory is counteracted by the Mao beehive huts. They have lost their erstwhile functionality for the Mao as a forest people, but instead of disappearing they have been frozen in time. The beehive huts have become a mnemonic device and the materialization of collective fantasy for the Mao. It is precisely their stasis – in contrast to their people's decline – that allows them to abolish time and preserve a sense of power and independence that is denied them in reality.

The non-linearity of time remains at the forefront in chapter three, where Carl Knappett takes seals and sealings of the Bronze Age Aegean as an occasion to push the boundaries of how the mobility of objects might be approached. He posits as a challenge to the historicist trajectory of motion the idea of an imprint, which hovers between seal and sealing. Sealings – the impressions of seals in clay – were only ever meant to be temporary. The imprint they leave behind, defined by its durable form rather than its changing substance, evokes both presence and absence. Knappett uses the term *anachronic* to capture this collapsing together of past and present, contact and loss. His discussion highlights the possibilities for objects to resist movement.

If Knappett introduces the collapsing of time conceptually, Jean-Pierre Warnier demonstrates it ethnographically. In chapter four, he explains how kings in contemporary Cameroon are reasserting their long-lost legitimacy because of new political alliances. This opens up a space for the reinvention of royal traditions through which the king can produce a virtual envelope to encompass his subjects who have gone away into the various diasporas. This ritual containment is enacted through material objects and physical substances that can combine to erase the interval between the old kingdoms and the present moment. Specifically, in the king's offerings, his bodily substances (breath, speech, saliva, semen) and their extensions (palm oil, camwood powder, raffia wine, medicines) are invested with the life and reproductive essence of the ancestors. This essence permeates subjects' lives, children, health, crops and livestock, who thereby incur a lifelong debt to their king.

Political containment can also apply directly to objects, as Peter Oakley shows in chapter five. Recounting the history of minting and hallmarking in medieval and modern England, he highlights the concerted social efforts – including legal instruments and material objects – to contain gold and silver both physically and conceptually. These efforts were perennially renewed and modified in the face of the persistent tendency of gold and silver to exert their identity as substances. Through the stabilization of the substances of gold and silver, political institutions inscribed the representations of their power and defined its boundaries. While the goals of hallmarking varied historically, the social identity of the object – its liquidity or singularization – was always at stake. Finally, as Oakley demonstrates, the institutions charged with hallmarking reflected this identity.

If hallmarking exemplifies the stabilization of meaning, in chapter six Anamaria Depner discusses the possibilities of its de-stabilization. Calling our attention to a single earring given to her by one of her subjects – an old lady in a nursing home – she launches into a meditation about what makes things worthless or meaningful. She observes how the negotiation of the object's meaning entails a reconsideration of one's own position with respect to the object, an exercise which both she and her subject undertake separately but in dialogue. It demonstrates how an object-centred methodology can alert us to how things are interwoven into our daily lives. As Depner shows, the evaluation and devaluation of things can be a deeply meaningful process in terms of personal biography.

Just as Depner insists on the meaningfulness of discarded objects, Selma Abdelhamid, in chapter seven, militates against what she calls a *throw-away-mentality*. The context of her discussion is the reuse of Roman amphorae in ancient maritime transport. She marshals evidence from shipwrecks to show that, contrary to the common assumption that antique amphorae were always discarded after shipment, amphorae were actually reused for transport on a grand scale. The phenomena of reuse is historically suggestive since it required a complex social organization, including a sufficient quantity of containers, work forces to collect, clean and refill the vessels, and a working and stocking space. Thus the transformation of amphorae over time becomes a model for objects' mobility over time and space as a factor in their value, as well as for the social goals and possibilities of this valuation.

The goals of reuse are not always so clear cut. This is the challenge confronting Gordana Ciric in chapter eight. Her data comes from the secondary use of Roman coins in medieval cemeteries from the territory of Serbia. As these coins were obviously no longer a means of exchange, the archaeologist is faced with a choice of which approach to take in determining their transformed meaning. Ciric criticizes numismatics for analysing coins in isolation and calls for a reintroduction of social context. Taking the idea of object biography as her starting point, she speculates about the possibility that, in the repositioning of the Barbarians with respect to the Romans, coins assumed symbolic powers. This leads her to assert that a full account of the meanings of reused coins would necessitate transcending the object-biographical perspective to include theories of exchange and social interaction.

Annelou van Gijn and Karsten Wentink are also pressed to explain the recurrence of objects in different contexts, but they have the advantage of being able to trace their use through laboratory study. In chapter nine, they use microscopic evidence to draw historical conclusions out of large retouched blades and other typical Michelsberg macrolithic tools found in the wetlands at a time when its inhabitants were gradually adopting a Neolithic lifestyle. Their evidence shows that, while in the early part of this period the Michelsberg tools were imported but no longer used, they were later incorporated into indigenous technological system and applied to special activities. Van Gijn and Wentink suggest that this indicates a change among the people of the wetlands, from affiliation with the Neolithic farmers to a gradual appropriation of a new identity. The objects thus reflect the negotiation and expression of a new, Neolithic identity.

Whereas van Gijn and Wentink present a synchronized consolidation of social identity through objects, in chapter ten Mario Schmidt shows that objects can also manifest divergent goals and identities. He focuses on the wampum beads of the Coastal Algonquian as objects that promise their owners self-completion and value. Yet this is a false promise. Schmidt suggests that decorating women and children with ornaments, redistributing beads to poor members of society and paying bridewealth in fathoms of beads blurred the difference between ascribed and achieved status. Political power was beyond the reach of ordinary individuals and women, and yet the circulation of wampum beads strengthened the position of political leaders and added prestige to individuals. They operated, therefore, to grant their possessors the illusion of agency, while actually reproducing existing hierarchies.

Questions regarding social identity can also appear in the value attributed to objects and the uses to which they are put. This is what Joseph Maran turns our attention to in chapter eleven with respect to amber objects in Mycenaean Greece. While amber – exported from a great distance and found in necklaces – is commonly interpreted as a decorative prestige object, Maran shies away from such insinuated semantic stability. Indeed, he finds evidence in Mycenaean male grave assemblages that amber was used in warrior equipment as a protective device that was perceived to be charged with supernatural power. This perception may have been related to amber's materiality: the Tiryns sun wheels of the post-palatial period show amber and gold being used as twin solar materials in objects that were not worn on the body of persons, but rather were integrated in ceremonies as religious paraphernalia.

If Maran raises the issue of Amber's materiality, Roberta Gilchrist places materiality at the forefront of her analysis of medieval heirlooms. In chapter twelve she presents evidence of objects associated with secular rites of personhood and family, such as pottery vessels or items of apparel linked with marriage, being gifted to the church. Gilchrist argues that objects were often selected for curation based on the social value that was placed on their physical materiality. It is by virtue of biographical objects' (social and physical) materiality, according to Gilchrist, that they were selected and endowed with spiritual power. Objects that were related to church sacraments were likewise selected to be *sacralised* by virtue of their engagement with life-course rituals. Medieval heirlooms were therefore not only *memory objects*, but also *sacred objects*.

Notes

1   However, the idea of a biography of a thing is much older and has long been used in popular texts about the material world (Tretjakov 2007 [1929]). For the Francophone tradition, see also Morin (1969).
2   This interest might not only originate from the uncertainty about what can legitimately be regarded as an objects end, but also in the potential transformation of objects into useful or harmful substances, or more generally in the cultural consequences of recycling (Norris 2004; Douny 2007; Thompson 1979; Strasser 1999). The distinction between a substance and an object is useful in this context, although this has hardly ever been a topic in material culture studies (Hahn and Soentgen 2010).
3   The same applies for the *beginning* of an object as has been recently discussed in studies about second hand objects (Hetherington 2004).
4   The notion of the *aura* of an object is closely related to the question of its uniqueness. According to Walter Benjamin's famous essay, the property of having an *aura* is threatened by the increasing practices of mechanical reproduction (Benjamin 1936). Marlen Stoessel (1983) concisely shows that it is not *uniqueness* as such, but merely the way things are perceived as something special, that matters. This is precisely the context of things coming from *far away*.

References

Appadurai, A. (ed.) (1986) *The social life of things: Commodities in cultural perspective*. Cambridge, Cambridge University Press.

Appadurai, A. (1990) Disjuncture and difference in the global cultural economy. *Theory, Culture and Society* 7 (2), 295–310.

Appadurai, A. (2006) *Fear of small numbers: An essay on the geography of anger* (= Public Planet Books). Durham, Duke University Press.

Assmann, J. (1992) *Das kulturelle Gedächtnis. Schrift, Erinnerung und politische Identität in frühen Hochkulturen* (= C. H. Beck Kulturwissenschaft). München, Beck.

Assmann, J. (1995) Collective memory and cultural identity. *New German Critique*, No. 65, 125–133.

Basu, P. and Coleman, S. (2008) Introduction: Migrant worlds, material cultures. *Mobilities* 3 (3), 313–330.

Belk, R. W.; Ger, G. and Askegaard, S. (1997) Consumer desire in three cultures: Results from projective research. *Advances in Consumer Research* 24, 24–29.

Benfoughal, T. and Boulay, S. (2006) Sur les traces de quelques objets sahariens. Pistes de recherche croisées. *Journal des Africanistes* 76 (1), 9–24.

Benjamin, W. (1936) The work of art in the age of mechanical reproduction. In H. Arendt (ed.) (1970) *Illuminations: Walter Benjamin: Essays and reflections. Edited and with an introduction by Hannah Arendt*, 219–253. London, Cape.

Biel, J. (1985) *Der Keltenfürst von Hochdorf*. Stuttgart, Theiss.

Buchli, V. and Lucas, G. (2001) The absent present: Archaeologies of the contemporary past. In V. Buchli and G. Lucas (eds) *Archaeologies of the contemporary past*, 3–18. London and New York, Routledge.

Chapman, J. and Gajdarska, B. (eds) (2007) *Parts and wholes: Fragmentation in prehistoric context*. Oxford, Oxbow.

Clifford, J. (1992) Traveling cultures. In L. Grossberg, C. Nelson and P. A. Treichler (eds) *Cultural studies*, 96–116. London and New York, Routledge.

DeSilvey, C. (2006) Observed decay: Telling stories with mutable things. *Journal of Material Culture* 11 (3), 318–338.

Douny, L. (2007) The materiality of domestic waste: The recycled cosmology of the Dogon of Mali. *Journal of Material Culture* 12 (3), 309–331.

Englund, H. (2002) Ethnography after globalism: Migration and emplacement in Malawi. *American Ethnologist* 29 (2), 261–286.

Garhammer, M. (2003) Die dritte Runde der Globalisierungsdebatte: nach der Entdeckung des Globalen die Ethnographie des Lokalen. *Soziologische Revue* 26 (1), 46–63.

Ger, G. and Belk, R. W. (1996) I'd like to buy the world a coke: Consumptionscapes of the 'less affluent world'. *Journal of Consumer Policy* 19, 271–304.

Gosden, C. and Marshall, Y. (1999) The cultural biography of objects. *World Archaeology* 31 (2), 169–178.

Greenblatt, S. (1990) Resonance and wonder. *Bulletin of the American Academy of Arts and Sciences* 43 (4), 11–34.

Greenblatt, S. (ed.) (2009) *Cultural mobility: A manifesto*. Cambridge and New York, Cambridge University Press.

Gregson, N.; Metcalfe, A. and Crewe, L. (2009) Practices of object maintenance and repair. *Journal of Consumer Culture* 9 (2), 248–272.

Hahn, H. P. (2005) *Materielle Kultur. Eine Einführung*. Berlin, Reimer.

Hahn, H. P. (2008) Diffusionism, appropriation, and globalization: Some remarks on current debates in anthropology. *Anthropos* 103 (1), 191–202.

Hahn, H. P. and Soentgen, J. (2010) Acknowledging substances: Looking at the hidden side of the material world. *Philosophy and Technology* 24 (1), 19–33.

Hancock, J. F. (1992) *Plant evolution and the origin of crop species*. Englewood Cliffs, (NJ), Prentice Hall.

Helms, M. W. (1988) *Ulysses' sail: An ethnographic odyssey of power, knowledge, and geographical distance*. Princeton, Princeton University Press.

Hetherington, K. (2004) Secondhandedness: Consumption, disposal, and absent presence. *Environment and Planning D: Society and Space* 22 (1), 157–173.

Hooper, B. (2000) Globalisation and resistance in post-Mao China: The case of foreign consumer products. *Asian Studies Review* 24 (4), 439–470.

Hoskins, J. (1998) *Biographical objects: How things tell the stories of people's lives*. New York and London, Routledge.

Kopytoff, I. (1986) The cultural biography of things: Commoditization as process. In A. Appadurai (ed.) *The social life of things: Commodities in cultural perspective*, 64–91. Cambridge, Cambridge University Press.

Küchler, S. (2001) Why knot? Towards a theory of art and mathematics. In C. Pinney and N. Thomas (eds) *Beyond aesthetics: Art and the technologies of enchantment*, 57–77. Oxford and New York, Berg.

Merriam-Webster (1913) *Webster's third new international dictionary of the English language: Unabridged with the seven language dictionary; in 3 vols*. Chicago, Merriam-Webster.

Morin, V. (1969) L'objet biographique. *Communications* 13, 131–139.

Niehaus, M. (2009) *Das Buch der wandernden Dinge*. München, Hanser.

Norris, L. (2004) Shedding skins: The materiality of divestment in India. *Journal of Material Culture* 9 (1), 59–71.

Nyamnjoh, F. B. (2004) Globalisation, boundaries and livelihoods: Perspectives on Africa. *Identity, Culture and Politics* 5 (1/2), 37–59.

Orlove, B. S. (ed.) (1997) *The allure of the foreign: Imported goods in postcolonial Latin America*. Ann Arbor, University of Michigan Press.

Rathje, W. and Murphy, G. (1992) *Rubbish! The archaeology of garbage*. New York, Harper Colins.

Schmidt-Linsenhoff, V. and Coskun, D. (2010) Einführung: Wandernde Objekte. Die Bedeutung der Mobilität der Dinge. In A. Karentzos, A.-E. Kittner and J. Reuter (eds) *Topologien des Reisens. Tourismus, Imagination, Migration. = Topologies of travel: Tourism, imagination, migration*, 164–167. Trier, Onlinepublikation der Universitätsbibliothek Trier. 8.06.2012, http://ubt.opus.hbz-nrw.de/volltexte/2010/565/pdf/Topologien_des_Reisens.pdf

Seremetakis, C. N. (1994) *The senses still: Perception and memory as material culture in modernity*. Chicago, University of Chicago Press.

Shils, E. A. (1981) *Tradition*. London, Faber and Faber.

Stam, R. (1999) Palimpsestic aesthetics: A meditation on *hybridity* and garbage. In M. Joseph and J. Fink (eds) *Performing hybridity*, 59–78. Minneapolis and London, University of Minnesota Press.

Stoessel, M. (1983) *Aura. Das vergessene Menschliche. Zu Sprache und Erfahrung bei Walter Benjamin*. München, Hanser.

Strasser, S. (1999) *Waste and want: A social history of trash*. New York, Metropolitan Books.

Svensson, T. G. (2008) Knowledge and artifacts: People and objects. *Museum Anthropology* 31 (2), 85–104.

Thompson, M. (1979) *Rubbish theory: The creation and destruction of value*. Oxford, Oxford University Press.

Tretjakow, S. (2007 [1929]) Biographie des Dings. *Arbeitsblätter für die Sachbuchforschung* 12, S. 4–8. 02.06.2012, http://edoc.hu-berlin.de/series/sachbuchforschung/12/PDF/12.pdf

Veblen, T. (1899) *The theory of the leisure class: An economic study of institutions*. New York, Macmillan.

Weiner, A. B. (1992) *Inalienable possessions: The paradox of keeping-while-giving*. Berkeley, University of California Press.

Weiner, A. B. (1994) Cultural difference and the density of objects. *American Ethnologist* 21 (2), 391–403.

Wilk, R. R. (1997) Emulation and global consumerism. In P. C. Stern *et al.* (eds) *Environmentally significant consumption: Research directions*, 110–115. Washington, DC, National Academy Press.

Wills, Jr., J. E. (1993) European consumption and Asian production in the seventeenth and eighteenth centuries. In J. Brewer and R. Porter (eds) *Consumption and the world of goods*, 133–147. London, Routledge.

Chapter 2

Houses of resistance: Time and materiality among the Mao of Ethiopia

Alfredo González-Ruibal

Introduction: Itineraries of stasis

Archaeologists and anthropologists are fascinated by anything that changes or makes other things change, whether material objects, institutions or ideas. In relation to material culture, things that circulate and networks of things are clearly privileged by researchers (cf. Malinowski 1920; Foster 2006; Knappett 2011). Those objects that do not have a passive role, but that actively channel movement, trigger social transformations or enable connections are particularly well regarded. This category of objects is often imported: guns among Polynesians (Thomas 1991), videos among Aboriginal Australians (Michaels 2002) or Greek pottery among Celtic communities (Dietler 1997). Much less attention has been devoted to those things that help stop movement, that sever connections with other actors (human or non-human) and that move only a little or not at all. Strangely enough, three of the defining characteristics of things tend to be overlooked: their physicality, including their bulkiness and weight; their capacity to stand for themselves in their uniqueness (Olsen 2010, 154–157); and their contribution to making society durable and stable (Latour 1991). This triple oblivion can be explained by the modernist bias of the social sciences and by current concerns with fluidity and connections in the globalized world (Friedman 2002). While these tropes might be useful in understanding late modern societies (or at least some groups within late modernity), I doubt that they are always of use in making sense of other rationalities and historical experiences. Thus, in this chapter I would like to defend the necessity to look also at material itineraries that are not geared towards change, but rather the opposite: stopping change, or at least denying its existence. These material itineraries are paradoxical in that they are not based on movement, but on stasis. Admittedly, this perspective might seem conservative. However, I would argue that, in fact, the reverse is the case: this is a counter-hegemonic position which tries to do justice to the ethos of subaltern communities.

Maintenance activities – that is routine, everyday activities oriented towards the reproduction and care of the community (Picazo 1997, 59–60) – are usually associated with groups marginalized for gender, sexual, racial or class reasons. They have been ignored in the social sciences, because their aim is to maintain society as it is, not to change it. History, anthropology and archaeology have traditionally privileged activities of transformation, which are often carried out by the powerful (Hernando 2008). Of course, not all material practices that are rooted in the past can be equated with tactics of resistance. They can be part of struggles for hegemony or strategies of domination. It is important to distinguish here between maintenance activities and revivals. While both are based on tradition, the itineraries that they enable are quite different. An emphasis on maintenance activities entails the denial of change, as is the case with the Amish in the United States. Some groups cling to the repetition of activities that are sanctioned by tradition and that may be extremely old, such as arrow-making (Levi 1998; González-Ruibal *et al*. 2011). Revivalism, conversely, does accept change; actually, it demands change, but of a particular kind, the idea being to transform the present in order to make it look like the past. It is an itinerary from present to past, not from present to future, as change is understood in modernist evolutionary terms. Revivalism can challenge power or reinforce it. Thus, indigenous groups have often engaged in revivalist activities to re-enact an idealized moment before colonialism altered their lives (Mendoza 2004). This often involves the rejection of modern technology and beliefs and a return to traditional practices, but also the emergence of new ideas of spiritual purity and community. However, totalitarianism and other oppressive forms of power can also resort to an idealized past to negate the liberal aspects of modernity and the social changes they bring about: this return to the past exists in both Nazism (Goodrick-Clarke 1985) and Islamic fundamentalism (Watt 1988). The object of this chapter is not to discuss revivalism, but tactics of maintenance. Although the line that divides the two can be thin, it is important to realize that, from an emic perspective, people who consciously engage in maintenance activities do not perceive that they are returning to any past: they simply consider they are living in the inalterable time of tradition.

To illustrate my point, I offer an ethnographic example from my fieldwork in Ethiopia. Between 2001 and 2010 I conducted research among a variety of minority groups squeezed along the borderland between Sudan and Ethiopia (Fig. 2.1). The aim of the research was to explore different forms of resistance to the dominant powers in the region and, more particularly, the role of things in these forms of resistance (González-Ruibal in press). In this chapter, I will focus on one of the groups, the Mao, and one category of artefacts, houses.

The Mao are a little-known and diverse cluster of peoples living in the western Ethiopian borderlands (Grottanelli 1940; 1966; Fleming 1984). Through their encounter with expanding hierarchical societies from the nineteenth century onwards, the identity of the Mao has been, and still is being, thoroughly reshaped: in fact, it has been the unequal contact with other peoples that has created the Mao as such – a hybrid and heterogeneous subaltern group. I will describe here how, in a context of asymmetrical cultural contact and forced change, certain objects have become crucial in stopping movement and anchoring Mao society in the past. This is particularly the case with the traditional house of the Mao. Although it was considered virtually extinct in the 1930s (Grottanelli 1940), I discovered that it still exists and that it plays a pivotal role in Mao society. In fact, it has become a crucial element in the cultural survival of the Mao as a people. Today, the traditional house works as a device that is capable of abolishing time and linking the Mao to a period in which they were not subject to more powerful groups. At the same time, it can be argued that this structure is a materialized fantasy, through which an ideal image of society is performed which is less and less in consonance with the Mao's current predicament.

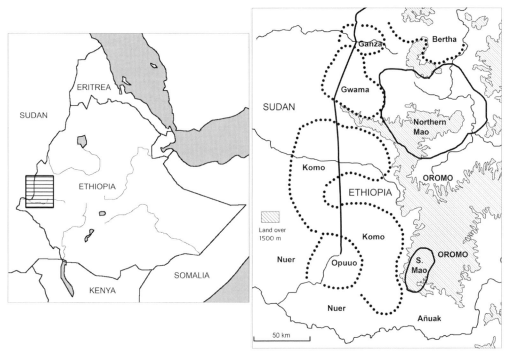

Figure 2.1. Present distribution of ethnic groups along the central Sudanese-Ethiopian border.

The making of the Mao (1550–1900)

The history of the Mao peoples is indissolubly linked to that of two dominant groups: the Busase and the Oromo. Whereas all communities that are traditionally included under the label Mao consist of egalitarian, slash-and-burn agriculturalists, both Busase and Oromo are intensive agriculturalists and cattle-herders, with remarkable differences in wealth and historically organized under chiefdoms. Other differences have to do with race and religion: the Mao are dark-skinned and tend to follow traditional beliefs, whereas the Busase and Oromo are paler with Caucasoid features and have massively turned to revealed religions. The history of the Busase, Oromo and Mao is a complex one, but it is important to understand it in order to comprehend both the current situation of the Mao and their forms of resistance (González-Ruibal 2012).

Around the early sixteenth century, the Busase were the rulers of a chiefdom established in southern Ethiopia. It was similar to other polities in the region, the most famous of which was the Kingdom of Kaffa, which survived until the late nineteenth century (Huntingford 1969 [1955]; Lange 1982). The Busase, the Kaffa and the peoples of the other neighbouring chiefdoms in southern Ethiopia were all related, as shown by their similar institutions, religious systems, social organization and closely related languages (all belonging to the Gonga branch of the Omotic family). These so-called

Gonga kingdoms (Lange 1982) were directly affected by the expansion of another society living further east: the Oromo.

The largest ethnic group in Ethiopia today, the Oromo were originally mobile pastoralists who profited from the situation of conflict existing in the country in the mid-sixteenth century to greatly expand their dominions. The brutal wars involving the Christian kingdom of Abyssinia, Muslim jihadists and the *pagan* Gonga chiefdoms severely weakened the latter, which became easy prey for the expanding Oromo (Hassen 1994, 30–31, 46–47). The ruling classes of some Gonga kingdoms, such as the Busase, decided to emigrate with their servants when the Oromo invaded their lands. Servants, dependants and subaltern peoples in general are known as *Mao*, *Manjo* or *Mawo* among the Gonga groups (Huntingford 1969 [1955], 136; Lange 1982, 264–268). These labels can refer either to peoples living on the periphery of a dominant group and maintaining master-client relations with it, or servants directly assigned to particular families and clans, as in a feudal system. In the first case, they provide game, honey and other forest products in exchange for agricultural products and manufactures; in the second case (which no longer exists), they have to offer work and tribute to their masters. The Busase emigrated towards the Sudan and eventually settled in the westernmost part of the Ethiopian highlands, where they subjected the native populations and founded a new polity, the Kingdom of Anfillo. The indigenous groups were incorporated into the subaltern class of the Mao (James 1980). Anthropologist Vinigi Grottanelli (1940) referred to this people as the Southern Mao. They adopted the (Omotic) language of their conquerors, which is usually called Anfillo by linguists because of the name of the kingdom (Yigezu and Yehualashet 1995).

The Busase, however, could not find peace in their new location because the Oromo kept expanding westwards and soon arrived at the gates of the Kingdom of Anfillo (Gidada 2001, 28–29). Some of the Busase, following an internecine conflict and under Oromo pressure, decided to emigrate with their Mao servants to the North. They settled in an area that was already occupied by a diversity of small-scale communities which shared a similar egalitarian ethos and an economic life based on shifting cultivation and the exploitation of forest resources. Once again, the Busase established master-servant relations with the egalitarian groups living in the margins of their new conquered land. These peoples also became *Mao* for the Busase. Unlike the Southern Mao, however, these Northern Mao always maintained an attitude of resistance, and their independent identities were not dissolved, but survived under the externally imposed homogeneous identity. Thus, we can still distinguish four distinct communities among the Northern Mao: the Sith Shwala (Nilo-Saharan speakers), and the Seze, Hozo and Bambasi (Omotic speakers) (Fig. 2.2).

The Oromo finally arrived in the newly acquired Busase territory as well. Through conquest and intermarriage, they ended up absorbing all Busase groups to both the North and South, and today Busase and Oromo consider themselves one people, which is how the different Mao communities also perceive them. The Oromo intensified the subjection of the Mao and other peripheral peoples already started by the Busase. They often transformed the master-servant or master-client relations that existed between Mao and Busase into a master-slave relationship. They raided Mao communities and forced them to deliver slaves from among their kin (usually orphans) as tribute. This

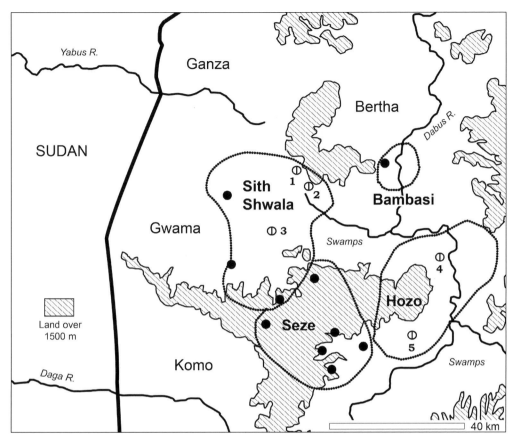

Figure 2.2. Location of Northern Mao groups. Black dots indicate Mao villages visited during the research. Divided dots indicate Mao villages with beehive huts. 1. Boshuma-K'ark'ege; 2. Boshuma; 3. Ishgogo Gedashola; 4. Folfoli; 5. Kuch'i. Oromo people live in most parts of Mao land, except in the western Sith Shwala and southern Hozo territories. The Busase live in Seze land.

further reinforced the subaltern identity of the Mao and simultaneously created a sense of solidarity between the different Mao communities. The marginalization of the Mao has not yet ended. Many live in the periphery of Oromo-Busase settlements and are considered an underclass of uncouth and primitive blacks. They have been gradually losing their cultural distinctiveness and adopting the hegemonic, state-sanctioned culture, a process that was already underway in the 1960s (Grottanelli 1966). These transformations are visible in the disappearance of specific Mao ways of building houses, the adoption among women of the one-piece dress that covers the entire body, the disappearance of technological skills (such as pottery-making, which has been monopolized by Oromo women), conversion to Islam (at least nominally), and the replacement of the traditional marriage system of sister exchange by the payment of a dowry. In the Oromo-dominated markets, the Mao crowd together in isolated, peripheral positions.

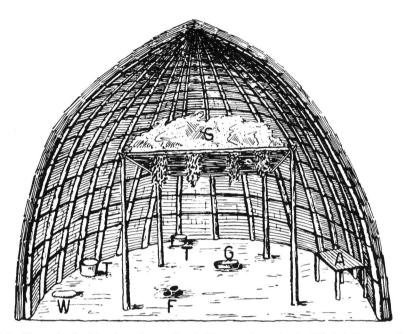

Figure 2.3. Plan of a beehive hut drawn by Italian anthropologist Vinigi Grottanelli in 1939 (after Grottanelli 1940).

Some Mao, however, still resist and cling to their traditions, especially in the margins of the territory occupied by the Oromo. It is in these margins that we can find the peculiar houses, which I will discuss in the rest of this chapter.

From the house to *our* house

The houses of the Mao were first described by the Italian anthropologist Vinigi Grottanelli (1940) in the colonial period of the 1930s. He called them *capanne alveare*, *beehive-shaped huts*, for their peculiar appearance, very different from the cylindrical houses with conical roofs that predominate in the region. Due to their archaic look, he considered them to be the original house type of the area: a dwelling of hunter-gatherers, which had progressively vanished under the pressure of more complex house types. Adopting a typically evolutionist perspective, he argued that these buildings, of which he saw only a few examples (Fig. 2.3), were condemned to disappear rapidly.

During my first travels to the region I could not spot a single *capanna alveare* and thought that Vinigi Grottanelli had been right to predict that the proto-house of the Mao would disappear forever. In December 2007, however, I saw my first beehive hut, a small structure used by a ritual specialist in the village of Ishgogo Gedashola. This could be the exception that confirmed the rule, but during 2009 and 2010 I had the chance to visit four more villages with *capanne alveare* (Kuch'i, Folfoli and Boshuma)

Figure 2.4. A beehive hut in use in the Hozo village of Folfoli (March 2010).

Figure 2.5. A beehive hut in use in the Sith Shwala village of Boshuma (February 2009).

belonging to two different Mao groups: the Nilo-Saharan-speaking Sith Shwala and the Omotic-speaking Hozo (Fig. 2.4). This proved that the beehive huts were, or had been, a pan-Mao phenomenon. More importantly, in one of the villages, Boshuma, there were dozens of beehive huts in use (Fig. 2.5). They did not look like the remnants of a fading tradition at all. On the contrary, I found out that this peculiar architecture plays a pivotal role among peripheral Mao communities, probably being more important than ever.

Not surprisingly, the Mao beehive hut has a biography which is as complex and hybrid as the Mao themselves. It could not be otherwise. Disentangling the precise itinerary of this structure is probably impossible, but we can at least identify the different traditions and practices that have informed it. The origin of the beehive hut is not clear: in Sudan and Ethiopia cylindrical structures with conical roofs are by far the most abundant house type. Beehive structures, however, do exist among a few communities. In southern Ethiopia, they are built and used by the Omotic-speaking Dorze. The great elaboration of their houses (Olmstead 1972), however, bears little resemblance to the Mao structures. Better parallels can be found among the Nilo-Saharan groups of the Sudanese-Ethiopian border zone. There are at least four Nilo-Saharan communities that use beehive structures: the Toposa of Sudan, near the southern Ethiopian frontier (Bodøgaard 1998); the Kunama and Nera, both living predominantly in Eritrea (Grottanelli and Masari 1943, 353–366); and the Kwama, who live mostly in Ethiopia, to the west of the Mao (Grottanelli 1948, 298). The Kwama, in fact, are directly related to the Sith Shwala Mao, the latter being Kwama who have entered into contact and hybridized with other societies (Oromo, Busase or Bertha). The name Sith Shwala (*Black Men*), in fact, represents an acceptance of racial difference as a defiant reply to the other's gaze.

The materiality of the Mao house is not trivial. As we will see, the Mao are as aware of the unique physicality of the house as they are of their own racial distinctiveness, and they use them both in the play of the differences that constitute their identity. However, the social meaning of these structures has, of course, an enormous relevance as well. In the entire region occupied by the Mao, it is common to find ritual structures beside the main house in each domestic compound. Externally, these structures are very similar to ordinary houses, except that they are smaller. They are found among both Omotic and Nilo-Saharan speakers, being called *swal shwombo* by the Sith Shwala Mao, *swe shwomo* by the Kwama and *doe kecho* by the Southern Mao (Grottanelli 1940, 321–322). The translation is the same: *house* (*swal*) *of the ancestral spirits* (*shwombo*). The use of the hut is very similar also: family and neighbours meet inside to celebrate harvest rituals in which they pray to god (*Yere*), drink beer and eat together. Indoors, one always finds large pots used to brew the ritual honey wine that is collectively drunk in the ceremonies (Fig. 2.6). In the case of the Kwama and Sith Shwala, hunting paraphernalia and first fruits (corn or sorghum) also hang from the roof to be blessed by the ancestral spirits that inhabit the house. Similar houses of spirits are used by ritual specialists, where they pray and perform their divinations and healing rites. There are two kinds of religious specialists: although their skills are similar, one of them is more concerned with propitiating fertility, of the fields and the people (called *kukulu* or *kugul* among the Sith Shwala Mao), the other with curing diseases and foreseeing the future (*sith bish*, literally, *the man who sees*). Whereas only men can be *kukulu*, both women and men can be *sith bish*. It is likely that the division between ritual and ordinary houses has been a later historical development and that originally the religious functions were incorporated into ordinary houses, except for the huts of ritual specialists. This lack of

*Figure 2.6. Inside a Kwama ritual hut (*swe shwomo*): ritual pots, calabashes and straws for drinking beer or honey wine.*

division between sacred and profane space occurs among other neighbouring groups, such as the Komo (Theis 1995, 91) and the Gumuz (Feyissa 2011, 335), and I have visited two Sith Shwala houses in the village of Boshuma mentioned earlier where ritual and ordinary functions coexisted in the same building. Significantly, they were the homes of older people. It is tempting to think that the idea of a separate ritual structure came to the area with the Busase, along with other religious institutions to which I will refer in the next section. To corroborate this point, it can be mentioned that in other Gonga kingdoms, such as Kaffa, there are special buildings, called *bare k'eto*, for conducting religious ceremonies (Huntingford 1969 [1955], 131). In all likelihood, though, the present division of functions (house/ritual house) has been influenced by the use of separate buildings for prayers by the hegemonic religions (Islam and Christianity). The Mao themselves, as we shall see, make a direct comparison between their ritual huts and the mosques and churches of other peoples.

Neither Busase nor Southern Mao had beehive huts in the Kingdom of Anfillo (cf. Grottanelli 1940): therefore, both their houses of spirits (*doe kecho*) and their ordinary houses (*kecho*) had cylindrical walls and conical roofs (Grottanelli 1940, 322). Among the Northern Mao, instead, both ritual (*swal shwombo*) and ordinary houses (*swal*) were beehive-shaped. I say *were* because the main house has gradually been losing its original shape and adopting the dominant style in the region. Thus, a large part of the remaining beehive huts today are houses of spirits. In Boshuma, for instance, most people had a large house with a conical roof and cylindrical walls for living in and a small beehive hut for conducting rituals. In this process, the materiality of the house has stopped being perceived as something ordinary, taken for granted, and has become a privileged vehicle of communication with the spirits and the past. This also explains why many *progressive* Mao who have converted to Islam, at least nominally, abandon the beehive huts where they used to live and build square or cylindrical houses. This was noticeable in the Hozo Mao village of Folfoli, where people were no longer maintaining their decaying beehive huts, had constructed cylindrical houses instead, and did not even want to talk about their old homes in front of strangers. The old house form has become too strongly associated with traditional practices and beliefs, which are despised by the dominant Oromo society.

That the Mao have come to realize that they possess a very particular kind of dwelling is proved by the local term for the beehive huts. When I asked the Mao what the constructions that used the beehive shape were called, the answer was revealing: *amo kera*: *house of the Amo*, or *swal kwama*: *house of the Kwama*, depending on the particular Mao group one asked, the Hozo (Amo is their self-denomination) or the Sith Shwala. The second case is striking because Kwama is *not* their self-denomination: the Kwama are the ancestors of the Sith Shwala. For them, *Kwama* refers either to their forebears or to a contemporary group living far away in Sudan to which they are related. An old Mao told me that originally Kwama and Mao were the sons of the same father: Bota Kwasa. When Kwama, the younger son, reached adulthood, he decided to move away towards the Sudan to marry, whereas Mao decided to remain where their descendants still live today. Some people only recognize the old ethnic name *Kwama* vaguely and are aware that it has something to do with them, but without actually knowing what it means, while others do not even identify the term at all. The original ethnic denomination of the Mao, therefore, has become fossilized in the description of a peculiar type of dwelling.

The name for the beehive hut shows that it has become a diacritical symbol of identity for the Mao, something linked to their very existence as a people. This strong relationship between the Mao and the hut was eloquently expressed by one of the elders I interviewed in the village of Boshuma. When I asked him about the *swal kwama* he told me:

> "The swal kwama and the Mao cannot be separated. They are the same. It is like the mosque for the Muslims and the church for the Christians. We pray there to our god. The swal kwama has to be perpetuated through the generations. The moment the swal kwama ceases to exist, there will be no more Mao"
>
> (Interview with Harun Rusk'alla, November 2009).

This is an impressive statement on the ontological relevance of material culture. What is perhaps more surprising, though, is not that the *swal kwama* plays such an outstanding role, but that the Mao themselves are aware of it, because technologies of the (collective) self or *core objects* are rarely conscious. Boesch (1991, 333) suggests that a "core object would be one which, by its usages and ritual connectedness, appears to be vital for the self-definition of a culture". He cites the example of the stone axes employed by a group of aboriginal Australians, the Yir Yiront (studied in a classical work by Sharp 1952). For them, the axe was not only a vital tool, but also a symbol of manhood, a vehicle for social interaction and a carrier of religious meanings. Boesch (ibid.) thinks that the Yir Yiront were not conscious of the relevance of axes, otherwise they would not have exchanged them for steel ones so readily: "Our consciousness tends to be unidimensional – we think of one aspect relevant to ongoing action concerns and tend to neglect other non-imminent ones". The same seems to occur with the Awá hunter-gatherers (Brazil) in relation to their bows and arrows: although they are ontologically inextricable from being *Awá*, they are not consciously perceived as such by the people themselves (González-Ruibal *et al.* 2011). What makes the Mao different? What makes them fully aware of the crucial relevance of beehive huts in their constitution as a people? I would argue that it is their long historical experience of contact with other peoples in which they have played a subaltern role. Australian aborigines and Awá Indians lack this experience: their contact was more sudden and with a more powerful entity (the modern nation state). They did not have time to reflect on the implications of radically altering their material itineraries, nor did they have much room for negotiation with the foreign powers. The Mao, conversely, have become acutely aware of their own cultural practices and their importance in their survival as a distinct people through three centuries of interaction with dominant societies, none of which had the power to meddle in other peoples' lives that the modern state has. In this process, the Mao have discovered in the beehive hut a vehicle for their self-preservation. This has changed from being an unconscious space for reproducing the collective to becoming a conscious space of cultural resistance, a space of self-assertion. This further represents a shift from *swal* to *swal kwama*, from a mere *house* to *the house of the people*.

House of resistance, house of the past

In the beehive hut, and more particularly in the house of ancestral spirits (*swal shwombo*), the Mao have also found a mechanism for bringing time to a halt, for denying change and for performing an ideal image of Mao society that is rooted in an unmovable past. This capacity for freezing time is perfectly expressed in the name of the building itself, *swal kwama*, a reference to an ancient ethnic identity. The ideal image of society that the beehive hut reproduces is predicated upon three oppositions: life in the forest versus the peasant life of the hegemonic Oromo society; *pagan* fertility rites versus Islam and Christianity (the religion of the hegemonic peoples); and a memory of open resistance versus the peaceful present, when violent resistance is no longer an option.

House of the forest

Vinigi Grottanelli was in a sense right when he described the beehive hut, the *swal kwama*, as the primitive dwelling of a hunter-gatherer. However, he did not imagine the Mao themselves to be playing with that idea. The material look of the structure

Figure 2.7. A beehive hut in Boshuma partially concealed by castor bean plants and other vegetation.

resembles the small shelters that the Mao and other borderland groups (Kwama, Komo) still make when they go hunting in the forest for several days. Besides, although the beehive huts are built today inside settlements, in locating such settlements people still choose places that are relatively isolated and surrounded with lush vegetation, as if to reproduce the forest environment (Fig. 2.7).

The Mao always describe themselves as a *people of the forest* and argue that the Oromo do not like forests but fell them to grow crops and creates pastures. The beehive hut, however, is a hunters' house or, more generally, the house of a forest people for other reasons. Hunters hang the bones, jawbones, horns and skins of the hunted animals indoors, on the wall opposite the entrance (Fig. 2.8), as an offering to the spirits and in order to propitiate them in respect of further hunts (as also among the Komo: Theis 1995, 91). Before a hunting trip, the hunters go to the beehive hut of the ritual specialist to receive his blessing; they put all the spears together on the floor and pray over them. When they return from the hunt, they go to the *swal kwama* and, if they have been successful, they give the ritual specialist part of the game. Some of these houses keep souvenirs of a particularly glorious hunt, such as an elephant's ear or the tail of a hippopotamus. Inside the beehive hut, domestic animals are sacrificed to the spirits by the ritual specialist, but they have to be killed with a spear – like the wild animals hunted by the Mao – because the beehive hut is the house of the forest, the house of

Figure 2.8. Jaws and horns of wild animals inside the ritual house of Nekura Dinze, a diviner (sith bish) *from Ishgogo Gedashola.*

the wild. The woodlands, though, are not only the place for hunting. People also go there to gather honey, one of the main riches of the Mao, as it is the case with other peripheral peoples of the Ethiopian forest (Tippett 1970, 44–49; Stauder 1972). Inside the *swal kwama*, one always finds old beehives and rings used in the making of beehives, gourds of honey and old pots in which honey wine is brewed and collectively drunk.

House of fertility

As I pointed out, religious specialists celebrate their rituals inside the *swal kwama*. These rituals have the propitiation of fertility (human and non-human) as their leitmotif. The most important celebrations are related to the agricultural cycle. There are three main festivals: the first, called *is*, takes place during the beginning of the rainy season (around May). Immediately before sowing maize, people bring corncobs, beer, food and two chickens to the beehive hut. The ritual specialist (*kukulu* in this case) slaughters the hens over the maize grains and mixes the blood with the grains, which are then distributed among the attendants to the ceremony. After that, they pray for a good rainy season and plentiful crops. At the start of the harvest period they have another ceremony, called *k'in siana* (feast of the sorghum). This is a working party, in which they all harvest together and at the end eat the first grains and fruits, except those that are reserved for the next

Figure 2.9. Offers of first fruits hanging from the entrance of a beehive hut in Boshuma.

year, under the protection of *Yere* (Fig. 2.9). After the harvest is over (December), there is another festival *(shul t'wa pʰwash)*: people bring their crops to the *swal kwama* to be blessed by the ritual specialist, drink beer *(shul)* and eat porridge *(pʰwash)* together. The blessing consists in prayers and the ceremonial spraying of beer or honey wine from the mouth of the ritual specialist. Both *kukulu* and *sith bish* (diviner) are thought capable of both bringing rain and stopping it, as well as of preventing hail from destroying the crops. These rituals also take place in the beehive hut or around it.

In addition, the ritual specialist blesses the beehives. Honey plays a crucial symbolic and economic role among the Mao because, as we have seen, it is a product of the forest and the main element of exchange with other groups, which allows them to obtain salt, iron, clothes and other goods that they cannot produce themselves. They have a festival of honey similar to the cereal harvest festival. It is called *k'obo gjandal, cut of the beehives,* because the ropes that tie the beehives *(gjandal)* to the trees are cut at that moment to pick up the honeycombs. After collecting the beehives, every family gives the first one to the ritual specialist, which he keeps inside the *swal kwama,* together with the ropes that are used to hang them (Fig. 2.10). The beehives are blessed and stones are put on top of the ropes, so that the beehives will be as heavy with honey as stones the following season. The beehives are returned to their owners when the time for planting comes. With the first honey of the season, the ritual specialist brews the honey wine that is later used in his healing, divination or fertility rituals.

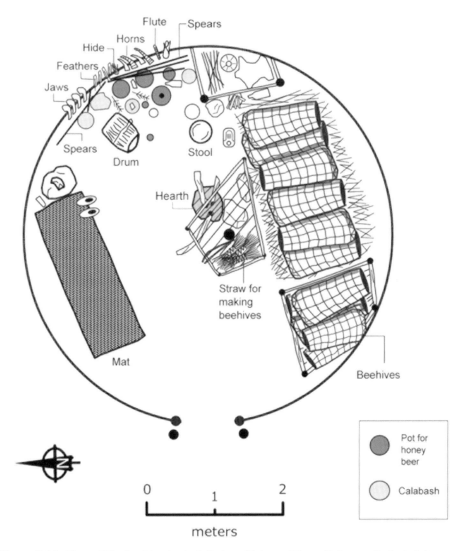

Figure 2.10. Plan of the beehive hut of diviner Nekura Dinze (Ishgogo Gedashola).

The *kukulu* also blesses people inside the *swal kwama*. During every harvest ritual (sorghum, maize or honey), he dips his finger in the blood of the sacrificed chickens, sheep or goat, and then uses it to anoint the arms of the men and the foreheads of the women. He also spits honey wine into their hands to multiply their wealth and fertility: more children and more abundant crops. Related to this, one month after a child is born, the parents bring the baby to the *swal kwama* to be blessed by the ritual specialist, sacrifice an animal (goat, sheep or chicken) and eat and drink together. Moreover, when a woman cannot bear children, she goes to visit the diviner (*sith bish*) in his or her *swal kwama*. One of the *sit bish*, Nekura Dinze, made women kiss a helical piece of wood that he keeps inside the ritual hut to make them fertile. The fertility ritual for people involves similar prayers, ritual spitting or spraying and the drinking of honey wine to those of the agricultural rituals. Apart from helping crops and people to multiply, the *sith bish* also has healing powers. The diviner cures people either through dreams or by throwing cowries (*payak*) on to the ground and seeing how they fall. In both cases, the nature of the illness is revealed. In sum, the *swal kwama* is strongly related to all rituals in Mao society that guarantee the healthy reproduction of the group: the harvest festivals (subsistence), the honey rituals (exchange with the gods and with foreigners) and the fertility rituals (children). It is not surprising, then, that old Harun Rusk'alla considered there can be no future for his people without *swal kwama*.

Finally, it is worth noting that the idea of praying and the concept of an autonomous god to whom one can pray, which are absent among most borderland peoples (James 1988, 180), have been assimilated by the Mao from their erstwhile rulers, the Busase. *Yere* or *Yero*, a divinity who resides in the skies, was the paramount god among the Busase (Grottanelli 1940, 311–312, 317), as among other Gonga peoples (Huntingford 1969 [1955], 132). However, the Busase, like the Oromo, have massively converted to either Islam or Christianity, and no one believes in the pagan deities anymore. In this way, *Yere*, a god of the powerful, has become a god of resistance against the revealed religions – a Mao god inextricably linked to the Mao house.

House of ancient wars

The Mao are very conscious of their subaltern situation with regard to the Oromo and the Busase. The history of conflict, encroachment and ultimate subordination that explains their current predicament is very present in their collective imaginary. The founding event of Mao cultural memory is the first escape from the advancing Oromo. All the Mao – irrespective of the group to which they belong – claim to have their origins in the Gibe basin in south-central Ethiopia, the area from where the Busase were originally expelled during the Oromo expansion of the mid-sixteenth century. While this origin might be historically correct for the Omotic-speaking Mao (Hozo, Seze and Bambasi), it is hardly the case for the Nilo-Saharan Sith Shwala, whose ancestors have been living in the Ethiopian-Sudanese borderlands for several millennia (cf. Fernández 2003). It seems that the history of the Busase migrations and the Oromo invasions have been conflated into a single episode that resonates with the present situation of the Mao, in which they are continually being pressed by the expanding Oromo. The important thing, though, is that, by borrowing from the collective memory of other Mao, the Sith Shwala strengthen their links with the entire subaltern community of Mao. The history of conflict that the Mao really share is a more recent one: during the nineteenth century, they had to fight Oromo encroachment from the South and East and Bertha encroachment from the West, as well as the slave traders coming from Sudan. The Mao achieved fame during that time as a redoubtable people. The Dutch traveller Juan Maria Schuver (cited in James *et al.* 1996, 50), who visited the area in 1881–1882, writes that during the 1850s:

Figure 2.11. Spears of the ancestors (shin shwombo) with ancestral beehive rings and calabash in the beehive hut of the ritual specialist (kukulu) Harun Rusk'alla (Boshuma).

"both Bashi-bazuks and Arab slave-hunters, after subjugating and devastating the Bertas, tried to invade the Amam [Mao] country, but were beaten back on each occasion with loss of men and guns. Up to the present moment every 'Turk' from the Hukumdar of Khartoum to the common soldier has a wholesome fear of the dreaded Amam [Mao]. The very word alone makes them shudder."

Later in the same text, Schuver (cited in James *et al.* 1996, 94) reports a "fierce tribe of Ma'o negroes" that are "the terror of the Bertas as much as of the Ganti and Shibu Galla [Oromo groups]". This story stands in stark contrast to the present pacifist attitude of the Mao. Not only do they not fight anymore, they also stress the need for conflicts to be solved peacefully: *The Mao do not conflict with other people, they just emigrate to empty land not occupied by others*, a Mao elder told me. He also insisted that: *They do not need to fight other peoples. We see them as brothers and sisters*. Other neighbours expressed themselves in similar terms. As a matter of fact, no ethnic fighting has been reported between the Mao and other groups for a very long time, in contrast with other communities of the western borderland, such as the Gumuz, Añuak, Nuer and Oromo (cf. Markakis 2011).

However, memory is not only transmitted orally, it is also present in things inside the *swal kwama*. And things tell of a time when the Mao did not simply escape from their enemies, but fought back. The Mao have kept the precious memories of that period in the form of relics, displayed inside the *swal kwama*: the spears (*shin*), with which their

*Figure 2.12. Bulgu Masad (*kukulu*) holding the shield of the ancestors (*kep shwombo*) inside his beehive hut (Boshuma). Also hanging from the wall, there are offerings of corn and a warthog hide (*Phacochoerus africanus*).*

ancestors killed their enemies (Fig. 2.11), the throwing sticks (*baŋa*) with which they performed the war dances and also fought, and the elaborated shields (*kep*), made of buffalo leather, with which they defended themselves (Fig. 2.12). They argue that some of the spears and shields belong to the earliest defensive wars, when the Oromo broke into the Gibe valley (that is, in the sixteenth century). They more likely date from the late nineteenth century, the period in which the Mao fought against slave traders and invaders of various kinds. But the historicist narrative is not important to the Mao, whose temporality is based on the repeated phenomena of aggression and dispossession by other societies. In a sense, the tools of war kept inside the *swal kwama* give the lie to the pacifist discourse of their owners.

It is not just the weapons that are from the past. All the artefacts displayed inside the *swal shwombo* constitute a sort of *wild museography* (Menard 2011, 47), as every item belongs to the ancestral spirits, either because it is dedicated to them (*pʰwashuŋ shwombo, the maize of the ancestors*) or because it has been transmitted from generation to generation, like the *dul shwombo* (a stick used in ritual dances), *koŋo shwombo* (the pot used for brewing beer and honey wine), *gen gjandal shwombo* (the rings employed in the making of beehives), *pamba shwombo* (drum) and *kóŋo shwombo* (stool). They are collectively called *gwama swal shwombo, the things of the house of the ancestral spirits*. The *gwama shwombo*, like the objects exhibited in a museum, make the past present. However, the things of the ritual house are not selected for reasons of aesthetics or age in the way they are in western museums. The things that are selected are those that resonate with the present concerns of the Mao: people from the dominant societies keep encroaching into Mao territory, felling down their forests, killing their wild animals and making the livelihood of the Mao unfeasible. The *gwama shwombo* are those things that relate the Mao to their historical experience as a free people of the forest.

Conclusion: The phantasmatic house

In this chapter I have explored the role that a particular kind of house has played among the Mao of Ethiopia. I have described how the meaning of the building, which is strongly associated with its material form, has changed with the gradual expansion on to Mao land of a hegemonic, hierarchical, alien society. What used to be a peculiar hut shape, used equally for ritual and ordinary purposes, ended up being something more: something of outstanding relevance for the survival of the Mao people. The beehive-shaped hut, the *swal kwama*, has become so entwined with being Mao that the people themselves cannot conceive their independent existence without it. The most important transformations undergone by the beehive hut are the virtual disappearance of its profane functions and its acquisition of a strongly mnemonic role. This function has only emerged through generations of contact with expanding groups and with the increasing external threats to Mao society. However, to say that the beehive hut now primarily serves the function of memory would be an understatement. What this kind of building does is to slow history down. The Mao discovered long ago what the philosopher Michel Serres (1995 [1982], 87) argues: that an object "stabilizes our relationships, it slows down the time of our revolutions […] The object, for us, makes our history slow". This is particularly true for those small-scale egalitarian peoples for whom keeping history slow – or *cold*, as Lévi-Strauss would put it – is fundamental to their survival in the face of more aggressive groups. Lévi-Strauss (1966 [1962], 234) said that *cold* societies "want to deny it [change] and try, with a dexterity we underestimate, to make the states of their development which they consider 'prior' as permanent as possible". This is clearly the case with the Mao. And what better way of making that *prior* permanent than curating the artefacts of the past in a museum? However, to say that the Mao house makes history slow or cold is not sufficient either. The work of the Mao house is more radical because it actually abolishes the distinction between past and present. It allows the Mao to live in their own time, which neither fits our concept of the present nor of the past, but includes both in the same ontological sphere.

The beehive hut, however, is also a phantom dwelling, the materialization of a collective fantasy. As I have pointed out, the fact that it is called *house of the Kwama* instead of *house of the Sith Shwala* or *house of the Mao* eloquently speaks of the denial of change. Although its very existence is based on the historical experience of the Mao as a subaltern people, it is also a denial of the negative circumstances that make them a subaltern people today. The *swal kwama* produces an idealized image of the Mao as an independent people of the forest, which is no longer tenable. It probably never was as they imagine it, but today is less so than ever. For this reason, they look after these fragile things that are gradually vanishing from their lives with the utmost care. The concern for a world that is falling apart is very present in the interviews I conducted with the Mao elders. Like other borderland groups, they are being engulfed by the dominant Ethiopian societies and successfully incorporated into the state (Markakis 2011). Unlike their ancestors, they have nowhere to go, no forest to which they can retreat. If the present trend continues, the Mao will become more and more a marginalized underclass and less and less an autonomous group with their own traditions, as it has happened to certain other groups in Ethiopia (Freeman and Pankhurst 2001).

Acknowledgements

This work could not have been carried out without the help of the Mao, Oromo and Busase communities of western Ethiopia that generously offered their knowledge and hospitality. Special thanks are due to my collaborators, Yonatan Sahle, Tesfaye Tekaliñ, Álvaro Falquina and Xurxo Ayán Vila, for their invaluable assistance in the field and their insights. Fieldwork for this project was funded by the Ministry of Culture of Spain (Archaeological Projects Abroad) and the Complutense University of Madrid. I would also like to thank an anonymous referee for his or her helpful comments and the colleagues at the Itineraries of the Material Conference for their feedback.

References

Bodøgaard, T. (1998) Toposa. In P. Oliver (ed.) *Encyclopedia of vernacular architecture of the world, Vol. 3: Cultures and habitats*, 2096–2097. Cambridge, Cambridge University Press.

Boesch, E. E. (1991) *Symbolic action theory and cultural psychology*. Berlin, Springer.

Dietler, M. (1997) The iron age in Mediterranean France: Colonial encounters, entanglements, and transformations. *Journal of World Prehistory* 11 (3), 269–358.

Fernández, V. M. (2003) Four thousand years in the Blue Nile: Paths to inequality and ways of resistance. *Complutum* 14, 409–425.

Feyissa, G. (2011) *Etnoarqueología, identidad y cultura material de un pueblo fronterizo africano. Los Gumuz de Etiopía occidental*. Unpublished PhD thesis, Complutense University of Madrid.

Fleming, H. C. (1984) The importance of Mao in Ethiopian history. In S. Rubenson (ed.) *Proceedings of the 7th international conference on Ethiopian studies, University of Lund, 26–29 April 1982*, 31–38. Addis Abeba, Institute of Ethiopian Studies; Uppsala, Scandinavian Institute of African Studies; East Lansing, MI, Michigan State University, African Studies Center.

Foster, R. J. (2006) Tracking globalization: Commodities and value in motion. In C. Tilley, W. Keane, S. Küchler, M. Rowlands and P. Spyer (eds) *Handbook of material culture*, 285–302. London and New York, Sage.

Freeman, D. and Pankhurst, A. (eds) (2001) *Living on the edge: Marginalised minorities of craftworkers and hunters in southern Ethiopia*. Addis Abeba, Addis Abeba University, Department of Sociology and Social Administration.

Friedman, J. (2002) From roots to routes: Tropes for trippers. *Anthropological Theory* 2 (1), 21–36.

Gidada, N. (2001) *History of the Sayyoo Oromoo of southwestern Ethiopia from about 1730 to 1886*. Addis Ababa, Mega.

González-Ruibal, A. (2012) Generations of free men: Resistance and material culture in western Ethiopia. In T. L. Kienlin and A. Zimmermann (eds) *Beyond elites: Alternatives to hierarchical systems in modelling social formations. International Conference at the Ruhr-Universität Bochum, Germany, October 22–24, 2009,* 67–82 (= Universitätsforschungen zur prähistorischen Archäologie). Bonn, Habelt.

González-Ruibal, A.; Hernando, A. and Politis, G. (2011) Ontology of the self and material culture: Arrow-making among the Awá hunter-gatherers (Brazil). *Journal of Anthropological Archaeology* 30 (1), 1–16.

Goodrick-Clarke, N. (1985) *The occult roots of Nazism: The Ariosophists of Austria and Germany, 1890–1935.* Wellingborough, Aquarian Press.

Grottanelli, V. L. (1940) *Missione etnografica nel Uollega Occidentale. Volume Primo. I Mao.* Rome, Reale Accademia d'Italia.

Grottanelli, V. L. (1948) I Preniloti. Un'arcaica provincia culturale in Africa. *Annali Lateranensi* 12, 280–326.

Grottanelli, V. L. (1966) The vanishing Pre-Nilotes revisited. *Bulletin of the International Committee of Urgent Anthropological Research* 8, 23–32.

Grottanelli, V. L. and Massari, C. (1943) *I Baria, i Cunama e i Beni Amer.* Rome, Reale Accademia d'Italia.

Hassen, M. (1994) *The Oromo of Ethiopia: A history, 1570–1860.* Trenton, NJ, Red Sea Press.

Hernando, A. (2008) Why has history not appreciated maintenance activities? In S. Montón-Subías and M. Sánchez-Romero (eds) *Engendering social dynamics: The archaeology of maintenance activities.* BAR International Series 1862, 9–16. Oxford, Archaeopress.

Huntingford, G. W. B. (1969 [1955]) *The Galla of Ethiopia: The kingdoms of Kafa and Janjero* (= Ethnographic Survey of Africa. Northeastern Africa, Part II). London, International African Institute.

James, W. (1980) From aboriginal to frontier society in western Ethiopia. In D. L. Donham and W. James (eds) *Working papers on society and history in imperial Ethiopia: The southern periphery from 1880 to 1974,* 37–67. Cambridge, Cambridge University Press for African Studies Centre.

James, W. (1988) *The listening ebony: Moral knowledge, religion and power among the Uduk of Sudan.* Oxford, Clarendon.

James, W.; Bauman, G. and Johnson, D. (eds) (1996) *Juan Maria Schuver's travels in North East Africa. 1880–1883.* London, Hakluyt Society.

Knappett, C. (2011) *An archaeology of interaction: Network perspectives on material culture and society.* Oxford and New York, Oxford University Press.

Lange, W. J. (1982) *History of the Southern Gonga (southwestern Ethiopia).* Wiesbaden, Franz Steiner.

Latour, B. (1991) Technology is society made durable. In J. Law (ed.) *A sociology of monsters: Essays on power, technology and domination.* Sociological Review Monograph, 103–131. London, Routledge.

Levi, J. (1998) The bow and the blanket: Religion, identity, and resistance in Rarámuri material culture. *Journal of Anthropological Research* 54 (3), 299–324.

Lévi-Strauss, C. (1966 [1962]) *The savage mind.* Chicago, The University of Chicago Press (first published in French, 1962) *La pensée sauvage.* Paris, Plon).

Malinowski, B. (1920) Kula: The circulating exchange of valuables in the archipelagos of eastern New Guinea. *Man* 20, 97–105.

Markakis, J. (2011) *Ethiopia: The last two frontiers.* Oxford, James Currey.

Menard, A. (2011) Comentario a A. Hernando y A. González Ruibal. *Revista de Antropología Chilena* 24 (2), 44–47.

Mendoza, M. (2004) Western Toba messianism and resistance to colonization, 1915–1918. *Ethnohistory* 51 (2) 293–316.

Michaels, E. (2002) Hollywood iconography: A Warlpiri reading. In J. X. Inda and R. Rosaldo (eds) *The anthrology of globalization: A reader*, 311–324. London, Blackwell.

Olmstead, J. (1972) The Dorze house: A bamboo basket. *Journal of Ethiopian Studies* 10 (2), 27–36.

Olsen, B. (2010) *In defense of things: Archaeology and the ontology of objects*. Plymouth, AltaMira Press.

Picazo, M. (1997) Hearth and home: The timing of maintenance activities. In J. Moore and E. Scott (eds) *Invisible people and processes: Writing gender and childhood into European archaeology*, 59–67. London, Leicester University Press.

Serres, M. (1995 [1982]) *Genesis*. Translated by G. James and J. Nielson. Ann Arbor, University of Michigan Press (first published in French, 1982, *Genèse*. Paris, Grasset).

Sharp, L. (1952) Steel axes for Stone Age Australians. In E. H. Spicer (ed.) *Human problems in technological change: A casebook*, 69–92. New York, Russell Sage Foundation.

Stauder, J. (1972) *The Majangir: Ecology and society of a southwestern Ethiopian people*. Cambridge, Cambridge University Press.

Theis, J. (1995) *Nach der Razzia. Ethnographie und Geschichte der Koma*. München, Trickster.

Thomas, N. (1991) *Entangled objects: Exchange, material culture and colonialism in the Pacific*. Cambridge, Harvard University Press.

Tippett, A. R. (1970) *Peoples of southwest Ethiopia*. South Pasadena, CA, William Carey.

Watt, W. M. (1988) *Islamic fundamentalism and modernity*. London and New York, Routledge.

Yigezu, M. and Yehualashet, T. (1995) Anfillo: A sketch of grammar and lexicon. *Afrikanistische Arbeitspapiere* 44, 97–123.

Chapter 3

Imprints as punctuations of material itineraries

Carl Knappett

Introduction

In the film *Alps*, by avant-garde Greek director Yorgos Lanthimos, a small circle of acquaintances (who call themselves *Alps*) decide to help those grieving the loss of a loved one by substituting for the deceased. One couple has lost their tennis-playing daughter to a car accident. The nurse who tends to her in her last days is a member of *Alps* and persuades the couple to let her fill in for their daughter, at least for a time, to ease their grief. She dresses in a tennis skirt, wears the dead girl's wristband, they lend her their daughter's tennis shoes, and she fills the role. One message the audience can take from this is that death leaves an absence that all we wish to do is fill with a presence, and we may go to extremes to do so. Rarely do we find another individual to fill the role quite so unconventionally, and material objects may do the job of providing at least some level of contact amidst the loss – the girl's favourite wristband she wore playing tennis, for example. Whatever precise form the substitution may take, there is a profound need to create continuity and stability, and substitution is one means to this end.

At one level, this desire for persistence over time seems to run counter to the message we often hear from material culture theory that materials are forever in motion through time and space, following itineraries and acquiring biographies (Kopytoff 1986; Hoskins 1998; Gosden and Marshall 1999; Joy 2009). Both itinerary and biography appear to suggest a linear, historicist trajectory for motion, with a beginning, middle and end. However, the editors of this volume counsel caution *about the linear evolution of things*. They want instead *to highlight the complexity of changing contexts*. Still, there remains the danger of assuming constant movement, even if not in straight lines. Addressing the temporal dimension more explicitly, they allude to the work of Edward Shils (1981), highlighting the longevity of objects, and how things appear, disappear, are forgotten and come back. With the potential complexity of material identity over long periods, they suggest that the biography metaphor is imprecise. This I would agree with, though I wonder if its replacement by the metaphor of an itinerary is an improvement. It still seems to indicate movement, from one point to the next – it is difficult to imagine a non-linear itinerary.

Temporality and the anachronic

Perhaps part of the problem lies in our conception of time. Archaeologist Laurent Olivier (2004; 2008) has written about the difficulties we face in escaping from the linear, historicist view of time that dominates archaeological thinking. In this view, we can easily fool ourselves into thinking that there is a hermetically sealed past immune from the present, if only we might find ways of accessing it. Olivier argues that we must move away from this melancholic quest by recognizing that the past can only be known to us in the present through a series of traces that have been worked on over time. This also means that we cannot bracket off, for example, an ancient Minoan past from a Classical Cretan past, or either from a Roman Cretan past, as each subsequent phase works on earlier ones. They are not in sequential order, the one isolated from the other like catalogue cards, or like stages in an itinerary. Olivier uses the idea of *memory-objects* to convey this sense of past objects being endlessly reconstituted, such that a Minoan artefact is an artefact with multiple pasts as well as a present. It is interesting that Olivier is strongly influenced by the work of Aby Warburg and Walter Benjamin, authors whom archaeologists have only sporadically cited (Olivier 2004), despite the apparent suitability of Warburg's idea of *Nachleben*, the notion that there is a survival of the past in a present object (e.g. Warburg 1999; Benjamin 1936).

Art historians, however, are much better acquainted with both Warburg and Benjamin, and this tradition is very effectively activated in "Anachronic Renaissance" (Nagel and Wood 2010). These art historians too are in search of a new way of contemplating the temporal dimension of objects, particularly the way in which they can seem to operate between past and present times. For this they use the term *anachronic* to capture the tension between times. The idea of the anachronic is also taken up in the work of art historian Georges Didi-Huberman (2008), again leaning heavily on Warburg and Benjamin. As is the case for Olivier, Warburg's idea of *Nachleben*, or *survivance*, is critical, as it indicates that many artefacts – and perhaps especially artworks – operate between times, between past and present. The survival of the past in the present artefact can be quite troubling, particularly to our historicist assumptions.

The term *anachronic* is not one that we may immediately grasp, but it encapsulates an idea that promises to be useful in trying to understand the nature of material movement across time. We need examples to penetrate the meaning of anachronic. Laurent Olivier (2008) uses the example of Oradour-sur-Glane to convey the strange ways in which the past inhabits the present. Oradour-sur-Glane was the scene of a World War II massacre of innocent villagers, a tragedy since marked by the preservation of the village ruins in a state as true to 1944 as possible. In the intervening decades, rotting wooden beams have been replaced and collapsing walls shored up. Constant work is needed to keep the village in the present looking like it was in the past. An example used by Nagel and Wood (2010) is uncannily similar – the Ship of Theseus. This ship, on which Theseus returned to Athens after his slaying of the Minotaur, was preserved by the Athenian state, for centuries according to Plutarch, with old planks being replaced as they decayed: "The Ship of Theseus is a paradigm of the object defined by its structure rather than by its material make-up" (ibid., 8). It is what Rosalind Krauss (1985) would call a *structural object*. Perhaps the materials that go into its upkeep are in motion, but the structural object is itself defined by survival and persistence, rather than by movement.

This point, of the object being defined by its form and not its materials, is an important one. Nagel and Wood (2010, 8–9) say that: "To think 'structurally' […] is to reject linear chronology as the inevitable matrix of experience and cognition." This one can understand in the strange case presented in the film *Alps* – if one casts the daughter as the *structural object* whose *form*, or *role*, is maintained even if the substituted *material* is completely different. Nagel and Wood (2010, 16) explore how in the Renaissance a dialogue emerged in art around this tension between past and present, between form and material, and they talk of substitution and "performance as two competitive models of creativity that are always in play."

Imprints

What is also fascinating in their work is the use of the woodcut to explore the character of processes of substitution. They thereby identify the imprint as an effective means of thinking about the anachronic – which is precisely what art historian Georges Didi-Huberman (2008) does in his book *"Ressemblance par contact"* (and Didi-Huberman is clearly an influence on Nagel and Wood). Whether a photograph, a Duchamp artwork, a stamped coin or a hand negative in cave art – all of which are discussed by Didi-Huberman – the imprint reveals the double temporality, or dialectic, in such images, which enact both a here-now and a there-then (see Platt 2006, citing Barthes). Oradour-sur-Glane and the Ship of Theseus both have/had a here-now and a there-then. Another way of thinking about this dialectic is in terms of presence and absence, or rather, how the one implies the other, so one may encounter a present absence (Runia 2006). Sometimes a presence can make an absence apparent – in its simplest form, this may be a footprint; the presence of a human body that is now absent nevertheless left a presence in the form of a trace, the footprint, which signals the body's prior presence. Other imprints, such as the photograph or cave art hand negative mentioned above, operate in the same way, whereby a temporary contact produces a trace that remains once contact has ended – so the contact reveals this *loss*. The trace is a presence that substitutes (metonymically) for an absence. In the case of an entire village, such as Oradour-sur-Glane, the process is more complex, but essentially it is the same: the ruins are traces that are maintained in order to signal what was in this case a devastating loss.

Didi-Huberman dedicates a whole book to this search for the complex meaning of imprints. He says there is an entire history lacking, in part tracing the reasoning back to Vasari (and simply exacerbated by particular readings of Benjamin's essay on mechanical reproduction – Benjamin 1936). Verity Platt (2006) also has a fascinating essay on seals as imprints. There are connections between this kind of work and recent use of Peircean semiotics in archaeology (e.g. Preucel and Bauer 2001; Preucel 2006; Crossland 2009). What I want to do is take elements of each of these and look at one particular body of material to try to examine this question of the anachronic, and to throw a different light on this issue of material *itineraries*, or rather, non-itineraries, through time.

Seals and sealings in the Bronze Age Aegean

The material I examine here consists of the seals and sealings of the Bronze Age Aegean. They are made and used for more than a millennium, from the Early to Late Bronze Age. The seals are made in a wide range of materials, including ivory, soft and hard stones, and metals in the case of the gold finger rings (Krzyszkowska 2005; Weingarten 2010). Sealings – the impressions of seals in clay – were only ever meant to be temporary, and we find them solely as a result of accidental destruction by fire, often in palatial settings; only occasionally do we find seal impressions on fired objects like pots or loom weights (Krzyszkowska 2005). To give an idea of the partial nature of the sample left to us, in not a single case has a sealing been found that can be matched to its seal (ibid.). And yet the seal corpus is very large, with more than 10,000 motifs known from seals and their impressions. While the sealings are found principally in settlements, the seals themselves most often turn up in burials – which may reflect not only their value in general terms, but also their close association with the individual body, personal identity, and perhaps also their magico-religious status. It is this combination of features – the impermanence of sealings and the extreme portability of seals – that makes for an appropriate case study here, as they would appear at first glance to be the perfect incarnation of the *itineraries of the material*. Yet, the quality of substitution lent by the imprinting process creates temporalities that resist this easy characterization, rendering seals and sealings conversely immobile and persistent. Indeed, we should note the very term itself, *seal*, connoting something being secured, fastened, closed off.

The seals, miniature in scale, little more than 2 cm across in many cases, are carved (*intaglio*) with a wide variety of motifs, very often animals, and sometimes of great complexity. Hence the finest examples are given extended treatment in accounts of Aegean Bronze Age *art* (e.g. Higgins 1967; Hood 1978). This art historical dimension to the seals has some particular local relevance in that their systematic study has been conducted for some 50 years in Marburg (with the entire *Corpus der minoischen und mykenischen Siegel*, CMS for short, soon to be moved to Heidelberg). Yet while the material and iconography of the seals attract an art historical audience, their clay impressions, the sealings, draw another kind of scholarly interest: as sealings very often occur side by side with early writing, whether Cretan Hieroglyphic, Linear A or Linear B, it is epigraphers who tend to focus on the sealings, in order to understand administration and bureaucracy, which is what these were largely used in, as indeed in the earlier cases in the Near East. However, it should be noted that there is an important strand of research that works on sealings that occur *before* writing, and which is therefore more functional than epigraphic in approach (Schmandt-Besserat 1996; Ferioli *et al.* 1994; Frangipane 2007). This approach has itself figured significantly in work on Minoan sealings too (e.g. Fiandra 1968; Weingarten 1986; 2010).

No doubt as a result of these disciplinary fault lines, the study of seals and sealings in the Aegean Bronze Age is divided. Torn between art historical, epigraphic and functional approaches, they rarely draw the attention of many *anthropological* archaeologists. Only in one or two instances have they been treated within an anthropological framework, as in Andrew Shapland's recent work focusing on their animal motifs (Shapland 2010a; 2010b; forthcoming). The occasional exception aside, this leaves many features of these *forms* and *counterforms* lacking much explicit consideration (though, theoretically, the tireless work of the CMS at Marburg makes this possible). What I consider here – and this as one of those Aegean archaeologists who feels *outside* the study of seals – are the complex temporalities, or *anachronies*, that these imprinting devices and their imprints create.

First, I take a leaf out of Didi-Huberman's book (who in turn has taken one from Marcel Mauss). He stresses the particular importance of *gesture* in understanding imprints. It is gesture that links the body to the substrate and the eventual trace. Thinking about this solely from the perspective of the body, without any intervening artefacts, one can see how this applies well to the taking of a fingerprint. With a particular gesture, a fingerprint impression can be made in a substrate, whether plasticine or ink on paper, leaving a trace. This is a biometric imprint. With sealstones, we have an artefactual intervention between skin and substrate; nonetheless, gesture remains important, with different shapes implying different actions: flat-ended seals call for a stamping motion, those with a convex surface require a rolling from side to side, while cylinder seals demand a rolling out across a surface (see Malafouris 2008 on the imbrication of a Mycenaean signet ring into bodily schema and peripersonal space). Each time an impression is made the outcome may be slightly different, depending on the precise pressure exerted through the course of the gesture and the malleability of the clay (Fig. 3.1).

This also means, as Didi-Huberman notes, that there is a degree of openness and indeterminacy in the process. One only learns the result of contact once the contact comes to an end and the seal leaves the clay surface: absence has to follow presence to leave a trace. And from that moment on the nature of the loss, the no-longer-present seal (or finger, for that matter), is potentially troubling. Is the body, the person, responsible for that sealing action, long gone? In both space and time? Or still present, ready to make another impression? Is this the only impression that will be made with this seal, or are many more impressions soon to be made, or to be made at some undetermined time and place in the future?

Perhaps even more troubling are the doubts that might arise around the uniqueness of the seal and hence the authenticity of the impression. Leaving aside the phenomenon of "replica rings" (Weingarten 2010, 323), no two Minoan seals, even in this huge corpus, are alike, though there may of course be multiple sealings from a single seal (Fig. 3.2).

While sealings may, therefore, in theory be commonplace, the seal may still be unique. Indeed, it *must* be unique if the sense of authenticity is to be maintained: the impression cannot be an imitation or forgery because it has that direct physical link with the original. Yet, as Platt (2006) argues, this somehow makes forgery and duplicity all the more tempting: because of the trust that is placed in the directness of the link between seal and sealing, duplicating the original can be very rewarding. Didi-Huberman (2008) discusses the theme of imprinting and authenticity in relation to coins bearing the image of Caesar – created from a single stamp in Rome, signifying contact, but also with the potential for dissemination across the Empire. He suggests there is something magical in this process, referencing Frazer's notion of *contagious magic*, magic through contact (Frazer 2009 [1922], 11). Of course, an issued coin is designed to be rather more enduring

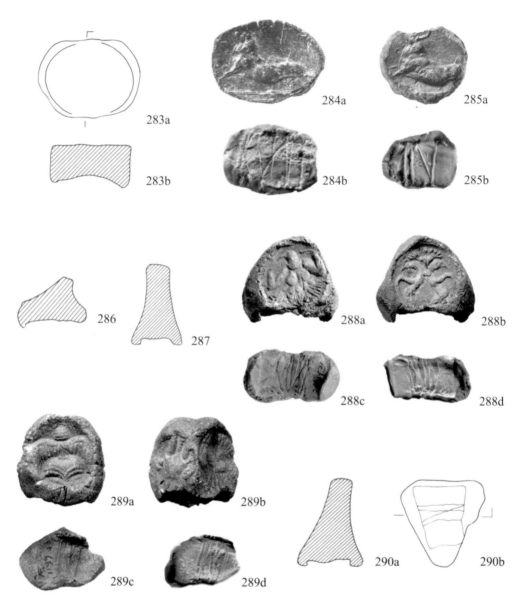

LM I flat-based nodules/'packets'. 283–285: Single-seal recumbent nodules from Ayia Triada (HMs 498 and 497) and Sklavokambos (HMs 628). These three nodules bear impressions of the same gold signet ring (see 368). 286: Two-seal recumbent nodule from Ayia Triada; section drawing. 287: Two-seal standing nodule from Zakros; profiles, reverse and impression of reverse. 289a–d: Three-seal standing nodule from Zakros; profiles, reverse and impression of reverse. 290a–b: Three-seal standing nodule from Zakros; drawings of section and underside.

Figure 3.1. Different kinds of Neopalatial sealings, with variable depth and clarity of impression (after Krzyszkowska 2005, 157).

than an Aegean sealing, with an intrinsic material value and an assumed universal applicability. Aegean sealings in clay not only had no such value, their meaning was restricted to a specific context, and they were only ever meant to be impermanent, lasting perhaps just one single administrative cycle (a matter of months?).

Even though Aegean sealings were less permanent than stamped Roman coins, they still must have held quite some weight for the duration of their existence. Perhaps their actual impermanence did not jeopardize their significance because the point is that they *could* last, no matter how long they might have actually lasted (just as fingerprints *may* last, even if often fleeting and sometimes erased). What is probably more important is the potential for replication: in the case of Caesar's coins, even if they were only kept in circulation for a matter of months, they would still carry weight because of the possibility of almost endless replication and the concomitant existence of multiple impressions. So whether the imprint lasts a day or a year is less important than the idea that the imprint indicates the existence of a stable, enduring form. This is important where authentication is concerned: when I sign my name, it matters less that the piece of paper is kept than it does that I can repeat the signature endlessly, in principle throughout my life. The same goes for my fingerprint – it can be reproduced endlessly and invariably if need be. Both have what appears to be the same advantage, of being intimately connected to one human body. But this can also be a disadvantage when contrasted with a portable artefact such as a sealstone or a signet ring, which can be passed down from one generation to another, promulgating a genealogy and extending authority inter-generationally. In this sense, then, the authority afforded by an imprint from a sealstone is more *stable* and *enduring* than an individual iconic sign written in Cretan Hieroglyphic or Linear A (in which we see quite some variation in the way the 90 different signs are inscribed). It is perhaps because of these complementary properties – which we may in a sense call the single generation individuality of a particular hand and the multi-generation communality of the seal impression – that the Minoan administrative system thoroughly integrated the two (Hallager 1996; Schoep 2002).

We can see that Minoan seals actually did have genealogies, in the example of multiple sealing episodes (see Fig. 3.2), as the Theran example dates from Late Minoan IA, and those from Crete occur in the following phase, Late Minoan IB, with a likely difference of at least a couple of generations. The inter-generational persistence of seals is also clearly seen in the Phaistos vano 25 archive: though dating to around 1700 BC, some seals in use were centuries old (Krzyszkowska 2005; see Fig. 3.3). Despite individual changes in the person, the *structural object*, whether family or elite status, goes on, held in place by the very permanence *and* transferability of the carved stone.

The seal's genealogical power is further accentuated in its iconography, materials and craftsmanship. Seal iconography is varied, with many different patterns and figures across the extensive Bronze Age corpus, but wild animals are especially prominent, as are supernatural figures such as griffins and Minoan genii, and complex scenes depicting hunting, bull-leaping and cult epiphany. As for materials, while in many cases local soft stones are used, numerous examples are carved in exotic hard stones imported from the Near East, not to mention the use of ivory and gold. In terms of craftsmanship, the extreme miniaturization of the scenes, with many seal surfaces only 1–2 cm across,

Ayia Triada (*CMS* Il.6 no. 43). 3 flat-based: 1 impression (HMs 497–499). Gournia (*CMS* Il.6 no. 161) 1 nodulus (HMs 101) Sklavokambos (*CMS* Il.6 no. 259) 2 flat-based: 1 impression (HMs 628–629) Zakros Palace (*CMS* Il.6 no. 39) 1 nodulus (HMs 1051)

Ayia Triada (*CMS* Il.6 no. 44). 1 flat-based: 1 impression (RMP 71974). Gournia (*CMS* Il.6 no. 162) 1 flat-based; 1 impression (HMs 102) Sklavokambos (*CMS* Il.6 no. 255) 1 flat-based: 1 impression (HMs 612)

Akrotiri (*CMS* V Suppl. 3 no. 391) 3 flat-based: 1 impression. Ayia Triada (*CMS* Il.6 no. 19). 1 flat-based: 1 impression (HMs 591); 1 flat-based: 2 impressions (HMs 516; combined with Il.6 no. 41); Sklavokambos (*CMS* Il.6 no. 260) 4 flat-based: 1 impression (HMs 628–629) Zakros Palace (*CMS* Il.6 no. 39) 1 nodulus (HMs 632–635)

Ayia Triada (*CMS* Il.6 no. 15). 3 flat-based: 1 impression (HMs 526/1–3); 2 flat-based: 2 impressions (HMs 595–596; combined with Il.6 no. 4, here 245). Knossos (*CMS* Il.8 no. 279) 1 nodulus (HMs 101) Sklavokambos (*CMS* Il.6 no. 259) 2 single-hole hanging (HMs 369, 1275)

Impressions from the same signet rings are attested at several Cretan sites in LM IB (368–371) and now at Akrotiri on Thera in LM IA (370). The known matches are listed here by site (with *CMS* numbers) and the specific nodules on which they are found.

Figure 3.2. Examples of multiple sealings at different sites made by the same rings (after Krzyszkowska 2005, 190).

coupled with the complexity of the motifs and the hardness of some of the stones, implies an extremely high level of artisanal skill that could surely only have been accessible to a select few. Krzyszkowska (2005, xxv) captures the larger-than-life aura of the finest Aegean seals when she describes them as "monuments in miniature".

Thus, the imprint, hovering between seal and sealing, is anachronic, in so far as it

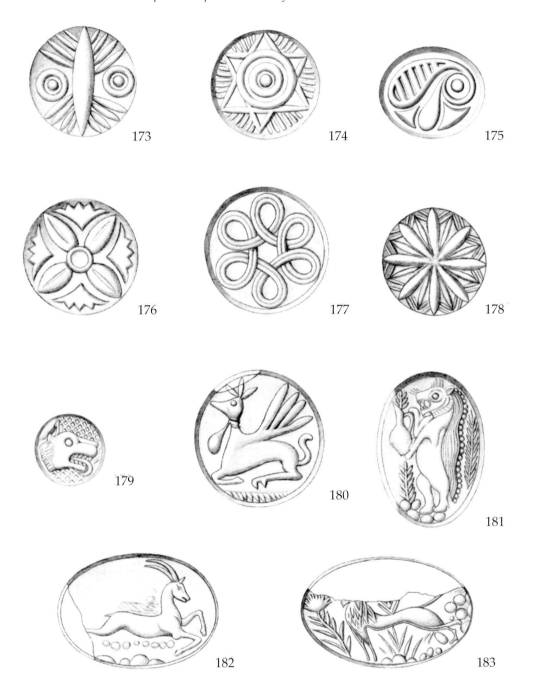

Figure 3.3. A selection of the sealings from Vano 25, Phaistos, showing the range of motifs and the continued use of much earlier seals (after Krzyszkowska 2005, 106).

collapses together past and present time. An imprint exists in the here and now but also presents quite blatantly another time, a prior time. It *presents* – not represents – both contact and loss. It presents an absence and shows its form. In this it highlights the possibilities for objects to resist movement; the imprint is anti-itinerary.

Other substitutions: Miniatures and skeuomorphs

Is this relationship to time something that comes out particularly in artworks (cf. Nagel and Wood 2010)? If so, one might try to examine the operation of similar processes of substitution in other categories of Minoan *art*. Two possible categories present themselves: miniatures and skeuomorphs. Both are extremely frequent in Aegean Bronze Age material culture, and both effect a form of substitution that might be considered anachronic. Let us briefly consider each of these categories in turn.

Miniatures could be taken to cover a broad range of material, from miniature figurines to stone vessels, not to mention the miniature scenes on seals. Here, for the sake of argument, I will only consider miniature ceramic vessels. While in Minoan Crete these are often found in burials and on peak sanctuaries, suggesting a close connection with ritual activities, they are also found in settlements. They take many forms, from cups and jugs to cooking pots and pithoi. Whether we interpret them as ritual artefacts, or toys, or in broader terms, they can readily be interpreted as *substitutes* for the full-scale, *real* vessels they mimic (Knappett 2012). Going further, these miniature substitutes may be considered anachronic because they condense, iconicise and hence stabilise form, partly by rendering the performance of function irrelevant. For example, if a full-scale pithos has the capacity to store hundreds of litres of olive oil, wine or grain, then a miniature pithos with a capacity of less than a litre is an afunctional, iconic substitute. Arguably, the miniature substitute is then an object *against* time, in the very sense of anachronic: it is an objectified version of a real thing, in suspended animation. Curiously, work on models and miniatures in other contexts has found some interesting temporal phenomena at play (Knappett 2012). Cognitive philosopher Andy Clark (2010) talks of the *temporal relaxation* at work in models; Susan Stewart (1993, 65) suggests that the miniature "skews the time and space relations of the everyday world"; and in a series of psychological experiments, Alton Delong (1983) shows that *spatial* compression (i.e. miniaturisation) can generate a proportionate *temporal* compression (see also Bailey 2005, 36–38). Each of these observations supports the notion of miniatures being anachronic, with complex temporalities blending together the past and the present.

Skeuomorphs are another distinctive category in Minoan material culture. Again, I focus here only on ceramic examples, that is to say, on pottery that mimics vessels more commonly made in another material, such as metal or stone. One of the clearest examples is a silver *kantharos* from Gournia that is very closely replicated in a ceramic version from Malia (Davis 1977). The latter can thus be said to operate as a substitute for the *missing* metal original. But in what way is this substitution anachronic? Most of these kinds of connections between crafts that we can identify in Minoan material culture seem to be synchronic rather than diachronic (Knappett forthcoming). However, the meaning of *skeuomorph* as first used in the 1880s was a little different; as Taylor (2010,

153) puts it, skeuomorphs are "carryovers from an older technology or way of doing things that had value, and are retained as a semblance, and expectation" (see also Frieman 2010). Taylor's example is *le voleur*, the distinctive indent in the bottom of a wine bottle, originally an inevitable feature of glass-blown bottles, but redundant now that bottles are mould-made. Still, it is retained as a carryover that has value. This is anachronic: a contemporary artefact carrying the past within it, as *survivance*. Can we see such cases in the material culture of Minoan Crete? Perhaps we can, though it has not been a focus of research. It may be that we should consider the long-term persistence of certain vessel shapes, such as rounded cups or bridge-spouted jars and jugs, in these terms. This would mean that the Late Minoan IA bridge-spouted jar would carry within it as a persistent survival the memory of the original bridge-spouted jars of Middle Minoan IA, continuously produced over the intervening five centuries or so.

We might easily turn to other emblematic forms of Minoan material culture to investigate the degree to which they are substitutional and anachronic. Yet it is arguably seals that best encapsulate the nature of Minoan art, not least in the eyes of Sir Arthur Evans (1894, 276), who wrote that "these minor relics of antiquity" are often "of greater archaeological importance than far more imposing monuments."

Conclusions

The move to think of artefacts as having biographies, social lives or itineraries has been a crucial development in the reinvigoration of material culture studies in the last 25 years. Arguably, it is one of the most stable points of common ground between archaeology and anthropology. But bringing artefacts to life and having them constantly in motion, both through time and space, can be rather dizzying and can at times make us forget some of their most critical features: durability, stability and persistence (Knappett 2011). This chapter does not seek to diminish the importance of the biographies or itineraries of materials, but rather seeks to counterbalance the common emphasis on movement with one that is grounded instead in non-movement, particularly the idea of persistence and survival over time. To this end, ideas of substitution and the anachronic, developed in both archaeological and art historical contexts, have proved extremely useful. This does not mean, of course, that I am advocating a return to the static view of material culture that so many scholars have worked hard to overturn, but rather, to find ways in which we might more fully grasp how artefacts are *actively durable* over time.

Acknowledgements

I would like to thank Annabel Bokern, Hans Peter Hahn and Hadas Weiss for the invitation to the conference, where we were all warmly received into an intellectually stimulating environment. I have discussed some of the themes in this chapter with Elana Steingart and thank her warmly for her input. I am grateful for the helpful comments of the anonymous reviewer. Olga Krzyszkowska very kindly provided the figures. Any errors remain my own.

References

Bailey, D. W. (2005) *Prehistoric figurines: Representation and corporeality in the Neolithic.* London, Routledge.

Benjamin, W. (1936) The work of art in the age of mechanical reproduction. In H. Arendt (ed.) (1970) *Illuminations: Walter Benjamin: Essays and reflections. Edited and with an introduction by Hannah Arendt,* 219–253. London, Cape.

Clark, A. (2010) Material surrogacy and the supernatural: Reflections on the role of artefacts in 'off-line' cognition. In L. Malafouris and C. Renfrew (eds) *The cognitive life of things: Recasting the boundaries of the mind.* McDonald Institute Monographs, 23–28. Cambridge, McDonald Institute for Archaeological Research.

Crossland, Z. (2009) Of clues and signs: The dead body and its evidential traces. *American Anthropologist* 111 (1), 69–80.

Davis, E. N. (1977) *The Vapheio cups and Aegean gold and silver ware.* New York, Garland.

Delong, A. (1983) Spatial scale, temporal experience and information processing: An empirical examination of experiential reality. *Man-Environment Systems* 13, 77–86.

Didi-Huberman, G. (2008) *La ressemblance par contact. Archéologie, anachronisme et modernité de l'empreinte.* Paris, Les Editions de Minuit.

Evans, A. (1894) Primitive pictographs and a prae-Phoenician script, from Crete and the Peloponnese. *Journal of Hellenic Studies* 14, 270–372.

Ferioli, P.; Fiandra, E.; Fissore, G. G. and Frangipane, M. (eds) (1994) *Archives before writing: Proceedings of the International Colloquium at Oriolo Romano, October 23-25, 1991.* CIRAAS, 1. Torino, Scriptorium.

Fiandra, E. (1968) A che cosa servivano le cretule di Festòs. *Pepragmena tou B' Diethnous Kretologikou Synedriou,* 383–397.

Frangipane, M. (ed.) (2007) *Arslantepe Cretulae: An early centralised administrative system before writing.* Arslantepe, 5. Roma, Edizioni CIRAAS.

Frazer, J. G. (2009 [1922]). *The golden bough: A study in magic and religion.* New York, Cosimo.

Frieman, C. (2010) Imitation, identity and communication: The presence and problems of skeuomorphs in the Metal Ages. In B. V. Eriksen (ed.) *Lithic technology in metal using societies: Proceedings of a UISPP Workshop, Lisbon, September 2006,* 33–44. Højbjerg, Jutland Archaeological Society.

Gosden, C. and Marshall, Y. (1999) The cultural biography of objects. *World Archaeology* 31 (2), 169–178.

Hallager, E. (1996) The Minoan roundel and other sealed documents in the Neopalatial Linear A administration: Volumes 1 & 2. *Annales d'archéologie égéenne de l'Université de Liège.* Aegaeum, 14.

Higgins, R. A. (1967) *Minoan and Mycenaean art.* London, Thames and Hudson.

Hood, M. S. F. (1978) *The arts in prehistoric Greece.* Harmondsworth, Penguin.

Hoskins, J. (1998) *Biographical objects: How things tell the stories of people's lives.* New York and London, Routledge.

Joy, J. (2009) Reinvigorating object biography: Reproducing the drama of object lives. *World Archaeology* 41 (4), 540–556.

Knappett, C. (2011) Networks of objects: Meshworks of things. In T. Ingold (ed.) *Redrawing anthropology: Materials, movements, lines.* Anthropological Studies of Creativity and Perception, 45–63. Farnham and Burlington, Ashgate.

Knappett, C. (2012) Meaning in miniature: Semiotic networks in material culture. In M. Jensen, N. Johanssen and H. J. Jensen (eds) *Excavating the mind: Cross-sections through culture, cognition and materiality,* 87–109. Aarhus, Aarhus University Press.

Knappett, C. (forthcoming) Materials, material worlds and materialities of the prehistoric Aegean. In R. Doonan, S. Sherratt and C. Tsoraki (eds) *Material worlds of the Aegean*. Oxford, Oxbow.

Kopytoff, I. (1986) The cultural biography of things: Commoditization as process. In A. Appadurai (ed.) *The social life of things: Commodities in cultural perspective*, 64–91. Cambridge, Cambridge University Press.

Krauss, R. (1985) *The originality of the avant-garde and other modernist myths*. Cambridge, MA, MIT Press.

Krzyszkowska, O. (2005) *Aegean seals: An introduction. Bulletin of the Institute of Classical Studies*, Supplement, 85. London, Institute of Classical Studies, School of Advanced Study.

Malafouris, L. (2008) Between brains, bodies and things: Tectonoetic awareness and the extended self. *Philosophical Transactions of the Royal Society of London, Series B: Biological Sciences* 363 (1499), 1993–2002.

Nagel, A. and Wood, C. S. (2010) *Anachronic Renaissance*. New York, Zone Books.

Olivier, L. (2004) The past of the present: Archaeological memory and time. *Archaeological Dialogues* 10 (2), 204–213.

Olivier, L. (2008) *Le sombre abîme du temps. Mémoire et archéologie*. Paris, Seuil.

Platt, V. (2006) Making an impression: Replication and the ontology of the Graeco-Roman seal stone. *Art History* 29 (2), 233–257.

Preucel, R. (2006) *Archaeological semiotics*. Oxford, Blackwell.

Preucel, R. and Bauer, A. A. (2001) Archaeological pragmatics. *Norwegian Archaeological Review* 34 (2), 85–96.

Runia, E. (2006) Presence. *History and Theory* 45 (1), 1–29.

Schmandt-Besserat, D. (1996) *How writing came about*. Austin, University of Texas Press.

Schoep, I. (2002) *The administration of Neopalatial Crete: A critical assessment of the Linear A Tablets and their role in the administrative process*. Minos, Supplement, 17. Salamanca, Ediciones Universidad de Salamanca.

Shapland, A. (2010a) Wild nature? Human-animal relations on Neopalatial Crete. *Cambridge Archaeological Journal* 20 (1), 109–127.

Shapland, A. (2010b) The Minoan lion: Presence and absence on Bronze Age Crete. *World Archaeology* 42 (2), 273–289.

Shapland, A. (forthcoming) *Over the horizon: Human-animal relations in Bronze Age Crete*. Cambridge, Cambridge University Press.

Shils, E. A. (1981) *Tradition*. Chicago, University of Chicago Press.

Stewart, S. (1993) *On longing: Narratives of the miniature, the gigantic, the souvenir, the collection*. London, Duke University Press.

Taylor, T. (2010) *The artificial ape: How technology changed the course of human evolution*. New York, Palgrave Macmillan.

Warburg, A. (1999) *The renewal of pagan antiquity. Introduction by Kurt W. Forster. Translation by David Britt*. Los Angeles, Getty Research Institute.

Weingarten, J. (1986) The sealing structures of Minoan Crete: MM II Phaistos to the destruction of the palace of Knossos. *Oxford Journal of Archaeology* 5 (3), 279–298.

Weingarten, J. (2010) Minoan seals and sealings. In E. Cline (ed.) *The Oxford handbook of the Aegean Bronze Age*, 317–328. Oxford, Oxford University Press.

Chapter 4

The sacred king, royal containers, alienable material contents, and value in contemporary Cameroon

Jean-Pierre Warnier

Introduction

This chapter deals with subjects, objects, substances and materialities, their mobility and their value in a contemporary Cameroon kingdom. The practical rules obtaining in the kingdom are, so to speak, as follows. The body of the king is a container. When the king performs libations to his ancestors, it is understood that his bodily substances are invested with ancestral life essence bestowed on him by the deceased kings. This is never said in so many words, but it is done in practice, it is performed. The king stores these substances in his body and gives them out to his people. These substances are his saliva, breath, speech and semen. Being of limited supply, they are increased by several other substances such as raffia wine, palm oil, various medicines and crimson camwood powder. The king does not only store such substances in his body. He makes use of various containers embodied in his *Körperschema* (see Schilder 1923; 1935). The containers are raffia bags, drinking horns, calabashes, clay pots, wooden drums and mortars, houses, the palace and the city.

These containers (body and objects) share a common structure of an envelope and one or several apertures. Any object belongs to one of two categories, either container or contents. Containers included in other containers belong to both categories, like Russian dolls. Motricity is essential to such a royal practice: bodies, objects and substances pass through the apertures, either when going into or coming out of any envelope/container, thus defining specific itineraries of the material. Subjects and objects such as a foetus, the new-born, children, people, houses, utensils, tools, subsistence goods, personal belongings, crops, livestock, bank notes, motorbikes and mobile phones belong to a broad category of material objects that circulate between various containers and are ultimately distributed between the kingdom as an envelope and what is outside it in general. When on the move, the king and his subjects implement technologies of the self and of power by making use of the bodily and material culture of containers and contents. These technologies of power outline a governmentality, that is, a network of actions on other people's actions, which results in shaping their subjectivity and subjecting them to a sovereignty.[1]

Itineraries

What matters in the governmentality of the containers and contents of this kingdom is the way subjects, material objects and substances are on the move. One would have to outline more precisely the notions of substances, objects, bodies and materialities – a point I will have to take for granted for lack of space, although I should not. They shift or are shifted from one place to another, from inside to outside and vice versa. In order to illustrate this point, let us consider a few ethnographic examples, past and present.

To this day, men seldom go about without a bag, nor women without a basket. Nowadays, older men favour a raffia bag manufactured locally. More acculturated people make use of various kinds of shoulder bags purchased in the market place. The more sophisticated go around with an attaché case. The more traditional raffia bags may have one or two compartments. Ordinary, untitled men use a one-compartment raffia bag of square or rectangular shape, with a shoulder strap attached to its two upper corners. The bag is open along the whole length of its upper side. Its owner always carries in his bag at least a drinking horn, a mug or a cup. He may take it out when sitting in a bar, a funeral or any get-together in order to have his share of beer, raffia wine or other drinks. He may also carry cigarettes, tobacco, kola nuts, snacks, a mobile phone or any other belongings in his bag.

Notables who enjoy a lineage or palace title have a different sort of bag. It is rectangular, just like the more ordinary one, but is made of three pieces of raffia textile of identical dimensions sewn together on three sides, leaving the upper side open. Consequently, it has two separate compartments, with their apertures running along the top. However, the apertures of the two compartments are of different sizes: a large one, running all along the width of the bag, and a shorter one, just large enough for one to pass one's hand through it. The notable stores different kinds of objects in the two different pouches. In the more open one, he puts things that anyone may have access to, such as kola nuts, cigarettes and snacks. In the less open one, he keeps his more personal belongings, like his drinking horn, powerful objects or medicines, and his wallet. The fabric of the notable's bag consists of finer raffia fibres than the ordinary bag. It is dyed in various colours, tightly woven and adorned with various attachments.

Men often address each other by saying: *What have you got in your bag for me?* Or *Where is my kola nut?* Unlike in Western countries, the cycle of exchange of gifts and counter-gifts begins with a request, not an offer. Requesting a gift conveys a message of friendship. But, more importantly, one may search the bag of a friend without warning and extract from it a kola nut or a cigarette. One may search the simpler bag of a commoner or the compartment provided with a larger opening in a notable's bag, but never the pouch of the latter provided with a smaller opening. A notable is someone who identifies with a bag with two inner spaces, one that contains alienable goods that can be shared out, and one in which the man of substance will keep his more restricted, inalienable contents. A notable is someone who enjoys some sort of interiority.

When I was doing fieldwork, my status entitled me to make use of a notable's raffia bag with two compartments. However, the latter was too small and inconvenient to contain my notebooks, camera, drinking cup, wallet and the like, in addition to miscellaneous gifts. My favourite bag was a kind of *Samsonite* shoulder bag with a smaller pouch in front for my wallet and two larger compartments each equipped with a zip. When calling on friends and informants, I used to put small gifts of kola nuts, soap bars, beer, tobacco and, once in a while, a fathom of cloth into one of the two larger compartments, and I would leave its zip open. The other compartment contained my notebooks, camera and personal belongings. Usually, I kept it closed. Most of the time, when approaching the compound I was about to visit, I announced myself by shouting *kwa kwa*, which is the equivalent of ringing a door bell or knocking on the door. There and then a couple of children would approach me, grab the shoulder bag, usually without saying much, and disappear into one of the houses with it. Once I was seated in the parlour, my bag would be promptly brought back to me, with all my personal belongings in the closed compartment and emptied of whatever I had stored in the larger compartment I had left open. It was taken for granted that the bag contained something for the household and that it could be appropriated without even waiting for me to offer the gifts. If I had planned to pay a visit and to give out gifts to other people later the same day, I had to parcel up the gifts in two different bags and inform the children of my intentions.

We are dealing here with several categories of material objects. The first, as already mentioned, are predicated on the distinction between containers and contents. Furthermore, we find two different categories of containers, accessible to all, or restricted. They are respectively related to two categories of contents, alienable or inalienable – an important distinction made by Annette Weiner (1992). Such distinctions match different kinds of itineraries and different kinds of subjects.

Let me now reflect briefly on the relationship between these containers/contents and itineraries on the one hand, and what Appadurai (1986) called different regimes of value on the other hand. Alienable goods are endowed with exchange value in a gift/counter-gift relationship or on the market. Inalienable goods are endowed with another kind of value, more related to the status of the king or the notable, his inherited belongings, and his relationship to the deceased elders and to his own successors. I will comment further on this point later.

Sacred kingship and the mobility of things and persons

Returning to the itineraries of the material, a full discussion would need to be fleshed out with more ethnographic descriptions. I will content myself with a general statement and a couple of examples. What is Grassfields sacred kingship all about? This region was and still is criss-crossed by marriage alliance and diplomatic networks, together with long-distance trading in luxury goods and regional exchanges of subsistence goods. This has been the case for centuries, if not millennia (see Warnier 1985). People and things are highly mobile on this 'African frontier', as Igor Kopytoff (1987) would call it, that is, a space open to the mobility of people and things, and to the production of new political entities. In such an open space, they roam at large and without restriction; 'unmoored' is the term used by Appadurai (1997, 31) to qualify them, because it conveys the idea of something that has lost the moorage it had in its local place of origin and drifts haphazardly on the oceans. Most kingdoms in the area, such as the kingdom of Mankon, include descent groups and individuals of multiple origins, and people speaking different languages. They are composite kingdoms. In an area the size of Belgium, linguists have identified some 50 genetically related but mutually unintelligible languages. Many women who married into the kingdom came (and still come) from other, neighbouring polities.

In such a regional context where people and things are constantly shifting place, the burden of kingship consists in producing locality, some sort of boundedness, with an inside and an outside, and in assigning people and things to the local, while maintaining exchanges and communications between the inside and the outside. Furthermore, the contents of the kingdom must be wrought into a unified polity by bestowing on them the royal, ancestral, unifying substances contained in the king's body, and by the constant maintenance of the kingdom's envelope, together with its apertures. The logic of the governmentality of containers, contents and fluxes, or itineraries, is a consequence of the historical situation I have mentioned. Needless to say it is constantly put to the test by all the fissiparous and centripetal forces at work within and outside the kingdom, such as conflicts over the succession, people, land and other resources, not to speak of witchcraft accusations.

Cases of itineraries

Having provided my general statement, I will now turn to a couple of itineraries of the material. The first is taken from market exchange. This is an old practice in the area under consideration. Currencies, local and regional market places, professional traders and rotating credit associations are well documented as having existed for at least the last two centuries (see Warnier 1985). However, well into the twentieth century the market economy was embedded in the local and regional hierarchies. In the twentieth century, and especially after World War II, market exchange increasingly escaped the control of the kingdoms' notables and became disembedded. Younger men migrated *en masse* to the major cities of Cameroon, Nigeria and Gabon, as well as further away to Europe and the United States. Their earnings and remittances in cash gave them access to things that were formerly considered luxuries reserved for the use of kings and notables and frozen into the corporate estates of the latter's descent groups. They also blurred the boundaries between alienable and inalienable goods. A material culture of success developed (see Rowlands 1996), together with the rise of businessmen and women who did not enjoy any adequate status in the kingdom hierarchy. The itineraries of material things were reshaped to include the coastal areas, labour migrations and men of commoner status.

The progressive shift from an embedded market economy to a more international, urban and salaried economy provided a whole range of itineraries of the material. In the mid-nineteenth century, slaves, trade guns, cloths, cowries, Toby jugs, brass rods, beads, etc. circulated between the compounds of high-ranking notables and kings along a few major trade routes. Except for slaves, all the goods were parcelled and wrapped up so as to keep them hidden from the gaze of ordinary persons. In the early 21st century, the political economy of such noble exchanges has been subverted by migrant labour and the rise of a category of businessmen and politicians who have been co-opted into the hegemonic alliance that has been ruling Cameroon since independence.

However, the kingdoms have not been disqualified by such deep changes in the political economy of Africa. Since the early 1980s, the kings have made a spectacular come back on the political stage (see Perrot and Fauvelle-Aymar 2003). They had been pushed aside at the time of independence by the construction of independent, modernizing states that endeavoured to move away from the more traditional forms of authority. Twenty years after independence, the failure of African states could not be denied. The kings offered alternative and more legitimate sources of authority that were more in tune with the neoliberal turn of the 1980s and the craze for civil society. They were therefore co-opted into the hegemonic alliance ruling Cameroon. This move has opened up a space for the invention of royal traditions and the siphoning off of the new class of wealthy business operators and politicians into the reinvented kingdoms. Posh cars can be seen in the car park in front of the palace. Wealthy people make ceremonial payments in order to acquire titles of nobility. They undergo the ritual called *miye* in order to obtain the right to address the king without resorting to the service of a speaker and go-between. They commute between the town where they work and the kingdom, in which they make it a point to build a house and will be buried when they die. The conservative modernization of many African states has created new forms of inequality and hierarchy.

Another ethnographic example of interest here is the development of the virtual envelope of the kingdom through the Internet. I would like to challenge the trope of the virtual as something immaterial. The *Mankon* diaspora in the USA, Europe and urban Africa is deeply entrenched in the material culture of success. It has computers, digital cameras, mobile phones and the Internet. It has acquired the bodily culture and the techniques of the body that are attuned to such material culture. Members of this diaspora know how to type, how to make the proper wired or wireless connections, how to transfer digital photographs on *Picasa*, etc. The migrations from the kingdom to urban centres in Cameroon and foreign universities, to the UK and the USA by medical doctors, lawyers, nurses and the like entail the acquisition of the corresponding urban material culture and the intertwining of the itineraries of people and things. At face value, this seems to challenge the capacity of the kingdom to encompass its population within its bounded territory. Yet, King Ngwa'fo of Mankon has been quick to react. Like many of his peers, he has developed means of producing a virtual envelope to encompass his subjects despite their dispersal into the various diasporas.

King Ngwa'fo succeeded his father in 1959, on the eve of independence. Being one of the first university graduates in the mandated territories (he had read agricultural engineering in Ibadan, Nigeria), he was co-opted by the British onto the committee in charge of preparing the independence referendum. Ever since, he has never left national politics at the highest level. In early 2000, he created an association, the *Mankon Cultural Development Association* (MACUDA), which was soon provided with several websites in different countries. In 2009, he celebrated his golden jubilee. Two years earlier, in 2007, he toured the *Mankon* diaspora in the USA in order to stimulate its support. As far as I can ascertain, it was his third journey outside Cameroon, with the exception of his university studies in Nigeria. His itinerary took him from Boston to Chicago via

Minneapolis, Houston etc., meeting MACUDA members along the way and performing the *miye* ritual with the leaders of the local groups.

The outcome of all these shifts in contexts is a constant reshaping of the itineraries of the material. The major shifts are the following: from regional networks and their socio-political hierarchies to a disembedded market economy; from regional hierarchies of kingdoms to a hegemonic alliance in an African state; from the material culture of the traditional village to that of an African modernity with its various components (money, banking, salaried or self-employment, imported goods, cars and mobile phones, and Christian churches with their specific and usually overwhelming material cultures). However, the king and the kingdom have survived these shifts in context, and the governmentality of containers, contents and fluxes has been redefined rather than destroyed and discarded, to such an extent that, in the early 21st century, one may identify recognizable regimes of value, however fragile and unstable they may be in a context of very rapid and deep change, together with growing political, social and economic inequality incorporating the old kingdom hierarchies into the new wealthy classes.

Value

In dealing with value, I will follow the interpretation of Georg Simmel given by Appadurai (1986) and the comments I have elaborated on its basis (see Warnier 2009). The gist of the argument relies on the fact that the value of goods and services does not pre-exist the act of exchanging them. Exchange takes place between two or more subjects. The value of the things exchanged results from the desire of each subject to acquire something that is owned by another subject. The value of a given item is measured by whatever one is willing to sacrifice (most clearly in terms of money) in order to acquire the desired good. Such an approach does not consider value as something that inheres in the good, as in the Marxist labour theory of value, but as something that depends on the relations between different people, that is, on various politics of value. I will take this approach as a touchstone in assessing the value of the material things and persons/bodies that circulate along given itineraries within and around the kingdom.

Let us return to what I described at the beginning of this article. The king goes every week and more formally every year to the ancestral graveyard, where he makes offerings to the dead kings. Whenever the offerings are accepted, *ipso facto* it is understood (but never said in so many words) that the bodily substances of the king (breath, speech, saliva, semen) and their extensions (palm oil, camwood powder, raffia wine, medicines) are invested with the life and reproductive essence owned by the ancestors. Theirs is the single spring of all life, production and reproduction in the kingdom. The burden of kingship consists in obtaining, storing and giving out such substances to the people while building up the envelopes in which people, substances and things are contained, and by controlling the apertures through which things, substances and people may circulate and be transformed in the process. Similarly, every descent group head does the same as regards his own ancestors and the members of his descent group.

Consequently, each and every subject in the kingdom is considered to owe his life and wealth (livestock, crops, salary, earnings, material belongings) to his own descent group head and to the king, and, through them, ultimately to the deceased elders, the source of all life and reproduction on earth. Each and every subject has contracted a life debt that cannot be paid back in any way. Therefore, the bodily substances of the king and of the descent group heads are priceless, endowed with a *value beyond any value*. They are the most desirable things that any subject might want to acquire. Anyone would be willing to make costly sacrifices in order to acquire them.

As regards the itineraries, let me sketch a few of them. During the annual festival, a palace steward pours raffia wine contained in a royal calabash into the buffalo drinking horn held by the king. The king takes the wine into his mouth, where it is mixed with his saliva. There and then, the king sprays the mixture on the people around him so that it can reach the skin of his subjects, that is, their bodily envelope. He may also give it to people to drink by pouring the raffia wine from his cup into their hands joined in front of their mouths as a sort of gutter or funnel. The king has his notables take camwood powder from the royal bag and smear it on the skin of his subjects on various occasions. Camwood powder is made from the wood of *Pterocarpus soyanxii*, a forest tree. It is harvested in the forest areas to the southwest of the Grassfields, cut into small pieces and traded by medicine men in all the market places in the Grassfields, where it can be purchased by anyone. Kings and notables have it purchased, ground with a grinding stone, put into a raffia bag and taken with them when they perform libations to the ancestors. When the libations have taken place, it is understood that the life essence of the deceased elders inheres in the camwood power contained in the bag. Pinches of it are then taken out of the bag, to be smeared directly on the skin of the king's subjects and on material things on various occasions, or mixed with palm oil in a mixing bowl called *azo'* to be smeared on people's skin.

Being considered the most fertile man in the kingdom, since his body is plugged straight into the ancestral source of life's essence, the king has many wives (*c.* 100 early in the twentieth century, some 30 around 2010). He has sexual intercourse with them following an elaborate court etiquette. His real or titular mother is in charge of designating the royal spouses who are expected to have intercourse with him on a given day or night. In the past, intercourse took place on a carved wooden bed lined with leopard pelts. Thus, each royal material substance (saliva, raffia wine, camwood, medicines, etc.) follows a specific itinerary from harvest or production, through various containers (including the body of the king or his subjects) and through their apertures. All of them, including the doors of the palace and the houses, and most orifices of the body, etc. are designated by the single lexeme *ntsu*, that is, *mouth*.

Within this category of *value beyond value*, one may distinguish between the inalienable containers and the alienable contents. The epitome of the inalienable containers is the king's body and all his embodied vessels: drinking horn, garments, palace, royal bags, wooden drums and mortars, calabashes, houses, courtyards and the city. Most of them cannot be touched by ordinary persons; they are sacred. This is the case with the king's body and the things and persons that are close to it (spouses, drinking horn, garments). People who attend to the king and have to touch his body must ingest the same apotropaic medicines he takes on a daily basis. Accordingly, we have two kinds

Figure 4.1. The king, his body, and his incorporated containers, Mankon, December 2009 (Photo by Manuela Zips-Mairitsch).

of *value beyond value*: the value beyond value of the inalienable containers, and the value beyond value of the alienable ancestral contents (Fig. 4.1).

Since the contents are alienable and given out by the king, they call for something in return. However, whatever is given to the king in return for his ancestral life substances cannot in any way match the value beyond value of the material substances inherent with life essence. It is not a counter gift or a payment, since a life debt cannot be extinguished. It is no more than a token that acknowledges the existence of the debt. In the past, people brought a number of bodily or material items to the palace: daughters of commoner status as spouses for the king, boys as retainers, servants, livestock, subsistence goods and money.

Exchange value

The life substances given out by the king and by the descent group heads to their subjects are deemed to irrigate their lives and activities. They provide the reproductive and productive principles of their daily lives. The outcome can be seen in their having many children (explicitly requested from the dead elders whenever libations are offered to them), good health, abundant crops, prolific livestock and lucrative activities. Children (men and women) fetch an exchange value in the sphere of rights in persons. Being endowed with exchange value, crops, livestock, manufactured objects and services fetch a given price in the market place. Over the last two centuries at least – and probably much longer – market exchange, together with market places, currencies, rotating credit associations, etc. have been common practice in the Grassfields, forming a regional system of economic specialization and trade above and beyond domestic production (see Warnier 1985). Nowadays, any man who earns money as a taxi-driver, salaried worker or street hawker feels the urge to give some of his earnings to the elder who channels the life essence of the ancestors towards him. How far this obligation is felt as regards the king is not clear at first glance. Ordinary persons seldom call at the palace. Obligations towards the king are met mostly by proxy through descent-group heads, notables and the modern elite. Wealthy members of the emerging middle and upper classes may call at the palace and pay their dues in money and kind to obtain the privilege of speaking directly to the king.

Accordingly, exchange value is not entirely disconnected from the value beyond value of the alienable ancestral life substances that are given to the people. It is perceived as a product of the latter, and should return to its source as a token of acknowledgment for the life debt contracted by any subject of the kingdom.

Spheres of exchange

In the mid-1950s, Paul Bohannan (1955) analysed a similar system of exchange, that of the Tiv of Nigeria. Later on, his analysis of various spheres of exchange was found to have some (if sometimes limited) relevance all over Africa and beyond or, at least, to provide a helpful trope in sorting out different kinds of exchange. Igor Kopytoff (1986) made it a key issue in his analysis of "the cultural biography of things" and people. At least four spheres of exchange can be identified in the case of the Grassfields kingdoms.

The first sphere concerns the ancestral sphere of the exchange of libations and speech given by the living to the dead, against life essence given by deceased kings and lineage elders to their lieutenants on earth, that is, the Pot-king and the notables-containers. The latter store the material life substances in their bodies, bags, calabashes, etc. The second sphere of exchange is concerned with rights in persons. The life substances given to the subjects produce children – male and female – who are considered to be the children of the notable who stores and provides the life essence of the descent group. The genitor is only seen as the *stud* who impregnates his partner on behalf of the man whom he considers his father (see Warnier 2007, 212). Rights in children may be negotiated for someone else. For example, in the past, commoner lineages provided girls as spouses and boys as retainers to the king without compensation since they are considered to be the product of the royal life substances, and the king would compensate by giving a wife to a retainer who had completed his time of service at the palace. Until the 1920s, the Grassfields were heavily involved in the slave trade with the coastal areas. The sale of slaves and the marriage alliance systems belonged to the same sphere of exchange, and in some cases (for example, that of Bangwa – see Brain 1972) they developed into a single system in which a notable would have control over the marriage rights of a number of girls that he would give out in marriage to low-ranking men without any other compensation than a similar marriage right over the girls to be born of these unions.

The third sphere is concerned with the exchange of ancestral life substances for goods and services that fetch a given price in the market place. In the words of Bohannan, this can be considered a kind of conversion between goods belonging to two different spheres of exchange, as opposed to the conveyance of goods belonging to a single sphere of exchange. However, the Tiv, studied by Bohannan, saw conversion as something shameful and exceptional. By contrast, in Mankon and the Western Grassfields, it is seen as something acceptable and even esteemed. Any young man must bring money and market goods to his maternal grandfather, who provided his daughter as the young man's mother. Sons must bring things and money to their father as return goods for the life debt they have contracted with him. Indeed, no equivalence is established between life substances and market goods: the latter are taken only as tokens of acknowledgment for the life debt. However, this type of transaction is practised on a routine basis. It is legitimate, although it combines some aspects of conveyance with some aspects of conversion. I am tempted to consider it the core practice of a specific sphere of exchange.

The fourth sphere of exchange concerns ordinary gift exchange and the market economy, whether embedded in the local and regional hierarchies or not, depending on historical circumstances.

On top of all four spheres of exchange, there is a layer constituted by the inalienable containers. This is not a sphere of exchange properly speaking since exchange is barred from it. It is made of the bodily and material containers of life substances. They are not given out or exchanged, but transmitted along the vertical axis of descent, between the dead and the living, and between one generation and the next.

Thus, to comment again on the contribution of Annette Weiner, no inalienable container is of any use unless there is an alienable content to be stored, kept, poured out and transformed in the process, and no content can be handled unless there is a suitable container to store it. This is a kind of embodied proof that alienable and inalienable things (persons and goods) are tightly intertwined. Neither of the two broad sets of categories (containers and contents, inalienable and alienable) makes any sense on its own. Furthermore, what I wish to underscore by stretching Bohannan's categories to fit the Grassfields case is the fact that container and contents are not all of the same kind: there is a hierarchy of containers and contents as regards their degree of alienability. Yet, there are systems of conversion between the different rungs of the hierarchical ladder corresponding to various regimes of value all the way from the life essence inhering in the dead elders that has no price to the mundane exchange of goods that fetch a given, limited price in the market.

Itineraries of the material in an African context and in Western societies

It could be said that such a system of itineraries and values is heavily embedded in the materiality of bodies, things and material substances because it is taken from an African (read *primitive*) civilization. I contend that this would be to misconstrue the data reflecting a Eurocentric bias to the effect that Africans are closer to nature, materiality and the body, whereas Westerners are closer to civilization, logos, speech and the intellect. Actually, our modern (some would say post-modern) Western societies are as deeply embedded in bodily and material cultures as is the kingdom of Mankon. In these two cases, however, the subjects are not conscious of their dependence upon the material and upon bodily substances. This requires an explanation.

In my view, the blindness of both African and European civilisations as regards their dependence on things material is the result of the gap between two different kinds of human knowledge: practical, procedural, embodied knowledge on the one hand, and verbalized, propositional knowledge on the other. The first is sealed away in what specialists in the cognitive sciences call the cognitive unconscious. I am conscious of the fact that I know how to ride a bicycle. I can say: *I know how to ride a bicycle*. However, I do not have any awareness of the billions of synapses in my nervous system and of the way my brain sends billions of impulses to the many muscles of my body, legs and arms, with the effect that I can steer the bike and peddle it in a highly coordinated way so as to move along without losing my balance. I would be at a loss to explain in so many words how I steer my muscles and nerves in order to obtain the desired result. Knowing how to peddle a bicycle effortlessly and without losing one's balance is acquired by non-verbal apprenticeship. Therefore it is possible to name it, but certainly not to express how it works. We simply do not pay attention to the way it works; we are satisfied with doing it and not talking about it.

Similarly, the king and his subject do not pay attention to the many things they do when they tap raffia wine, collect and grind camwood, manufacture and make use of drinking horns, bags, mixing bowls etc. All this seems to belong to the ordinary and mundane logistics of life that hardly surfaces to the awareness of the subjects, except when it fails. It belongs mostly to procedural, non-propositional knowledge. As the saying goes in Sri Lanka, *Fish don't talk about the water*. Similarly, Michel Foucault (1976; 1984a; 1984b) has emphasised how the techniques of the self and of power address the body and make use of material *dispositifs* outside any sophisticated awareness on the part of the subject. As a result, they may be smuggled into the subjectivity of people without much discussion. Speech and verbalized knowledge often play the role of a decoy attracting the gaze of people away from the material and bodily practices that impinge on their subjectivity.

Another aspect of this question of awareness comes from the fact that neither the king nor any of his subjects can conceive of any other way of doing things; it is the only one they know and practice. Until recently, they had no access to other, alternative ways of doing things. This ethnocentric bias does not favour any critical awareness of the cultural and local dimensions of their own practice. The same remark could be made as regards contemporary Western societies: in spite of the globalization of cultural fluxes, Europeans remain parochial in the knowledge of their idiosyncrasies when it comes to their own bodily and material practices.

This type of bias and the duality of human knowledge on which it rests are sufficient to disqualify any ethnographic enquiry based exclusively on the statements of one's informants. One has to develop a praxeological enquiry and assess it against the vernacular verbal knowledge shared by the members of a given society.

The present contribution acknowledges the existence of some kind of agency exercised by material things, as does Bruno Latour (1991). In the present case, the things that may be considered as exercising an agency of sorts pertain to the material and bodily culture of containers and contents. However, I depart from Latour when he considers all the components of a human/non-human collective as being equally endowed with agency. The only capacity to act that I would take into consideration is that of the human subject. The agency of material things only comes from the fact that the latter are incorporated in the *Körperschema* of any subject thanks to the acquisition of the appropriate procedural knowledge. For example, camwood power may indeed be considered as having some kind of agency, but only in so far as it is contained in royal containers embodied by the king and put into motion by him or any surrogate, therefore being imbued with ancestral life essence, that is, as being in transit through the king's body.

This approach to agency has some implications as regards value. Embodied procedural knowledge belongs with motricity, the senses and emotions, and therefore with the desires or drives of the acting subject. Consequently, I am pulling value away from the valuation of things in terms of its verbal expression in computations and equivalences (as regards quantities, monetary counts, speech and representations, etc.) and bringing it close to the senses, the body and the way the subject moves, perceives and desires in a material world – in the present case, a world of containers and contents, among which are the body and its bodily substances. This is what I have attempted to suggest in the present chapter in order to bring out the itineraries of bodies, substances and material things and the way these itineraries result in the construction of different regimes of value in people and in things.

Note

1   I have given a fuller account of this version of African sacred kingship in: Warnier (2007) *The pot-king: The body and technologies of power*. Leiden and Boston, Brill.

References

Appadurai, A. (ed.) (1986) *The social life of things: Commodities in cultural perspective*. Cambridge, Cambridge University Press.

Appadurai, A. (1997) *Modernity at large: Cultural dimensions of globalization*. Minneapolis, MN, University of Minnesota Press.

Bohannan, P. (1955) Some principles of exchange and investment among the Tiv. *American Anthropologist* 57 (1), 60–70.

Brain, R. (1972) *Bangwa kinship and marriage*. Cambridge, Cambridge University Press.

Foucault, M. (1976) *Histoire de la sexualité. Vol. 1. La volonté de savoir*. Paris, Gallimard.

Foucault, M. (1984a) *Histoire de la sexualité. Vol. 2. L'usage des plaisirs*. Paris, Gallimard.

Foucault, M. (1984b) *Histoire de la sexualité. Vol. 3. Le souci de soi*. Paris, Gallimard.

Kopytoff, I. (1986) The cultural biography of things: Commoditization as process. In A. Appadurai (ed.) *The social life of things: Commodities in cultural perspective*, 64–91. Cambridge, Cambridge University Press.

Kopytoff, I. (1987) *The African frontier: The reproduction of traditional African societies*. Bloomington, Indiana University Press.

Latour, B. (1991) *Nous n'avons jamais été modernes. Essai d'anthropologie symétrique,* Paris, La Découverte.

Perrot, C.-H. and Fauvelle-Aymar, F.-X. (2003) *Le retour des rois. Les autorités traditionnelles et l'état en Afrique contemporaine,* Paris, Karthala.

Rowlands, M. (1996) The consumption of an African modernity. In M. J. Arnoldi, C. M. Geary and K. L. Hardin (eds) *African material culture,* 189–213. Bloomington and Indianapolis, Indiana University Press.

Schilder, P. (1923) *Das Körperschema. Ein Beitrag zur Lehre vom Bewußtsein des eigenen Körpers.* Berlin, Springer.

Schilder, P. (1935) *The image and appearance of the human body: Studies in the constructive energies of the psyche.* London, Kegan Paul.

Warnier, J.-P. (1985) *Échanges, développement et hiérarchies dans le Bamenda précolonial (Cameroun).* Studien zur Kulturkunde, 76. Stuttgart, Franz Steiner.

Warnier, J.-P. (2007) *The pot-king: The body and technologies of power.* Leiden and Boston, Brill.

Warnier, J.-P. (2009) Les politiques de la valeur. *Sociétés Politiques Comparées* (11), (janvier 2009), 1–67. 14.05.202, http://www.fasopo.org/reasopo/n11/warnier.pdf

Weiner, A. (1992) *Inalienable possessions: The paradox of keeping-while-giving.* Berkeley, University of California Press.

Chapter 5

Containing precious metals: Hallmarking, minting and the materiality of gold and silver in medieval and modern England

Peter Oakley

Introduction

For over half a millennium, newly-made gold or silver objects have been taken to the Goldsmiths' Hall in London to be submitted to material testing and stamped with symbols before being offered for sale; this process is called *hallmarking*. Using information gathered during fieldwork and from library research and object collections, this chapter will consider the extent to which the justifications currently offered for hallmarking differ from the rationale behind its early development. It will provide evidence to support the claim that from the sixteenth to the twentieth century hallmarking was closely related to the minting of coinage, with both practices having a similar aim: restricting the movement of precious metals, both geographically and between different classes of object. Through a discussion of what these practices were attempting to achieve and the level of their success, it will demonstrate the tension between coherent form and constituent substance that is a permanent feature of all gold and silver objects. The impact on hallmarking of comparatively recent social changes, namely the demise of precious metal coinage and establishment of a common trading market amongst European states, and how this illustrates the UK hallmarking system's current relationship with contemporary material itineraries, will also be considered.

Terms and concepts

The following argument is conceptually underpinned by a foundational perspective of material culture: objects can be considered to have *social trajectories*, and categorization is linked to a concurrence of individual *object biographies* (Appadurai 1986; Kopytoff 1986). It does, however, problematize aspects of this perspective, questioning whether its acceptance that 'things-in-motion' (Appadurai 1986, 5) are continually socially coherent is a methodological blind spot. Challenges to the inevitability and stability of object definitions have previously been made by Mary Douglas (1966; 1994) and Bruno Latour (1987; 2004). Douglas (1994, 10) flagged up the role of diverse localised interactions and intentions in the construction of object identities and showed how established conventions regarding a particular object's coherence (or disaggregation) align with individual subjects' needs and social position. Latour (2004, 234–235.)

added the insight that stable objects, or 'matters of fact' (Latour 2004), always contain the potential to conceptually explode, becoming a collection of disbanded things, or 'matters of concern' (ibid.).

In the case under discussion, this potential for conceptual dissolution is enhanced by the nature of the materials from which the objects are made. Even when constituting objects, both gold and silver can still be recognised as *substances*. Unlike objects, substances can be divided repeatedly but still retain their identity. Substances also exhibit tendencies, properties held in common by all of that substance (Hahn and Soentgen 2010). This divisibility and commonality are antagonistic to the singularization required by *objectness*, even when objects are considered interchangeable. Even worse, as substances gold and silver share the specific tendencies of workability and recombination. Not only can they be divided, they can be recombined, holding the potential for an infinite number and range of future amalgamations that undermines the stability of any current object; any existing gold or silver object can all too easily be perceived as a mass of raw material for the manufacture of a future object-in-waiting. Consequently, keeping any gold or silver object in its current form (both conceptually and physically) requires continual and concerted social effort.

For most of recorded history, gold and silver as substances have constituted one half of a dualistic material classification: *precious metals* as opposed to *base metals.* These terms are founded on social perceptions rather than inherent material properties. Being a precious metal is not dependent on relative market price; silver is far cheaper than many of the rarer base metals. The categorization rests on a metal's capacity to act as a material store of wealth with a high liquidity and its widespread use in the manufacture of luxury goods. These criteria explain why platinum and palladium are today often also classified as precious metals, and the term is occasionally extended to include all of the platinum group metals (PGMs). In the UK, once a metal is included in the hallmarking legislation it becomes legally defined as a precious metal. By this convention, gold and silver have always been precious metals; platinum became precious in 1975 and palladium in 2010 (HMG 2012).

Within the following discussion, hallmarking is considered holistically rather than just the physical act of stamping a set of marks into precious metal. It is conceived as a *system*, a social entity created by an assemblage of physical, performative and conceptual elements, including legislation, tools, defined spaces and the activities of practitioners. The central feature of systems is that they are constructed and managed to produce a specific outcome. Over time initial intentions may be reconfigured by the introduction of new imperatives resulting from social changes, including longer-term responses to the properties of non-human elements. Though these lack conscious intention, they can be influential due to the impositions they make on other non-human elements and human actors, reshaping entire systems in unanticipated ways (Hodder 2011; cf. Gooday 2004; Clark 1997).

A system's outcome may be a physical product, or it may be intangible, such as systems that confer authenticity or identify properties. Alternatively, systems may be directed towards the management and control of specific groups, individuals or non-human actants. The Panopticon, the military drill and handwriting instruction are all clear examples of such systems of control (Foucault 1977 [1975]). One of the systems under discussion, the minting of coins, is usually considered a manufacturing process, with the output being new objects. The other, hallmarking, is a process of technical observation that defines composition and, while making only minimal physical changes, significantly alters the social identity of pre-existing objects.

Hallmarking in 2011

In the UK, any item offered for sale that is described as made of precious metal (with the exception of very small items, industrial or medical objects) is legally required to be hallmarked. A hallmark is a set of symbols that identify where the object was assayed, the person or company that submitted the object for marking and the precious metal composition (Fig. 5.1).

The only institutions legally able to apply a hallmark are the four registered Assay Offices: London, Birmingham, Sheffield and Edinburgh. These are legal entities all created or confirmed by Acts of Parliament. If a hallmarked item is significantly altered, it cannot be offered for sale before being submitted for remarking. UK law now also recognises marks from member states of the International Convention for Hallmarking, though these are legally termed *convention marks* rather than hallmarks (HMG 2012).

Hallmarking assays are conducted using one of three techniques: touch assay, fire assay, or x-ray fluorescence spectrometry. Only items that pass are marked. The most commonly used and longest established method of hallmarking is stamping by hand with steel punches. Semi-automated machinery is used for large batches of identical pieces, and laser marking has been recently introduced for small or delicate items. Each sponsor (the individual or business submitting work) owns a unique design, inscribed on a punch kept at the Assay Office. Though the punch is said to be owned by the sponsor, they cannot physically remove *their* punch from the Assay Office.

Individually and collectively through the UK Hallmarking Council, the Assay Offices actively promote the hallmarking system as a consumer protection service. They claim that hallmarking also indirectly benefits jewellery and silverware retailers by supporting consumer confidence in the authenticity of precious metal items. The Offices consistently emphasise the longevity of the hallmarking system, claiming it is part of British heritage. These two aspects are frequently combined, as in the introductory lines

Figure 5.1. A modern hallmark. From left to right: The sponsor's mark (LAO); the mark for sterling silver (a rampant lion); the purity mark (925); the assay mark (a leopard's head indicating the London Assay Office); the date letter ("k" indicating 2009). © The Goldsmiths' Company.

to the Hallmarking Council booklet explaining hallmarking: "In the UK, hallmarking has a long history, dating back nearly 700 years, and representing the earliest form of consumer protection. The consumer benefits in many ways" (The Assay Offices of Great Britain n.d., 2).

The extent to which this rationale is accepted by the public was demonstrated by responses to the *Red Tape Challenge*, a 2011 UK government initiative to identify and scrap redundant or poor legislation (HM Cabinet Office 2011a). Acts slated for removal were listed on a website where any individual with a specific interest could post an opinion prior to the committee stage. The first 257 laws listed covered retailing and included the 1973 Hallmarking Act and its ten amendments. Public responses to the hallmarking legislation numbered 5,894, over half of the responses for all the retailing legislation (HM Cabinet Office 2011b). The comments submitted were overwhelmingly supportive of hallmarking, with most identifying customer protection, longevity and heritage as justifications for retention. In July 2011 the Minister for Business and Enterprise Mark Prisk announced that the Hallmarking Acts were to be reprieved, stating: "We've listened to what people have said [...] we are preserving good regulation, such as the hallmarking regime, for which there was strong support" (Prisk, cited after Department of Business, Innovation and Skills 2011).

The Assay Offices' promotional literature and the comments submitted to the Red Tape Challenge link the hallmarking system's roots with its validity as a protection for consumers. However, a close examination of the earliest hallmarking legislation indicates that the system was created primarily to meet other needs, the protection of purchasers being an incidental outcome.

The first hallmarking in England: 1300

The genesis of the British hallmarking system is generally taken to be a statute issued by Edward I in 1300 (Forbes 1999; Jackson 1921; Tann 1993). This statute states that all silver should be as good as sterling (92.5% silver), and gold at least *the Touch of Paris* (80% gold). It placed responsibility for assaying gold and silver wares on the guardians of the craft, who were instructed to visit goldsmiths' shops in order to test the wares for sale (Forbes 1999, 16). The statute included a crucial innovation: satisfactory silver items were henceforth to be stamped with a leopard's head mark (Fig. 5.2).

The *guardians of the craft* were given more formal status in 1327, when Edward III granted the goldsmiths' guild a royal charter, creating the Worshipful Company of Goldsmiths, one of the City of London's first Livery Companies. At the time any craftsman working in gold or silver was called a goldsmith. The charter explicitly stated that the guild's appointed leaders, the Wardens, had direct authority over goldsmiths in London. The Goldsmith's Company also became responsible for maintaining the hallmarking system for the Crown.

In Edward I's statute the identified standard for silverwares is sterling, the same as for English coinage. This was a reconfirmation of existing legislation: in 1238 Henry II had issued a statute stating that silverware should be as good as *the King's money* (Forbes 1999, 16). Both statutes make explicit references to the currency in preference to the method for describing silver content used by contemporary goldsmiths and assayers: the ratio of silver to base metals in the alloy expressed as a troy weight (Challis 1978). In contrast to the stability and local relevance of the silver standard, the gold standard was both novel and foreign. The Touch of Paris, defined by the Lord Provost of Paris in 1260 for gold wares, bore no relation to any coinage in circulation in France or England.

Figure 5.2. The first type of hallmark, a leopard's head, representing royal authority. © The Goldsmiths' Company

These points, namely explicit referral to the silver currency standard, the requirement to mark silver items and the lack of a comparable approach to gold items, all indicate the real intention behind the statutes. In 1300 the English currency consisted only of silver coins. Demanding that all other silver objects had an equivalent or better silver content and identifying tested items by marking them with the king's symbol helped curtail the destruction of English coins. The statute increased the financial and personal risks associated with selling plate or vessels made out of alloys containing less silver than the sterling standard. Consequently goldsmiths would be less inclined to melt down coins to make such substandard silver alloys. Making sterling ingots out of sterling coins became financially unviable. As each coin's face value was slightly higher than its material value, ingots made from coin were worth less than the coins they were made from. The perfunctory treatment of gold can be seen as a reflection of its peripheral role as an economic instrument in England in 1300. The first English gold coin to go into wide circulation was introduced in 1354, over half a century later.

Living with *specie*

Establishing that medieval English kings were concerned with protecting English coins raises the question of why this should occupy their attention. Today's world is dominated by symbolic fiat currencies, a reality that makes it difficult to fully appreciate the material aspects of living with precious metal currency coins, or *specie*. The Greek city states, the Roman Empire and European kingdoms of the High Middle Ages and Renaissance all relied on specie. Specie was also the fundamental element of what is today called *the gold standard*, the system of international exchange mediated through gold coin that first developed in Europe. The gold standard expanded to envelop most of the world during the nineteenth century and collapsed at the beginning of the twentieth (Eichengreen 1985).

During this period specie was conflated with money, an error evident in classical economic thought, including Marx's major texts (Frankel 1977; Ingham 2004; cf. Marx 1976 [1876], 186–188). This conflation was identified by Simmel (1978 [1900]), who understood money as an abstract idea. Despite this he believed there were reasons that made "tying monetary value to a precious metal desirable and indispensable, and there are enough causes that make the conditions for a symbolic money unfulfillable" (Simmel 1997 [1889], 237–238). The eurocentrism of this approach has since been exposed by ethnographies that reveal the multitude of alternative objects that function in the same manner, including salt (Godelier 1977 [1973]), raffia cloth (Douglas 1958) and grain (Fuller 1989). But Simmel's insight, that value was attributed to rather than inherent in specie allows us to recognise specie as a type of legal-material object that was open to manipulation, and that controlling its production was a source of power.

Throughout the medieval period the prerogative to create specie almost exclusively belonged to the territorial ruler. This monopoly included the right of rulers to enforce the exclusive use of their specie throughout their territory as *the coin of the realm* through legal procedures. This right enabled rulers to collect *seigniorage*, an indirect form of taxation that depended on the materiality of the coins. By making the material value of the metal content slightly lower than the face value of each coin, a ruler could create wealth from nothing. To collect seigniorage required a recoinage. All the coin of the realm was recalled and melted down so that new coins could be minted. Recoinages were common occurrences across medieval Europe (Porteous 1973). The extant precious metal coins we see today in collections are escapees from these recalls, survivals due to accidental loss or hoarding.

If the difference between the face value and metal content of coins was too great, the coin was considered *debased*. Debasement was attractive to rulers as it allowed them to vastly increase the number of coins they could make from the same stock of gold or silver. Theoretically, subjects had to accept the coin of the realm at face value, whatever its material constitution. But in practice a debased coinage inevitably led to rampant inflation and a degree of economic collapse. Sellers who were in a position to do so would demand enough coin to acquire the same amount of precious metal as they received before debasement. Foreign traders (who were not subjects of the ruler) could refuse to accept debased coin. Reviving specie once it had been debased was costly, requiring a recoinage that gathered no revenue as well as an input of bullion.

The ability of medieval rulers to maintain a sound coinage for their subjects was considered an indicator of their fitness to rule; the material condition of the realm's specie was invested with moral connotations. Henry VI of France was given the insulting nickname *le roi faux-monnayeur* for debasing the French currency (ibid.). After Henry VIII debased the English coinage in 1542, its revival by his daughter Elizabeth I in the great recoinage of 1560 helped cement her subjects' loyalty despite an ongoing religious schism. Elizabeth publicly signalled her continued commitment to maintaining the new standards by instituting quarterly assays of the Royal Mint's production (Challis 1978). The very material nature of specie both required such physical acts and invested them with a symbolic importance that granted prestige.

Edward I displayed a similar interest in managing his specie. In 1292 he issued three money statutes, followed by another in 1299 that prohibited the importation or use of foreign money. Over the same decade he first consolidated the management and then the physical location of minting, closing the provincial mints and making the Tower of London the sole site of production (Mayhew 1992). The 1300 hallmarking statute neatly fits into his strategy of closely controlling the production and protecting the circulation of specie.

The hallmarking system expands: 1300–1500

The 1300 statute only required a single mark, the leopard's head. This was a symbol of royal authority, showing that the object was subject to the king's will, but it was simultaneously a royal guarantee of authenticity. Over the following two centuries the number of marks being applied incrementally increased. Each addition extended the amount of information being recorded and improved the precision of the system's oversight. At the same time the original mark demonstrated a slippage in meaning.

The first development occurred in 1363, when a further royal statute required every master goldsmith in the city to register a unique mark with the Goldsmiths' Company. This mark, along with the leopard's head, was now to be stamped on each piece of silver the goldsmith submitted after it had passed assay. These first *maker's marks* were heraldic symbols; much later two initials in a shield became conventional. The maker's mark was introduced to allow the Goldsmith's Company to identify who had made any piece of silverware in circulation, ushering in a form of *Foucauldian* continual oversight.

In 1478 the Company's Wardens engaged a full-time assayer to assay the items to be hallmarked. He was given lodgings and an assay office in Goldsmith's Hall, in the middle of London's goldsmithing district. Following this appointment, all the master goldsmiths of London were required to bring their silverware to the Hall for assaying and marking, the derivation of the word *hallmarked* (Hare 1996). In order to monitor their employee, the Company decided that an additional mark, the *date letter*, should be applied. As the letter was changed each year, the Wardens could identify in which year, and so by which common assayer, any item had been passed. If the post-holder changed before the end of a year, the letter was altered accordingly (Forbes 1999; Fig. 5.3).

Whilst the Goldsmiths' Company controlled the trade in London, major provincial cities had their own assay offices working under the immediate control of the city leaders (though nominally under the authority of the Goldsmiths'

Figure 5.3. A hallmark from 1478–1479. From left to right: the date letter (a 'B' indicating 1479); the assay mark (a crowned leopard's head); the maker's mark (this example is believed to represent a leather jug). © The Goldsmiths' Company

Company). As the leopard's head had become synonymous with the Goldsmiths' Company's assay office, these offices started to mark the pieces they tested with a symbol derived from the arms of the city instead (Jackson 1921). This mark, indicating where the item had been assayed, became known as the *assay mark*.

Together these three marks, the assay mark, maker's mark and date letter, built up a picture of the place and time the item was assayed, its precious metal content and the individuals involved in its making and assay. Originally intended to signify that the object met the demands of the royal statute, over two centuries hallmarking evolved to become a much more encompassing system able to directly monitor all of the human actors who made or tested silverware. Though the marking system expanded further over the following centuries, these developments followed the pattern established by 1500.

After 1478 hallmarking necessitated the creation of a whole range of new, dedicated objects, the punches used to make the marks and entire assay offices, all of which became established elements of the system. At the same time the practice also instigated new (and enduring) object pathways, with the assay offices becoming physical and social nodes through which all pieces of silverware were expected to pass before they could begin more individual geographical and social trajectories.

Medieval minting and hallmarking as related technologies

The principles behind the expansion of the hallmarking system, and the use of symbols to identify the maker and place and time the object passed through the system, were prefigured in minting. This link was not only conceptual: during the medieval period minting made extensive use of steel punches to produce the marks themselves.

In medieval Europe minting coins was a manual process, with each stage separated physically and temporally. Squares of metal were clipped out of a flat sheet or bar. Each square was then either trimmed or forged into a disk and filed to the precise weight. Lastly, each disk was hammered between two dies, called a trussel and a pile, which impressed a design on both sides simultaneously (Cooper 1988; Fig. 5.4).

Figure 5.4. A medieval moneyer minting coins. The trussle is in his left hand, resting on the pile which is set into a block on the floor. © Peter Oakley

The trussels and piles were made by skilled metalworkers called engravers and die-sinkers. They cut the positive relief punches that carried each element of the overall design and used these to build up the design on the heads on each of the dies. Some elements, such as the central portrait, might remain the same for many years, with the same punch being used on successive dies. Other elements were changed on an annual basis and some designs (though not all) incorporated the year of issue as a number. Another symbol, called the *initial mark*, was specific to each trussel and pile (which could last less or more than a year depending on the amount it was used). The initial marks were a shape or heraldic symbol, such as a castle, coronet, star or lion. The *mint mark* was specific to each mint and appeared on all the coins minted there (Challis 1978; Cook 1998; Fig. 5.5).

These marks allowed any overseer to *read* the symbols embedded into the overall relief design on each coin and so identify where and when that specific coin had been minted and which dies had been used. This would also enable him to identify who was responsible for the coin's

Figure 5.5. A silver threepence from the reign of Elizabeth I. The Tudor rose next to the queen's portrait was only included as part of the design on alternate years. © Peter Oakley

manufacture. Those directly involved with the mint would also have been familiar with the mechanics behind this achievement, namely the collections of relief punches used to build up the designs on the dies and the groups of visual symbols that were utilised as identifiers.

Considering the contagion between specie and silverware that hallmarking had initiated and the commonality of substance, it is not surprising that the recording technologies already used in minting were adopted in response to similar issues around monitoring hallmarking activities. Each development has a close correlation to minting: the assay mark equates to the mint mark, the maker's mark to the royal portrait (both lasting an adult's lifetime) and the date letter to the initial mark.

The argument relating to technology transfer is strengthened by evidence that individuals were sequentially or even simultaneously working within both systems. The typical background for a die-sinker would be goldsmithing (Challis 1978). Assayers often undertook work for both the Goldsmiths' Company and the Mint or moved between them (Forbes 1999). Unlike in many other European states, English mint employees were not kept permanently confined on site (Cooper 1988). One individual found the time to draw a mint salary as a die-sinker and develop a business as a scientific instrument maker, making his finest examples from silver (Cook 1998). The skilled workers needed to support both the hallmarking and minting systems were being drawn from the same pool of talent, and contacts between experts were being continually renewed, assisting the flow of experience and spread of conventions of practice.

Minting and hallmarking diverge

After the sixteenth century, minting and hallmarking diverged. Minting became increasingly industrialised in response to the need for ever increasing amounts of specie and more detail and regularity to deter forgers and clippers. In contrast, hallmarking remained virtually unchanged in its technology and underlying principles.

The expansion of the national economy and trade with the growing empire required vastly increasing amounts of specie. Ever greater recoinages repeatedly placed sudden and immense strain on mint facilities and work forces. In response minting adopted the latest technologies. Presses and rolling mills were in use at the Royal Mint by the seventeenth century (Gaspar 1993). In the 1790s Matthew Boulton's steam-powered coin presses, with the power to stamp designs and mill the edges of a coin in a single action, revolutionised minting (Doty 1993).

Forgers making fake coins from base metal were a perennial problem. The crisper the relief detail and the more regular the shape, the more difficult it was to forge. But a skilled forger could be as good at engraving dies as a mint employee. During the nineteenth century, pantograph technology led to dies being produced using a different form of prototype, a large-scale model of the entire design (Cooper 1988). This procedure, which produced a level of detail far in excess of what could be produced directly by hand, differed both mechanically and conceptually from the process of building up the design using multiple punches.

Hallmarking was under much less pressure to innovate. Though the UK Assay Offices eventually adopted mechanised equipment such as fly presses and pantographs, take-up lagged centuries behind their appearance in mints. An observer comparing the two systems after the early 1600s would see little similarity. In contrast to the manual and individual nature of hallmarking practice, minting was technologically cutting-edge, highly mechanised and internally integrated.

A bi-metallic currency and gold hallmarking

Despite the technological divergence of hallmarking and minting, precious metals still provided a conceptual link. This was reinforced during the first half of the nineteenth century as gold items became subject to increasing levels of legislation, culminating in the compulsory hallmarking of gold items in 1854 (Forbes 1999; Beasley and Dove 2012). The interest in hallmarking gold related to the new importance of gold in the English currency. The growing use of gold coins was gradual and unplanned, but by the late seventeenth century England was running a fully bi-metallic currency. At this point a shift in the price ratio between the two precious metals precipitated an economic crisis. The face value of silver coins (a set fraction of the gold coins) dropped below the financial value of the mass of silver they contained and opportunists started melting down silver coins to make bullion. The lack of sufficient silver coin to pay wages and rents or make day-to-day purchases started to threaten social stability (Levenson 2009). The great recoinage if 1696–1697, undertaken to counter this threat, fixed the gold–silver ratio in the coinage at a level that privileged gold, turning it into the *de facto* standard (Craig 1946; Eichengreen 1985).

Hallmarking after specie

The fundamental break between hallmarking and minting occurred when Britain left the gold standard in 1922, severing the direct link between circulating currency and gold and silver. Though the Royal Mint still produced small runs of gold coins and used silver alloys to make smaller denomination coins until 1947, the Mint no longer made specie.

Since 1922 there have been repeated calls to abandon hallmarking and to make significant changes to the legislation. The most serious crisis for the system came in 1969, when the UK government actively considered abolishing compulsory hallmarking, claiming that the extensive 1968 Trade Descriptions Act could become the foundation for standards (Forbes 1999). Following a campaign by the manufacturing trades hallmarking survived, but the 1973 Hallmarking Act introduced fundamental changes (HMG 2012). Instead of it being illegal to manufacture or sell any article under standard, after 1975 it was only illegal to describe such items as made of gold or silver. In addition, policing the legislation was passed from the Assay Offices to the Trading Standards Departments and Weights and Measures Authorities.

This restructuring took place within a context of preparation for entry into the European Economic Community (EEC). Meanwhile, the UK Assay Offices had been supporting an alternative international agenda through active involvement in the creation of an International Convention on Hallmarking through the European Free Trade Association (EFTA). The Convention, signed in 1972, privileged the standards of each importing country in the assessment of imports, but made the assay marks of any convention country valid across all signatories.

Britain's accession to the EEC in 1973, combined with the near complete collapse of the UK jewellery manufacturing industry over the following decade, meant the level of imports rose inexorably, from 6% in 1976 to 40% in 1996. Major jewellery exporters in EEC member states who were not Hallmarking Convention signatories contested national rulings, claiming such hallmarking legislation was protectionist. A test case, the 1994 the European Court of Justice Houtwipper judgement, broadly supported the validity of national hallmarking legislation over the principle of removing barriers to trade between EU member states (European Union 2011). But the ruling did require the UK government to pass amendments that removed the obligation to identify the year of manufacture (National Measurement Office 2011).

Not all attacks have come from outside the UK. Following the election of a right wing-led coalition government that espoused neoliberal free-trade values, the parts of the system most exposed to government influence have been subject to assaults. The Hallmarking Council has been investigated as a potentially superfluous quango, and the hallmarking legislation was included in the Red Tape Challenge. Recent promotion of hallmarking as a form of consumer protection can be considered a response tuned to a social environment in which consumption and unimpeded trade have become established as the dominant policy principles.

The hallmarking system still retains the potential to influence the trajectories of gold objects subjected to it. The continual and dramatic rise in the gold price since the economic crisis of 2008 has led to a thriving market in scrap gold in the UK. Pawnbrokers, jewellers, scrap-dealers and *postal gold* companies all compete, advertising their willingness to purchase gold objects from the public. This market is heavily reliant on hallmarks for initial *spot* valuations by appraisers, as well as being a strong influence on owner's expectations of their object's value as scrap. A hallmark, by emphasising and quantifying the nature of a precious metal object's composition, allows that object to be conceived as substance rather than object, increasing its social velocity and speeding the of destruction of a gold object by making it more liquid as a financial asset.

Hallmarking has also acquired a new and contrasting role in the construction of an alternative regime of value for a specific sub-culture. Since the mid-eighteenth century, age value has played a major role in the cult of antiques (Rosenstein 2009). The existence of the date letter in old hallmarks has enabled antique collectors and dealers to date gold and silver items precisely, this becoming the means by which age value is attributed. This has played a fundamental role in the aesthetic appreciation and financial valuation of antique silverware and jewellery, helping reinforce each item's identity as a singular object rather than as a mass of substance.

Material containment and circulation

In economics, descriptions of currency frequently employ the word *circulating* to describe wide dispersal. The word also has an older meaning of travelling in a circle, inevitably returning to the beginning. The anticipated physical trajectory of specie in medieval Europe encompassed both meanings: after being created at the mint it was dispersed amongst the ruler's subjects, but later completed a circuit when it was recalled to the mint for its destruction during recoinage. The limits of this dispersal were envisioned as being coterminous with the physical boundaries of the kingdom. The impermeability of these borders, with coin of the realm contained and foreign coin excluded, was, like the coin itself, a material representation of royal power.

The hallmarking system created a mirror of this: precious metal goods were also required to materially conform to the will of the sovereign and to pass through Goldsmiths' Hall to be marked before they entered circulation. They were similarly banned from moving across territorial borders, echoing the geographical limits imposed on specie.

But these imagined subservient object itineraries were contradicted by many of the actual pathways of specie and hallmarked vessels and plate. Infractions included cross-border forays and sudden terminations due to unsanctioned object destruction in order to gain access to the substance they conceptually confined. Each time a coin was clipped, a little more silver-as-substance was released from the constraints of the object, to start an alternative trajectory as a new one, bullion.

Minting and hallmarking can be seen as systems concerned with socially anchoring or securing objects. These systems attempted this stabilisation in the face of the persistent tendency of gold and silver to exert an identity as substances, a property that inevitably compromised the integrity of the objects they constituted and that confined them. Eruptions of precious metal substantiality indicated the beginning of alternative physical and social pathways leading to the physical destruction of an existing object form in order to realise a more socially useful alternative.

In order to protect a specific class of object – specie – in which they had invested financial wealth and social prestige, the hegemonic institutions of medieval government became engaged in repeated skirmishes with the individuals who were attempting to create such alternative pathways. In the process other classes of objects were drawn into the fray. This never-ending contestation was conducted using a combination of legal instruments and apparatus and material technologies: refining, alloying, assaying and impressing marks.

Hallmarking, a system created initially as a means of checking the propensity of precious metals to migrate between object forms by removing the advantages that drove this, had the consequence of constructing an equivalence based on a conflation of object qualities. This conflation raises an intriguing question: during the later medieval period, were minting and hallmarking considered separate systems by practitioners? Anyone studying material culture quickly becomes wary of assuming that two physically similar objects are considered identical by the people that interact with them. But this wariness, together with the security blanket of linguistic distinctions of object types, may be distracting us from considering how extensive a level of concurrence existed between the systems during the period in question. As has been identified, during the fifteenth and sixteenth centuries, the same group of technical experts, using the same types of tools, used similar systems of marking to monitor these manufacturing practices using the same substances, both times in the direct service of the sovereign. These activities took place in different sites, but the process and sites were described using similar linguistic constructions: minting took place at the Royal Mint, hallmarking at Goldsmiths' Hall. The terms acknowledge the nodal function of each site in its respective system, being the fundamental anchor point in anticipated circulation, and housing the definitive acts of authentication required for the objects to be included in the established social categories. These circumstances, together with the ethnographic evidence that demonstrates that money need not equal coinage, allows us to conceive of hallmarked precious metal objects being regarded as *para-money* in medieval Europe.

We live in a post-specie world, only able to directly experience the remaining half of this pairing, and that only within an alternative economic structure. Today hallmarked items are regarded as commodities during the period of their production and initial sale. This, together with the ideology of free-market economics, means that the UK hallmarking system now has to offer an alternative justification for its existence: consumer protection. But hallmarking can still influence an object's social identity: depending on the context, it can either increase its social liquidity or conversely, through the date letter, enhance singularization. That the UK's hallmarking system has so far survived the destabilising effects of the demise of specie and the restructuring of sovereignty that followed entry into the EEC is remarkable. That, following the political rise of free-trade ideals, it has come under repeated attack from the same institutions that once relied on its capacity to restrict the geographical and social flows of precious metals is inevitable.

References

Appadurai, A. (1986) Introduction: Commodities and the politics of value. In A. Appadurai (ed.) *The social life of things: Commodities in cultural perspective*, 3–63. Cambridge, Cambridge University Press.

Beasley, D. and Dove, A. (2012) Hallmarks on Gold. In H. Clifford (ed.) *Gold: Power and and Allure*, 84–97. London, The Goldsmith's Company.

Challis, C. E. (1978) *The Tudor coinage*. Manchester, Manchester University Press.

Clark, C. (1997) *Radium girls: Women and industrial health reform, 1910-1935*. Chapel Hill and London, University of North Carolina Press.

Cook, B. J. (1998) Humphrey Cole at the mint. In S. Ackerman (ed.) *Humphrey Cole: Mint, measurement and maps in Elizabethan England*. British Museum Occasional Paper, 126, 21–26. London, British Museum Press.

Cooper, D. R. (1988) The art and craft of coinmaking: A history of minting technology. London, Spink.

Craig, J. (1946) *Newton at the Mint*. Cambridge, Cambridge University Press.

Department of Business, Innovation and Skills (2011) Red Tape Challenge sets retailers free from regulations. 30.04.2012, http://nds.coi.gov.uk/content/Detail.aspx?ReleaseID=420597&NewsAreaID=2&utm_source=feedburner&utm_medium=feed&utm_campaign=Feed%3A+bis-news+%28BIS+News%29

Doty, R. G. (1993) The industrialisation of money: Three examples. In M. M. Archibald and M. R. Cowell (eds) *Metallurgy in numismatics. Volume 3*. Special Publication, 24, 169–176. London, Royal Numismatic Society.

Douglas, M. (1958) Raffia cloth distribution in the Lele economy. *Africa* 28 (2), 109–122.

Douglas, M. (1966) *Purity and danger: An analysis of concepts of pollution and taboo*. London, Routledge and Kegan Paul.

Douglas, M. (1994) The genuine article. In S. H. Riggins (ed.) *The socialness of things: Essays on the socio-semiotics of objects*, 9–22. Berlin and New York, Mouton de Gruyter.

Eichengreen, B. (ed.) (1985) *The Gold Standard in theory and history*. New York and London, Methuen.

European Union (2011) Database of European law: Opinion of Mr Advocate General Gulmann delivered on 9 June 1994. Criminal proceedings against Ludomira Neeltje Barbara Houtwipper. Reference for a preliminary ruling: Arrondissementsrechtbank Zutphen – Netherlands. Free movement of goods – Precious metals – Compulsory hallmark. Case C-293/93. 30.04.2012, http://eur-law.eu/EN/Opinion-Mr-Advocate-General-Gulmann-delivered-9-June,267810,d

Foucault, M. (1977 [1975]) *Discipline and punish: The birth of prison*. London, Allen Lane (first published in French, 1975. *Surveiller et punir. Naissance de la prison*. Paris, Gallimard).

Forbes, J. S. (1999) *Hallmark: A history of the London Assay Office*. London, Unicorn Press in conjunction with the Goldsmiths' Company.

Frankel, S. H. (1977) *Money, two philosophies: The conflict of trust and authority*. Oxford, Basil Blackwell.

Fuller, C. J. (1989) Misconceiving the grain heap: A critique of the concept of the Indian jajmani system. In J. Parry and M. Bloch (eds) *Money and the morality of exchange*, 33–63. Cambridge, Cambridge University Press.

Gaspar, P. P. (1993) Coining and die-making techniques in the 17th century. In M. M. Archibald and M. R. Cowell (eds) *Metallurgy in numismatics. Volume 3*. Special Publication, 24, 130–142. London, Royal Numismatic Society.

Gooday, G. J. N. (2004) *The morals of measurement: Accuracy, irony, and trust in late Victorian electrical practice*. Cambridge, Cambridge University Press.

Godelier, M. (1977 [1973]) *Perspectives in Marxist anthropology*. Cambridge, Cambridge University Press, [First published in French: (1973) *Horizon, trajets marxistes en anthropologie*. Paris, Maspero].

Hahn, H. P. and Soentgen, J. (2010) Acknowledging substances: Looking at the hidden side of the material world. *Philosophy and Technology* 24 (1), 19–33.

Hare, S. M. (1996) *Goldsmiths' Hall in the City of London*. London, The Goldsmiths' Company.

HM Cabinet Office (2011a) Red Tape Challenge. 30.04.2012, http://www.redtapechallenge.cabinetoffice.gov.uk/home/index/

HM Cabinet Office (2011b) Red Tape Challenge: Hallmarking. 30.04.2012, http://www.redtapechallenge.cabinetoffice.gov.uk/hallmarking/

HMG (2012) Hallmarking Act 1973 [revised version]. London, The National Archives. 30.04.2012, http://www.legislation.gov.uk/ukpga/1973/43

Hodder, I. (2011) Human-thing entanglement: Towards an integrated archaeological perspective. *Journal of the Royal Anthropological Institute* 17 (1), 154–177.

Ingham, G. (2004) *The nature of money*. Cambridge, Polity Press.

Jackson, C. J. (1921) *English Goldsmiths and their marks: A history of the goldsmiths and plate workers of England, Scotland and Ireland*. New York, Dover Publications.

Kopytoff, I. (1986) The cultural biography of things: Commoditization as process. In A. Appadurai (ed.) *The social life of things: Commodities in cultural perspective*, 64–91. Cambridge, Cambridge University Press.

Latour, B. (1987) *Science in action: How to follow scientists and engineers through society*. Cambridge, Harvard University Press.

Latour, B. (2004) Why has critique run out of steam? From matters of fact to matters of concern. *Critical Inquiry* 30 (2), 225–248.

Marx, K. (1976 [1876]) *Capital: A critique of political economy. Volume 1*. Harmondsworth, Penguin, [First published in German: (1876) *Das Kapital. Kritik der politischen Ökonomie. Erster Band*. Hamburg, Ernst Meissner and New York, L. W. Schmidt].

Levenson, T. (2009) *Newton and the counterfeiter*. London, Faber and Faber.

Mayhew, N. J. (1992) From regional to central minting 1158-1464. In C. E. Challis (ed.) *A new history of the Royal Mint*, 83–178. Cambridge, Cambridge University Press.

National Measurement Office (2011) Hallmarking. 01.05.2012, http://www.bis.gov.uk/nmo/regulation/hallmarking

Porteous, J. (1973) *Coins*. London, Octopus Books.

Rosenstein, L. (2009) *Antiques: The history of an idea*. Ithaca, Cornell University Press.

Simmel, G. (1978 [1900]) *The philosophy of money*. London, Routledge (first published in German, 1900. *Philosophie des Geldes*. Leipzig and München, Duncker & Humblot).

Simmel, G. (1997 [1889]) On the psychology of money. In D. Frisby and M. Featherstone (eds) *Simmel on culture: Selected writings*, 233–242. London, Sage (first published in German, 1889. Zur Psychologie des Geldes. *Jahrbuch für Gesetzgebung, Verwaltung und Volkswirtschaft im Deutschen Reich* 13, 1251–1264).

Tann, J. (1993) *Birmingham Assay Office 1773-1993*. Birmingham, Birmingham Assay Office.

The Assay Offices of Great Britain (n.d.) *Hallmarks: On gold silver and platinum*. London *et al.*, The Assay Offices of Great Britain. 30.04.2012, http://www.britishhallmarkingcouncil.gov.uk/publications/hallmarks2.pdf

Chapter 6

Worthless things? On the difference between devaluing and sorting out things

Anamaria Depner

1. Introduction

Several months ago, this earring (Fig. 6.1) made a pause on its journey to land in my wallet. Its itinerary, of which I know only a little, is irrelevant to any other earring in the world – except maybe for its counterpart. The story how this came about is, however, relevant, since it shows the criteria that play a role in our everyday experience when dealing with things. In this chapter, I want to illustrate how an object is situationally newly defined by coincidentally encountering it and dealing with it accordingly. Analysing how things emerge due to what we know or what we think we know about them provides us with the hermeneutic key to the question of how the relationship between human beings and things is constituted. As we shall see, this knowledge is not only text-bound, not only a socio-cultural dimension, but also haptic knowledge, knowledge about corporal interaction with material objects and their physical constitution.

The earring depicted left and the story of how it entered into my possession are incidental to the interviews I conducted in the course of my research for my doctoral thesis. In my thesis I focus on the moment when things enter into motion, as is the case with moving house: I talked to people who had decided to move to a retirement home, even when it was not required from a medical point of view.[1] What I focus on within this context is the conflict with things that becomes necessary when the whole of one's personal belongings have to be reduced to a fraction. Things enter into motion, and none of them remains in

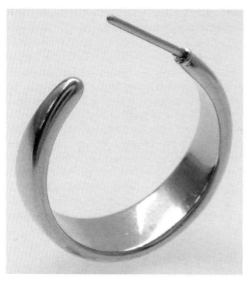

Figure 6.1. Earring handed over to the author by the old lady (Photo by Peter Steigerwald, Frankfurt on Main).

its place: they are being taken along, left behind, given away, thrown away, treasured and destroyed.

During my research, there have been some irritating and surprising moments regarding the semantic levels of things, as discussed in the literature and also in section 2 of this chapter. It is these moments that must be understood. They not only occur within the moving process, but are part of our dealings with things and of the emotions that things evoke. In order to illustrate this, I shall discuss the previously mentioned earring. A short part of its itinerary is traced in a conversation I conducted with one of my informants, though it was not one of the interviews I conducted in the course of my fieldwork (section 3). Finally this conversation will be confronted with the observations I made in the field (section 4). The detailed ethnographic description takes account of a *double irritation* and offers a better chance to reveal its context. I talk about a *double irritation* because of what I suffered in my role as the questioning researcher on the one hand (regarding the behaviour and answers of my informants), and because of the irritation that emanates from the objects on the other hand. Finally, I want to use the reasons for these irritations as a basis for further thoughts concerning the role of materiality, its perception and perceptibility, in order to make a plea to shift the perspective of the dialogue within cultural science in favour of these categories (section 5).

This chapter deals with our thing-oriented actions, a phenomenon we constantly encounter in our everyday lives and upon which we rarely reflect. It is vital to show how the findings concerning the earring and their relation to the empirical findings made in the field led to a deeper understanding of the research I conducted in the course of my doctoral thesis. This chapter reflects upon that cognitive process, rather than dealing essentially with the analysis of a partial aspect of a superordinated study. Perception, material, materiality and the evocation of strong feelings play a vital role therein. It will be emphasized that neither the question of whether a thing is worthwhile or worthless, nor the question of its whereabouts can be answered definitively.

2. Theory: Things in between being treasured and thrown away

One might imagine the rooms in the retirement home being overflowing chambers of biographical marvels, full of objects telling people's life-stories, if only one could understand the *language of things*. In material culture studies, there is a long tradition of questioning the symbolic or figurative function of things and the meanings that adhere to them regarding private living areas. The individual's interconnection with society is almost exclusively established by Pierre Bourdieu's reliable categories, like *habitus, lifestyle* or *distinction*. In his work, Bourdieu (1982 [1979]) shows us that taste, as the condition of possible appreciation, is constituted by socio-cultural frameworks and coherences. In this way, he refers to the cultural dimension of possible attributed meanings.

Confirming and psychoanalytically supporting the paradigm that could be called the *Bourdieuian approach*, the sociologist and psychoanalyst Rolf Haubl (2000) stresses the identity-making role of things, their emotional value and their function as carriers of memories. A significant *discovery* for research that is focused on meanings are *biographical objects*, like the ones Janet Hoskins (1998) found when she was exploring biographical novellas. Instead of stories she found things that could represent the biographies or even their owners. She therefore focused on material culture as a research object to examine the biographical meanings of things. This aspect is crucial to material culture studies, and even the collecting concepts of museums draw on the circumstance that things might refer to their owners, as the anthropologist Nina Hennig (2004) shows in exemplary fashion in her study of the correlation between biography and objects.

Despite all the profitable potential that the *Bourdieuian approach* was and still is contributing to ethnographic research, it might also mislead one into inverting the argument and claiming that some things always refer to a certain, unambiguous, culturally determined meaning. Hans Peter Hahn (2010) has recently stressed the concomitant difficulties and blocking effect of this interpretation on research. As he has repeatedly shown, the semiotic approach to things is neither adequate nor satisfactory as a way of approaching the things themselves (Hahn 2005a; 2012). The aspects discussed above must be complemented by the dimensions of loss, letting go and destruction, which receive no further attention from the authors mentioned. One of the leading theoreticians of ethnography of the Germanophone cultures, Martin Scharfe (2005; 2009), pointed out the importance of these aspects, which are central to my chapter. In addition to the fundamental connection between meaning and body (*Leibgebundenheit von Sinn*) (Scharfe 2009, 19–21), Scharfe (2009, 28–29) also stresses the consequence that, by destroying the material, the meaning that *adheres* to the object is also destroyed. Like Scharfe (2009), but from quite a different perspective, the chemist and philosopher Jens Soentgen (1997) also recognizes that discarded things and their materiality, as well as the material physicality of the perceptive human being, are inextricably intertwined. This scientific enhancement and absorption of the correlation of body, object, meaning, perception and knowledge is of equal importance for both a comprehensive conception of habitus, and an essential understanding of human actions on and with things. Soentgen makes a substantial contribution to that end, so that it becomes possible to associate the *Bourdieuian approach* with the 'phenomenology of perception' of Maurice Merleau-Ponty (1962 [1945]), as well as with scientific insights into the constitution of things.

Questions concerning the process of things becoming carriers of meaning, as well as questions concerning the value of memory, certainly belong to the heart of ethnographic research. Beyond doubt, I do see this level of meaning and the invaluable sentimental value of things in the context of my research as well. But I also see innumerable bagfuls of garbage, or better: things declared to be garbage, countless, forgotten, discarded, ignored and destroyed things, things that are transformed into unspecific piles of garbage once they are taken out of the cupboard. Are these *worthless things*?

Rubbish has in fact become a common object of research, so the problem here is not that things that apparently lack a certain meaning will be neglected by science in general. The problem rather is that rubbish itself is usually researched as something which lacks meaning. This concept of garbage is explicitly explained by Sonja Windmüller (2004, 292–299), one of the leading theoreticians of rubbish within cultural anthropology. The title of her study, '*Die Kehrseite der Dinge*' (Windmüller 2004), already implies that rubbish is the contrary of *things that matter*. Windmüller does recognize that garbage is not necessarily worthless, but she also implies that anything that is thrown away consciously has been thrown away because it is considered worthless. On the other hand, in his mathematically oriented rubbish theory, the anthropologist Michael Thompson (1981 [1979], 117–120) emphasises the contingency of the circumstances that lead to something being considered rubbish. Yet, Thompson sees the context in which an object is considered rubbish solely as a socio-cultural matrix determining its possible meanings. This, however, paradoxically excludes the object itself from its own itinerary.

In both approaches it still is the meanings of things that qualify them as objects of research. In his study 'In defense of things' Bjørnar Olsen (2010) argues that "THINGS MATTER – ALSO BY THEMSELVES" (ibid., 154; capital letters in the original), which is one reason for questioning approaching things exclusively for their attributed meaning. This requires the researcher to stick to certain things as an object of interest, even if – as in many cases – the things examined turn out to be attributed less meaning or simply have a different meaning than what was expected. What makes me even more suspicious about the idea that rubbish has no meaning are the convincing statements of Thompson (1981 [1979]) and Igor Kopytoff (1986) that, in certain societies, objects are constructed in much the same manner as people. Assuming this notion is valid not only for entire societies, but can be transferred to individuals as well, it can easily be observed that people abandon certain individuals not only because they have lost their meaning to them, but often enough because they have acquired a certain meaning (for example, in serious quarrels, or because of a deception, or maybe even because of unrequited love). Could things too be turned into rubbish for similar reasons?

To sum up, we can note that, as long as only the socio-cultural dimension as a quasi-transcendental background of meaning is taken into account, the mere focusing on the meanings of things might lead to things themselves being disregarded. Furthermore, research concerning material culture remains blind, or at least unilateral, regarding the phenomenon of rubbish, of throwing away and destroying, as long as this aspect is only seen as a manifestation of a loss of meaning, of the withdrawal of meaning, of devaluation. The destruction or throwing away of things is every bit as much a meaningful act as treasuring and caring for things. In order to avoid the mentioned reductions, it is inevitable that the material presence and constitution of things are attributed a role within the process of the emergence of things which is equivalent to that of the socio-cultural dimension of meaning.

3. Ethnography: How things emerge

3.1. Negotiating culture and material

This brings us back to the earring in my wallet. We can note from the beginning that it is worthless, because it is cheap and made of inferior material and because it is a single earring, torn out of its context. I do not know where its counterpart is, nor have I ever seen it. The situation in which it was encountered is not even typical for my research. Nevertheless, the story of how it came to be in my wallet clearly shows a pattern of behaviour that is valuable for my research but that extends beyond my particular case. It ultimately confirms my suspicions about the equation of use and worth of things and the meaning of emotions towards them.

The lady I acquired the earring from was one of the first persons I got to know in the course of my research, whose moving I could witness almost from the very beginning. Mrs Miller, as I will call her for the purposes of this chapter, is in her mid-eighties, lost her husband several years ago and has no children. Since she immigrated to Germany from Eastern Europe, she has no other relatives here and few friends because she never really learned German properly, even though she is relatively affluent and well educated. Although she is quite steady on her feet and quite active, her social isolation is very evident. As chance would have it, Mrs Miller and I were born in the same country, as a result of which I saw her a bit more frequently than the other informants.

When I visited her in spring 2011, she took the earring mentioned at the beginning of the chapter out of a drawer, saying: *Come! I'll show you what I have found.* She told me the earring lay on the stairs in the house she used to live in. She had found it as she went visiting her tenant some days before. She said she wanted to give it to me as a present for my son and that I could let him get his ear pierced. *I like it so much when men wear earrings. You know, only one, that looks so smart. I have seen them wear small simple round ones like this one here.* I found myself in a complicated situation. This earring was neither *small* nor actually *simple*, and technically speaking it was not even round! Instead it was an adaptation of the traditional form of the closed Creole, which was transformed by the fashion jewellery industry into an open form and provided with a clasp, which is cheaper and easier to produce. Obviously, this is not an earring a man could also wear – or would wear – at least the majority of men would not do so today, and much less is it one that a baby should wear.

What has happened here? Mrs Miller has seen a cultural practice that was new to her and transferred it to an already familiar object. This phenomenon is known very well among younger generations: it often occurs in the immediate family circle, when parents, grandparents or aunts try to pass things on to younger family members, saying, *I've seen that this is modern (again) at the moment.* The similarity with the things that *people wear/have at the moment* is actually given in most cases. But really using these things in an environment where people have *today's originals* would indicate: *I did not quite understand what it's about!* Recently bought retro-style things always seem kind of cool and romantic, while their prototypes often appear stuffy, old-fashioned and brittle. It is not about *still* having something; it's about having it *again*. It seems as if this distinction is harder to make with advancing age.

Presumably without any reason, I began to fear that Mrs Miller would expect my son to wear this earring on our next visit. What should I do? By saying, *Oh, but he is far too small for an earring,* I tried to avoid scandal quarrel, not anticipating that I was on my way to a battlefield of culturally shaped beliefs about things and material. That was the beginning of a long debate about this simple object, in which I was always one step behind, even though I should have been able to predict Mrs Miller's arguments. *Too small*, for example, was no argument to her – her only contact with this topic took place in a surrounding in which it was common for babies, meaning girls, to have their ears pierced only a few days after birth, often before even leaving the hospital. This was so natural that in some cases their mothers were not even asked to give their permission.

3.2. Ways to perceive an earring

I soon noticed that I needed something that was able to resist her culturally shaped perspective. I looked at the object carefully and finally found something: the earring had a pin on which a child could hurt itself. That was something well-founded, a material part of the earring; it could neither be denied nor culturally relativised. At first Mrs Miller did not even react to this argument. Rather, she supposed that I could sell the earring and use the proceeds to buy something for my son I considered more appropriate.

Although I recognized that I had not managed to avoid offending her, since she pointed that out clearly by suggesting turning her gift into a commodity (Appadurai 2006, 19–20), I made another mistake by wondering how she could actually think that the earring was made of real gold. In turn she could not believe that I considered the earring worthless. She assured me that she had examined its realness. Having tried to scratch and bend the earring out of shape carefully, she came to the conclusion that it must be gold! The colour, she said finally, is the surest indication.

But even in this case her cultural background was the reason for her error. In Southern and Eastern Europe the proportion of silver to copper, both of which are added to pure gold within the manufacturing process, is clearly in favour of the copper. This creates a more intense redness to the gold, which in Southern Germany is called *Turkish gold*. Being used to the yellow colour of gold in Germany, which comes closest to the colour of pure gold, one even tends to consider high-grade jewellery from the East as a forgery, whereas Eastern Europeans consider *western gold* to be of poor quality because to them it seems too pale.

I decided to talk about the earring pin once more. I showed it to her, saying that it was very unlikely that such a rough, malfunctioning clasp would be attached to a real piece of gold in such a poor way, using such cheap material. I could tell from her reaction that she had not yet noticed the earring pin for the simple reason that it did not fit her idea of an earring. She did not perceive it consciously because for her it was not meant to be there. I showed her my ear studs and how they are becoming closed. She silently nodded as I explained to her that it is much cheaper to manufacture a clasp like the one on the earring. The more she realized that the earring was fashion jewellery, the harder she scratched it and tried to bend it out of shape or to dent it – without result. This didn't appear like an attempt to determine further the earring's true material, but more as if she was trying to destroy it. *What a good quality fake things have nowadays!* she marvelled. She kept on talking about this small, not quite round object in her hand for a while. Finally she asked me to show the piece to a jeweller anyway, even though she knew it was pointless, as she said. Afterwards, I could throw it away.

Ultimately, the earring illustrated very clearly that the ways of interpreting dealings with things – especially their disposal – go beyond considerations of their lack of use or appreciation or the space they occupy. This insight is also crucial for the interpretation of several other informants of mine. How it can be transferred to questions about the material presence of things (Soentgen 1997), their perception (Hahn 2012) and the consequential pressure for action in general will be shown in the next section.

4. Interpreting unlooked-for research findings

4.1. Coping with the loss of things

When I started my research, I must confess that I expected to meet people clinging fast to their belongings. I thought they would try anything and against all reason take as much as possible into their comparatively small rooms at the retirement home. I expected my question, *What are you going to take with you?* to be answered with *Everything!* or at least with *As much as possible!* As the first person responded with a simple *Nothing!* and as I received the same answer in subsequent conversations with different persons, I was admittedly puzzled. Seeing that the interior of one of my informants' apartment being folded together to five cubic metres by the house clearance company caused me disorientation regarding how things are loaded with meaning and the value of memory. To make things worse, the wedding picture of her second marriage lay there with all the things that had been sorted out.

Of course, there are sometimes more, sometimes fewer things from the former apartment in all the rooms of my informants, sometimes even in the same arrangements. Furthermore, some things are given to loved ones or to charity organizations, mostly crockery or home textiles. But that is only a fraction, since for a lot of things, moving to a retirement home involves their last journey, which they do not start in the luggage of the elderly – for then it would not be a last journey – but rather in waste containers, being in a condition in which they cannot serve as whatever their specific function was. They are completely detached from those who had a relation to them, as well as those they might have had one with in the future.

You must not think about it! That's the way it is! This will all be dumped! – These are sentences I often heard during my conversations with the elderly. One could receive the impression that they do not really care, at least not as much as about their creeping frailty, which worries them a lot. This is different from Mrs Miller. She also suffers from the fact that *it does not work as good as before,* but she also suffers visibly from the loss of her things and feels somehow trapped in her room at the retirement home. In contrast to the other old persons she has designed her room the way one would have expected. It is filled with her old furniture and decorative objects: a lot of self-painted pictures, photos and little things that mean something to her can be found there. Even a corner that you could interpret as an altar, with icons in Orthodox style hanging on the wall and framed photos of her husband and her mother on the dresser underneath, can be found in her room.

Since we were undisturbed most of the time, I was able to observe her very intensely and thoroughly during the move. This circumstance, and perhaps the fact that her behaviour meets the idea one has of people in such a situation, are probably the reason why, in a way, it was she who provided me with the hermeneutic access to the startling answers and attitudes I was confronted with. It is precisely against such a background that unlooked-for statements or actions can discard their exotic status and lead to the understanding of higher-level contexts. So Mrs Miller gave me a lot to think about when she told me: *And actually this is not my altar, but my bar.* Of course I did not see any alcoholic beverages; the effect of the apparent arrangement was the basis of my judgement. The bottles of alcohol in the dresser were not visible to me, despite my knowledge of their existence. What is more important for the evaluation of the ensemble: the bottles, the icons, or maybe the photos?

4.2. *The disposal of things that matter*

The non-visible often turns out to be the decisive factor. Also in my research, there are things that disappear, that become invisible, things that matter. Mrs Miller also showed me this when she sorted out some important things in my presence and destroyed them or at least rendered them useless before throwing them away. Sensitized by this experience, I could also recognize the willingness and attempts of other informants to destroy their things. At first this remained hidden from me, as I could not observe them so closely when they moved. The woman who had deliberately brought her wedding picture into the room for the things that had been sorted out, for instance, left the physical destruction to the moving company. Strictly speaking, in this way the elderly passively destroyed the things they did not take with them. Most of these things became worthless in the moving process because they lost their context, their sense, their sentimental value. This seems to be easier to bear, because one does not have to think about where they are.

Mrs Miller did not have that option. She could not leave the half-furnished apartment to her relatives, the buyers or to a moving company responsible for removing what she did not want to keep. Thus she experienced her move to the retirement home much more intensely. Her conspicuous relatedness to things, as I would call it, was derived from the absence of any relatives. The things she left behind remained with no one: there was no one who knew her and who could make a connection between her things and herself. In my opinion this is not so much about living on, in or through the things that remind one of oneself, but rather about a feeling of unease regarding the idea that specific personal things might go on existing beyond one's grave. These are the things that stand out from the mass: some are so precious that they must be taken along; others are so precious that their owner wants to pass his/her verdict on their history him-/herself. These two criteria become mixed up in another case, in which an informant wanted to destroy a certain object in case he was not able to take it with him to the retirement home. This example illustrates that the destruction of things is a drastic form of our power over them, over their material existence and presence.

To sum up the aspect of the destruction of things, it can be stated that the process of decontextualisation, devaluation and the loss of meaning for their former owners does not make things worthless, but rather unbearable. The mass of objects is then simply ignored, cut out, abstracted to a heap – one just *does not think about it* and accepts it! In the case of moving house, it is often surprising to see what kinds of things unexpectedly belong to this mass. In this context, *protocolar objects* (Morin 1969, 133) surprisingly become mixed with things we would expect to be *biographical objects*, which, according to Hahn (2005b, 44), are the opposite of the former. Some things, however, *will be dumped*, some being given away deliberately and thus being made capable of undertaking new functions and being attributed new meanings within the biographical context of another person. Their itineraries can then be continued. Others are thrown away or left behind as single pieces to be disposed of by somebody else, and sometimes they are actively destroyed. At this point a last interaction with the thing in all its aspects, especially its materiality, is carried out. Afterwards the thing ends up in the trash, having now indeed become a piece of useless (but still not meaningless) rubbish. In their owners' perspectives these items are so strongly entangled with their biographies that it is their need, and perhaps even seems to be a necessity to them, not to let them continue to exist. Usually there are only a few things that end up in this way, just as there are only a few things that find a new place in the apartment at the retirement home.

As we have seen, the *value* or *worthlessness* of a thing cannot be linked directly to criteria like *keeping* or *throwing away*. The correlations extend far beyond a clear duality. The observations presented highlight the multiple ambivalence of the question of worthless things being put in the heading of this chapter. The great mass of discarded things, as well as informants' decisions to leave them behind, indicate a general worthlessness of things, even of those which one has possessed for a lifetime. The observed practices of destruction emphasise individual objects, but simultaneously they show that the concept of worthlessness must be completed. I have explained that the handling of things that one expects because of the paradigm of *meaningful things* is often not given. This consideration will be discussed further in the conclusion, combining it with (Miller/Olsen-oriented) reflections about the material presence of things and our knowledge of them. Turning back to the specific case presented at the beginning of this article, the influence of object-related perception on the potential desire to destroy or dispose of things can be deduced from Mrs Miller's dealings with her earring.

5. Further thoughts about the materiality of things

The destinies of things, where they go, where they come from and when they disappear, is determined by humans for the most part, a little by coincidence. But even though we have the power to influence the itineraries of things, we cannot influence what things *are*. They are there, present, they constitute permanent requests for action, they are a counterpart. In our daily lives, most of them are irrelevant to us. Others, in turn, can disturb us, make us sad or jealous. The particular situation we find ourselves in, as well as the information we have about a certain object, determines the corresponding effect. This aspect shapes our everyday thing-oriented actions.

When I say things *make us sad*, I certainly do not mean that they do that consciously or intentionally. But for all that, it is too short-sighted to think that things are only *charged up* with meaning, with our memories, with attributes of distinction, social conventions or the knowledge needed within the manufacturing process. Our knowledge of these aspects should not mislead us into thinking that we have gained complete knowledge of an object. Cultural factors do constitute the framework of our cognition, but the objects of cognition are the existing things. I would like to put it differently once more: Mrs Miller's background was crucial to her regarding whether the earring was valuable or worthless, presumably even to her seeing it at all as it lay somewhere she accidentally passed by. But does that lead to the conclusion that the earring itself did not play a role in this? Of considerable importance in the situation as portrayed was the fact that this specific earring was there in its material existence, which made it possible for us to look at it, touch it and deal with it in a variety of ways.

This example illustrates how closely we have to look at individual things in order to understand them – and by what means. Further, it is a plausible argument to support the claim to acknowledge substances and to "look" at the hidden side of the material world (Hahn and Soentgen 2010). Following Arnold Gehlen (1961 [1936], 28), we can note that it is only by experiencing a thing as sensory and interacting with it that a relationship can emerge, a relationship in which we are anxious to remain the dominant part. When Mrs Miller found out she was mistaken, she did not try to check the material carefully any more, but to destroy the earring. This was an action which shows how things evoke emotions to which we respond with a need to negotiate these emotions with them. The trouble caused by realizing one has made a mistake about the materiality of a (ostensibly known) thing becomes plausible considering Olsen's affirmation of the stabilizing function of things that are perceived as permanent (Olsen 2010, 159).

When the subjective opinion and evaluation linked to objective criteria are not congruent, it often seems easier to overlook obvious indications than to reconsider one's own position. However, being confronted with the earring, its sensory properties and its sensory perceptibility offered Mrs Miller an opportunity to reflect on her position. What she learned through accurate sensory analysis made her feel uneasy. She transformed her discomfort about it into an attempt to damage the earring. This relates to the already mentioned destruction of meaningful personal things. In both cases it is all about working up an insight and channelling a closeness, dismay or disappointment of whatever kind (or any other intense emotion) and retaining control over the object causing the emotion. Once more we can see that if objects were subjected only to the logic of semiotics, one would react differently but with aggression towards their physical existence.

It is significant that the material presence of a thing is experienced at its plainest when one sets one's hand to it. As mentioned at the beginning, the relevance of the material and its sensory perception is increasingly being discussed and emphasized in material culture studies. Acknowledging Merleau-Ponty's 'phenomenology of perception' (Merleau-Ponty 1962 [1945]), I would even say that the basal momentum is not only the perception but also the perceptibility of things, as well as the parallels that can be drawn between one's own corporal presence in this world and the physical presence of things. Connected with this, one can also find a lot of publications dealing with the body and its perception which try to overcome the dichotomy between constructivism and naturalism (e.g. Bogusz and Sørensen 2011).

As shown in the case of the earring, it is by means of the material presence of things that we acquire information about them. This information points far beyond the material characteristics. They give us the ability to explain the earring's peculiarities, its use, its form, and its historical and cultural contexts. I showed earlier how, in arguing for the *realness* of the earring, Mrs Miller relied greatly on her sensory perception: the colour, the resistance to scratching, and the flexibility. By the way, the jeweller just had to weigh the earring in his hand for a brief moment to know it was not made of gold (Hahn 2012, 8–10). Moreover, the intrinsic information we have about a certain object determines our relationship with it and our behaviour towards it.

We can therefore conclude that a person consciously sorting out a certain thing may do so for a variety of reasons. In connection with the empirical findings of my research, and given a holistically oriented theoretical foundation, as initially outlined in section two and then explained further, four possible types of scenario can be distinguished regarding the conscious sorting out of things:

1. The everyday case	Because it lost its function or context: the object is damaged or life circumstances have changed – the most usually assumed reason.
2. The complement to the *everyday case*	Because of an error.
3. The usual case with house moving or clearing	Because of an arbitrary selection, facing huge quantities of things to move or to dispose of (which, for several reasons, cannot be handled).
4. The *contrary case*	In order to gain a distance from a thing's uncomfortable presence.

The scenarios of the first and second type broadly correspond to the usual approaches to research in material culture studies, as represented, for instance, by Windmüller (2004) and Thompson (1981 [1979]). Both the aspect of a loss of meaning (type 1) and the aspect of contingency (type 2) are taken into account here. Types 3 and 4, however, widen the range by means of a strongly thing-oriented perspective. Type 3 foregrounds the challenging, or in this context even threatening, material presence of things. Faced with the practical impossibility of meeting the mass of calls to action, one is confronted with the piles of things in the course of moving house, while the dimensions of the ascription and withdrawal of meaning shift towards a selected part of things. Given this overwhelming pragmatic necessity, most of them are sorted out without further regard to their possible meaning. So the meaningful things remain, some of which again will need to be sorted out. Accordingly, it is not a *lack* of meaning that plays a role in this, but only the process of negotiating meanings and dealing with them, with the possibility or willingness of integrating these and exposing oneself to them in a now newly constituted everyday life. Thus, the aspect of creating a distance (type 4) is crucial, and within the negotiating process it is perhaps even more important and more serious than the aspect of integration, that is, treasuring etc.

Just like the appropriation or individualisation of a thing (Hoskins 1998), its disposal too may be an act constitutive of its owner's biography. Olsen (2010, 160–172), for instance, describes how things can represent something from which the owner wants to emancipate himself – even if it is only a conscious past that is willingly being discarded. In addition, focusing on a thing's materiality is an approach capable of revealing an unexpected variety of meanings which otherwise would be ignored. Choosing things because of their meaning (which is often assumed to be certain) can never guide the way to a new perspective. But as my own research has shown, a strictly thing-oriented understanding has proved to be useful, making possible not only a better approach to things themselves and thus taking account of their complex interweavings in our everyday lives, but also comprehending connections that are easily misunderstood. Accordingly practices of destruction, littering and loss – also and especially of valuable things – not only prove to be a sign of ignorance, mistake, chance or even irrelevance. Windmüller (2004, 292–299), who explicitly deals with this side of material culture, takes only these aspects into account. But object-oriented research does not overlook the fact that the destruction or discarding of valuable things can also be a deeply meaningful and meaning-creating process that has both an identity-establishing function and significant (object-)biographical implications and consequences.

Note

1   Focusing on people moving to the retirement home independently, I chose one that specialized in taking people who are not in need of intensive care. In a period of 18 months, the first six new arrivals were interviewed and attended to. The examination was inspired by the dialogue method used in Selle and Boehe (1986), while the interpretative theory is based on the method of "thick description" developed by Clifford Geertz (1973).

References

Appadurai, A. (2006) The thing itself. *Public Culture* 18 (1), 15–22.

Boehe, J. and Selle, G. (1986) *Leben mit den schönen Dingen. Anpassung und Eigensinn im Alltag des Wohnens.* Reinbek bei Hamburg, Rowohlt.

Bogusz, T. and Sørensen, E. (eds) (2011) *Naturalismus – Konstruktivismus. Zur Produktivität einer Dichotomie.* Berliner Blätter, Sonderheft, 55. Berlin, Panama Verlag.

Bourdieu, P. (1982 [1979]) *Die feinen Unterschiede. Kritik der gesellschaftlichen Urteilskraft.* Frankfurt am Main, Suhrkamp (first published in French, 1979. *La distinction. Critique sociale du jugement.* Paris, Les Editions de Minuit).

Geertz, C. (1973) Thick description: Toward an interpretative theory of culture. In C. Geertz *The interpretation of cultures: Selected essays*, 3–30. New York, Basic Books.

Gehlen, A. (1961 [1936]) Vom Wesen der Erfahrung (1936). In A. Gehlen (1961) *Anthropologische Forschung. Zur Selbstbegegnung und Selbstentdeckung des Menschen.* Rowohlts deutsche Enzyklopädie, 138, 26–43. Reinbek bei Hamburg, Rowohlt.

Hahn, H. P. (2005a) Dinge des Alltags – Umgang und Bedeutungen. Eine ethnologische Perspektive. In G. M. König (ed.) *Alltagsdinge. Erkundungen der materiellen Kultur.* Studien und Materialien des Ludwig-Uhland-Instituts der Universität Tübingen, 27; Tübinger kulturwissenschaftliche Gespräche, 1, 63–79. Tübingen, TVV-Verlag.

Hahn, H. P. (2005b) *Materielle Kultur. Eine Einführung.* Berlin, Reimer.

Hahn, H. P. (2010) Von der Ethnografie des Wohnzimmers zur 'Topografie des Zufalls'. In E. Tietmeyer, C. Hirschberger, K. Noack and J. Redlin (eds) *Die Sprache der Dinge. Kulturwissenschaftliche Perspektiven auf die materielle Kultur*, 9–21. Münster, Waxmann.

Hahn, H. P. (2012) Words and things: Reflections on people's interactions with the material world. In J. Maran and P. W. Stockhammer (eds) *Materiality and social practice: Transformative capacities of intercultural encounters*, 4–12. Oxford, Oxbow.

Hahn, H. P. and Soentgen, J. (2010) Acknowledging substances: Looking at the hidden side of the material world. *Philosophy and Technology* 24 (1), 19–33.

Haubl, R. (2000) Be-dingte Emotionen. Über identitätsstiftende Objekt-Beziehungen. In H. A. Hartmann and R. Haubl (eds) *Von Dingen und Menschen. Funktion und Bedeutung materieller Kultur*, 13–36. Opladen, Westdeutscher Verlag.

Hennig, N. (2004) *Lebensgeschichte in Objekten. Biografien als museales Sammelkonzept.* Kieler Studien zur Volkskunde und Kulturgeschichte, 3. Münster, Waxmann.

Hoskins, J. (1998) *Biographical objects: How things tell the stories of people's lives.* New York and London, Routledge.

Kopytoff, I. (1986) The cultural biography of things: Commoditization as process. In A. Appadurai (ed.) *The social life of things: Commodities in cultural perspective,* 64–91. Cambridge, Cambridge University Press.

Merleau-Ponty, M. (1962 [1945]) *Phenomenology of perception.* Translated from the French by Colin Smith. London, Routledge and Kegan Paul (first published in French, 1945. *La phénoménologie de la perception.* Paris, Gallimard).

Morin, V. (1969) L'objet biographique. *Communications* 13, 131–139.

Olsen, B. (2010) *In defense of things: Archaeology and the ontology of objects.* Plymouth, AltaMira Press.

Scharfe, M. (2005) Signatur der Dinge. Anmerkungen zu Körperwelt und objektiver Kultur. In G. M. König (ed.) *Alltagsdinge. Erkundungen der materiellen Kultur.* Studien und Materialien des Ludwig-Uhland-Instituts der Universität Tübingen, 27; Tübinger kulturwissenschaftliche Gespräche, 1, 93–116. Tübingen, TVV-Verlag.

Scharfe, M. (2009) Kulturelle Materialität. In K. C. Berger, M. Schindler and I. Schneider (eds) *Erb. gut? Kulturelles Erbe in Wissenschaft und Gesellschaft.* Buchreihe der Österreichischen Zeitschrift für Volkskunde, N. S., 23, 15–33. Wien, Selbstverlag des Vereins für Volkskunde.

Soentgen, J. (1997) *Das Unscheinbare. Phänomenologische Beschreibungen von Stoffen, Dingen und fraktalen Gebilden.* Berlin, Akademie Verlag.

Thompson, M. (1981 [1979]) *Die Theorie des Abfalls. Über die Schaffung und Vernichtung von Werten.* Stuttgart, Klett-Cotta (first published in English, 1979. *Rubbish theory: The creation and destruction of value.* Oxford, Oxford University Press).

Windmüller, S. (2004) *Die Kehrseite der Dinge. Müll, Abfall, Wegwerfen als kulturwissenschaftliches Problem.* Europäische Ethnologie, 2. Münster, LIT.

Chapter 7

Against the *throw-away-mentality*: The reuse of amphoras in ancient maritime transport

Selma Abdelhamid

Introduction

Three concepts are often evoked in discussions about ancient ship itineraries: travellers, ideas and objects. Of these three, the material objects are easiest to trace, even though they represent a particular challenge when they are removed from their cultural context and meaning. Setting aside the innumerable items that have disintegrated, those that have been preserved can be interpreted in various ways, though unfortunately, many shipwreck studies still rely on preconceived interpretations. The recovered objects are examined neither neutrally nor carefully, and choices in interpreting them are made much too soon.

Amphoras in particular are rarely questioned. They will therefore be taken as a prime example for discussion in this paper, partly because they occur frequently, but also because they sometimes followed multiple itineraries. This assumption might appear controversial, at least in Roman archaeology, since Monte Testaccio in Rome – a hill made of innumerable amphora sherds – as well as waste deposit studies have established the acceptability of a *throw-away-mentality* where antique amphoras are concerned. A further assumption is that these objects were conceived as transport containers for a specific purpose and became worthless once the journey was over, therefore experiencing a generalized and idealized history with a beginning and an ending. Yet, in light of the huge amount of amphora reuse attested in land excavations (e.g. Lawall 2000 for Classical Greece; Callender 1965, 23–36 and Peña 2007 for the Roman world), it becomes obvious that empty amphoras were not always regarded as useless in antiquity. From the moment they were produced, a long time could pass until they were finally discarded, recycled or lost.

There can be no doubt that the primary function of amphoras was their use in maritime transport (e.g. Twede 2002). It is therefore legitimate to ask whether they were reused for shipping before serving other purposes.

Careful examination reveals several indications of the reuse of amphoras within the maritime sphere, as I will demonstrate in the first part of this paper. I will then discuss the criteria indicating these situations before finally developing further theoretical thoughts about amphoras, their use and value.

The basic principles of the amphora trade

Antique amphoras differed greatly according to the area in which they were produced: not only did their type and size present distinctive features, so did the clay. We can therefore retrace the provenance of an amphora, if not to a single kiln, at least to a broader geographical area and culture. In the same way, it is possible to determine the period in which the amphora was produced because amphora morphology evolved with time. With regard to shipwrecks, an essential question to ask is whether the shipped amphoras form a typologically and chronologically homogeneous group. Indeed, it is to be expected of prime-use containers that they were made in the same place, filled, closed with a stopper often made of cork and covered with chalk or resin, and then shipped together. On the other hand, if the recovered amphoras appear heterogeneous, this suggests either that these jars were marketed following different and complex itineraries involving several stop-overs and diversifications of the cargo, or that they were reused and therefore responded to functional requirements, being incidentally collected, refilled, randomly stoppered and then distributed. Even though noted in the past, the reuse of amphoras has often been attributed to the storage methods of the crew, who had to stock the ship's supplies, as with an amphora that is supposed to have contained water on the Mazarrón-2 in Spain (Negueruela Martínez *et al.* 2004, 477, 480). However, the idea that jars could be reused as a commodity is often overlooked.

Empty amphoras were accorded a value. Ancient literary sources repeatedly show evidence of trade in empty containers, for instance, in Athens (Amyx 1958, 175–178). There are several examples of old and new empty jars being imported into Egypt, as demonstrated by the Ahiqar scrolls (Yardeni 1994; cf. Briant and Descat 1998, however, who stresses that these containers may not be amphoras). Furthermore, an ostrakon (O. Bodl. I 346) makes reference to Kolophonian amphoras being reused as containers for local wine (Kruit and Worp 2000, 82–83). There may also be evidence for Alexandria (Fraser 1972, 165–168). Last but not least, the often quoted passage in Herodotus, III. 6, even though it might not report a historical fact, confirms the realistic possibility of the collecting and refilling of amphoras in Egypt. However, as Lund (2004 211, note 1) points out, this may not be typical of the situation elsewhere. For the Roman world, Diocletian's price edict issued in the AD 301 (Peña 2007, 27 f.) states that the price of ceramic containers should be proportional to their capacity, ranging from 2 *denarii communes* for a small vessel of 2 *sextarii* (approximately 1.1 litres) to expensive 1,000 *denarii communes* for a large *dolium* of a capacity of perhaps 1,000 *sextarii*. Small amphoras referred to as *lagonae* with a volume of 24 *sextarii* cost 12 *denarii communes*. Compared with wine prices, it appears that the jar itself was valued at only 1% to 6% of its content. In addition, it has been suggested that some amphoras were exported to be filled elsewhere, for example, vessels traded in Lebanon (Mallowan 1939). It has also been argued that the kilns of El Rinconcillo near Algeciras provided the city of Baelo Claudia with amphoras and that a kiln in Los Matagallares supplied workshops in Almuñecar (Bernal Casasola 1999). Moreover, amphoras produced on Ebusus/Ibiza were used to carry Majorcan wine (Etienne 2006). Even shipwrecks may show traces of the transport of empty amphoras.

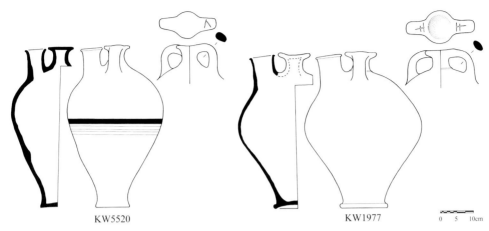

KW5520   KW1977   0   5   10cm

Figure 7.1. Marks applied on the handles of transport stirrup jars recovered from the Uluburun shipwreck are interpreted as signs for a previous diffusion by Cypriot merchants (Drawings by Doug Faulman and Julia Pfaff).

Amphoras reused in commerce: The evidence from underwater finds

In listing the known cases of amphora reuse in the widest possible range of shipping, my aim is not to point out similarities between cultures, practices and periods – specific amphora findings can only be considered within their cultural and chronological contexts. Nonetheless I would like to demonstrate the situations that may potentially arise on shipwrecks in order to broaden our perspective and discussions.[1]

Already mentioned some 30 years ago (Haskell 1981, 236, footnote 35), the theme of the possible reuse of transport jars in the Bronze Age has subsequently been provided with fresh data. The *Uluburun* wreck, found in Turkey but probably sailing between the Levant and the Aegean around 1300 BC, was carrying a large amount of raw materials, as well as manufactured goods and some artefacts interpreted as personal possessions (e.g. Pulak 2010). A group of 18 Aegean stirrup jars from the LH/LMIIIA2 period was recovered showing use wear, suggesting that they had already been in use previously (Bachhuber 2006, 347). This is confirmed by the observation of marks applied after firing on the handles of four vessels, interpreted as indicating previous diffusion by Cypriot merchants (Hirschfeld 1993; 2001; Fig. 7.1). Moreover, the stirrup jars form a heterogeneous group, some of them having been produced in western Crete, others in the centre of the island (Ben-Shlomo *et al.* 2011, 339). In a broader sense, it should be noted that a wide range of vessels of multiple origins was in use (and some of them in re-use) in the Eastern Mediterranean during Late Bronze Age, including Aegean stirrup jars, short-necked amphoras, Cypriot pithoi, Canaanite and Egyptian vessels (e.g. Day *et al.* 2011).

A varied picture is also provided by the *Giglio* wreck, which sank off the Tuscan coast around 600 BC. Amphora contents revealed the probable reuse of more than

130 vessels (Bound 1991). The majority are identified as having been produced in the Etruscan sphere and can be divided roughly into a flat-bottomed and a round-bottomed amphora type. They contained a large quantity of olives, pitch and maybe wine. Probably they were all coated with resin or pitch, which was usually done to make them impermeable while holding wine or fish conserves but is rather surprising in this context, since coating was even observed on amphoras proved to have held up to 70% of pitch. The hypothesis of their reuse is reinforced by the broad variety of fabrics, rim profiles, proportions and capacities. Besides, two amphoras showed "deep scratch marks that had been worn smooth well before the ship sank" (ibid., 24).

On the 7th–6th c. BC *Coltellazzo A* wreck near Nora, at least one amphora had been mended, indicating previous use (Parker 1992, 151–152). Moreover, a group of Punic amphoras belonging to the Bartoloni B, C and D forms were found to contain animal bones, mostly of lambs or sheep, again suggesting their reuse (Lawall 2011b, 30, footnote 31).

Rare contents are also attested on a shipwreck at *Tektaş Burnu* in Turkey, dated to around 425–400 BC (Carlson 2003). Indeed, nine Mendean amphoras were found to be filled with pitch. A further amphora of the same type and a pseudo-Samian jar revealed a large quantity of cattle bones. Pitch residues on the inside of the Mendean amphora led Carlson (2003) to suggest its having been formerly lined with pitch, inducing a secondary use for at least this amphora. However, it is possible that all the Mendean amphoras, which are generally thought to be wine containers, were being reused here. Yet the question should be raised whether at least the meat could be interpreted as the crew's provisions. The author argues against this on the basis that Athenaeus (*Deipn.* i 27. e) reports the importation of Thessalian beef in classical Athens, proving meat to have been a trading good. This amphora would then have been re-employed for commercial use. Additional indications of the reuse of jars on this shipwreck are the differences in dating certain vessels, in particular two Chian bulbous-necked amphoras dated respectively to 450-440 and 440-430/25 BC, as well as two Samian amphoras of types dated to within 20 to 25 years' time difference, indicating a long period of use and reuse and/or a temporary interruption and revival of trade.

A much shorter but still notable difference in dating has been reported for amphoras from the *Kyrenia* shipwreck, which sank off Cyprus in the 4th c. BC (Swiny and Katzev 1973). The stamps of the *c.* 345 Rhodian amphoras refer to four different years. Holes and important use-wear such as "completely worn off rims, worn down handle breaks, etc." (Lawall 2011a, 44) clearly reveal their reuse (Fig. 7.2). The same can be stated for other amphora types carried by this ship (ibid.).

As well as being dated to the 4th c. BC, the *El Sec* shipwreck is located in the mouth of Palma bay on Majorca. Although there might have been more than one wreck on the site, if all the amphoras belonged to the same ship, their great diversity of types, origins and above all dating, in combination with *graffiti*, suggests that they were reused (Lawall 2011b, 30–31).

Concerning the 2nd c. BC *Heliopolis II* wreck found in the south of France, Lawall reports "Graeco-Italic amphorae of a wide range of dates [with] missing handles and toes [...] and all filled with resin" (Lawall 2011b, 31, footnote 31), this indicating their reuse.

The same rare content was noted for the Lamboglia 2 amphoras on the nearby *Sud-Caveaux 1* wreck (Long and Delauze 1996). These amphoras from the end of the 2nd–1st

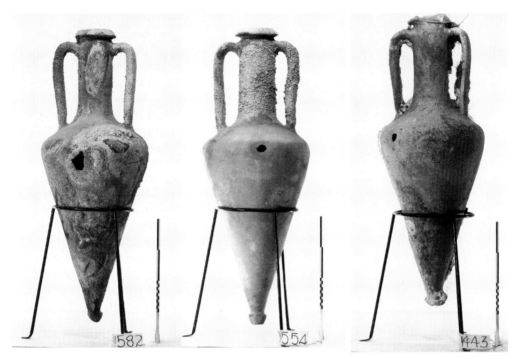

Figure 7.2. Use-wear and holes indicate that amphoras aboard the Kyrenia ship had already been used on a previous journey (Photo by S. W. Katzev).

c. BC often held wine and were attested as a complementary cargo. In this case, however, they seemed to have constituted the main freight and are proved to have contained resin.

A Brindisi-type amphora found on the *Maïre A* site next to Marseille held pozzolana (Benoît 1956, 25, fig. 2, 28.), volcanic ash which was widely employed in building. However, it is difficult to imagine how these could be useful on a ship, except maybe as ballast. Another surprising aspect is the 3 × 1 cm rectangular stamp on one handle, which seemed to have been erased. In addition, the original closure was apparently missing, having been replaced by a stopper carved out of an amphora sherd.

A similar situation may occur in Pisa on the late-Augustan wreck *San Rossore B*, which was loaded with Dressel 6A and Lamboglia 2 amphoras containing various substances (Bruni 2000). Besides volcanic sand, arsenic sulphide and red ochre, an assortment of fruits like peaches, plums and cherries were also found, as well as hazelnuts and chestnuts. These might, however, be the crew's supplies, not exchange goods.

Culip IV or *Culip D*, a ship sunk off the Spanish coast in Vespasian times, contained 76 Dressel 20 amphoras, which were suggested as having been filled with oil (Nieto Prieto *et al.* 1989, 59–83). Most interesting from our perspective are the great diversity of the 22 stamps that have been identified, as well as the rough-fitting stoppers made of amphora sherds, which were observed on about half of the amphoras. The excavators stress that they could not detect any traces of pozzolana, suggesting that the stoppers

Figure 7.3. The solid content consisting of scales and fishbones revealed that the amphoras of the Grado shipwreck did not hold oil, as expected, but preserved sardines (Photo by courtesy of R. Auriemma).

would not have been airtight. As oil rapidly goes rancid in contact with the air, they suggest that this oil could have been intended for the production of other goods, for instance, cosmetics.

The best example for Roman times is probably the shipwreck found near *Grado* in the Adriatic Sea, which sank in the early to mid-2nd century AD (Auriemma 2000). It was loaded with approximately 350 amphoras, of which more than 200 belonged to the African I type, which is largely attested as an oil container, but in Grado scales and fish bones revealed the presence of preserved sardines (Fig. 7.3). The amphora stoppers were carved out of the same amphoric material, probably being made of containers broken during a previous trip. Similar phenomena were observed for *c.* 20 Tripolitanian I amphoras, also known as oil containers but here filled with mackerel, and Aegean-type wine amphoras containing sardines.

Dated slightly later, the *Procchio* wreck on the island of Elba also contained amphoras amongst which stand out African IA specimens containing fig seeds. An additional amphora of the same type held an unidentified yellow liquid (Zecchini 1982, 162–166).

Similar vessel types were retrieved from the *Plemmirio B* shipwreck off the Sicilian coast, dated to AD 200 (Gibbins and Parker 1986, 279, 290). African IIA amphoras and a single pear-shaped Mauretanian amphora, though usually considered oil containers, were in this case found to be lined on the inside, perhaps having been subjected to secondary refilling.

The *Cabrera III* shipwreck off Majorca, dated to the middle of the 3rd c. AD, carried at least 124 amphoras which could be categorised into nine classes, among them 32 African II amphoras. The latter surprisingly turned out to belong to the African IIA, IIC and IID types, that is, to distinct categories which are usually assumed to have a different chronology (Bost *et al.* 1992, 137–144). The fabrics were similarly heterogeneous, and 13 of these amphoras presented distinct stamps, thus suggesting their production in different workshops. All amphoras were lined with pitch; two contained fish residues and two others olive pits, indicating that they had probably been collected on the Iberian Peninsula and refilled with local products.

Heterogeneous material is also revealed by the *Dor D* shipwreck found near the southern end of Mount Carmel and dated to the last quarter of the 6th c. AD (Kingsley 2003a; 2003b). Of 749 recovered amphora fragments, 89% were bag-shaped

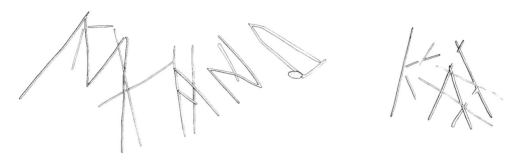

Figure 7.4. Some amphoras recovered from the Yassıada shipwreck show overwritten and scratched out graffiti. © Institute of Nautical Archaeology

LR 5 amphoras, including three subtypes and five different clay fabrics. Petrological evidence of domestic wares, tiles and ballast stones indicates that the ship started from or went via Cyprus. All the amphoras were lined with pitch, and grape seeds found in the resin of LR 5 specimens suggest that they had at one time been filled with wine. On basis of their heterogeneity and five tons of ballast stones intended to increase the cargo's weight, Kingsley proposes the rather unconvincing hypothesis that the ship was freighted with empty amphoras produced in several parts of southern Palestine that were destined to be returned and refilled or sold there. He supports this thesis by noting the strong consumer demand for the wine of the Holy Land in times of economic decline. Although we cannot exclude the possibility that other goods had been carried in these amphoras, their reuse seems certain. An additional indication is provided by an LR 5 vessel on which a lead plug was found closing an opening which could have served to release fermentation gas (Kingsley 2003b, 128) or to pour out the liquid the vessel contained (Adan-Bayewitz 1986, 92–97).

Only a few decades later, around 600-625 AD, the *Saint-Gervais 2* shipwreck sank in the south of France. Amphoras found in the aft of the ship contained pitch, which Parker (1992, 372–373) interprets as a local product of southwest Gaul.

The most obvious evidence comes from the Turkish coast. A 7th c. AD shipwreck found in *Yassıada* had more than 800 amphoras loaded, of which 719 belonged to globular types, with four main classes and various subtypes, some of the latter being dated considerably earlier than the rest (van Doorninck 1989). Examining these amphoras, more than 100 *graffiti* applied after firing were discovered, the overwhelming majority of them on globular amphora subtypes. Some pieces even had two to four *graffiti*. These inscriptions were identified as owners' names, digits, content indicators and sometimes allusions to the Christian religion. In several cases, *graffiti* were scratched out and overwritten, attesting to a change of ownership or content (Fig. 7.4). On the ship's last voyage, a majority of the amphoras were carrying wine; some, olive oil; and a few, sweet liturgical oil. The more recently made globular amphoras had precision-made mouths that accommodated bark stoppers of standardized sizes. The remaining amphoras with less precisely made mouths had stoppers made of rounded sherds. The more recently made globular amphoras provide a unique testimony for amphoras being made for multiple use as military transport jars. In a soon to be published paper, van Doorninck (in press) rejects the thesis of a commercial voyage: referring to the war between the Byzantine Empire and Persia from 603 to 628, he postulates a church ship transporting emergency supplies of wine and olive oil, most probably in the summer of 626, to troops then campaigning against the Persians in the East.

A shipwreck sunk around 1025 in *Serçe Limanı* off southern Anatolia provided similar evidence (van Doorninck 1989; Bass *et al.* 2009, 3–4). It was carrying a total of 104 Byzantine amphoras varying in type and capacity. Most of them had *graffiti*, many two to five *graffiti*. A majority of the *graffiti* have been interpreted as being the marks of at least twelve owners and of makers of the jars. In addition, more than half of the amphoras had been damaged before this ship sailed. Even though surface erosion and discoloration often occur after the jar's recovery, van Doorninck was able to make out five jars with surfaces showing wear prior to sinking, in particular at the maximum body diameter, thus inducing that these amphoras had at some time been transported in an upright position while touching other jars. In some cases, ridges had been completely worn away, which suggests that they had been transported several times. In addition, more than 50 jars had been damaged by previous stopper removal or by blows. In some instances, complete rims, necks or handles broke away (Fig. 7.5). Remaining rim parts or handle stubs were then carved smooth in order to prevent further tear. Supplementary

Figure 7.5. Like several jars, an amphora retrieved from Serçe Limanı had lost its neck prior to the ship's wreckage. © Institute of Nautical Archaeology

maintenance work is seen in the repair of a hole, which had its edges carved down and was then mended with a pitch plug. The fact that three severely damaged amphoras were found together at the stern might be an indication for their separate function, which might not have been transport. It is indeed difficult to imagine how jars without neck were used for carriage, whether they were closed or not. Significantly, a considerable amount of glass cullet was also on board, demonstrating a general awareness of material exploitation and recycling. Van Doorninck further points at piriform amphoras like those on the wreck recovered from other underwater sites, and which are on display in museums in Athens, Sozopol, Varna, Constanța, Bodrum, Çanakkale, Istanbul, Amasya and Taşucu. They particularly often show use wear, which leads him to the conclusion that such amphoras were widely reused for transport, maybe in a period in which they had, for reasons not yet entirely clear, become more expensive (F. H. van Doorninck, Jr., personal communication).

Clues to recognizing reused amphoras

As these examples demonstrate, amphora reuse is in some cases obvious, in others more difficult to discern. It is not revealed by recurrent features (see Table 7.1, which lists the observations I could find concerning the amphoras retrieved from the wrecks cited above).

First of all comes the often reported unusual content. But can we always determine what is usual content and what is not? And can we know for sure what the amphoras we find in wrecks actually contained? Generally speaking, it can be stated that Roman

	Uluburun	Giglio	Coltellazzo A	Tektaş Burnu	Kyrenia	El Sec	Heliopolis	Sud-Caveaux 1	Maïre A	San Rossore B	Culip IV	Grado	Procchio	Plemmirio B	Cabrera III	Dor D	St-Gervais	Yassı Ada	Serce Limani
Unusual content		▒						▒					▒				▒	▒	▒
Heterogeneity of types	▒	▒				▒												▒	
Use-wear		▒					▒												▒
Applied marks/indications	▒				▒													▒	
Heterogeneity in dating			▒	▒											▒				
Surface treatment		▒											▒						
Repair			▒																▒
Replacement of stoppers									▒		▒							▒	
Heterogeneity of stamps										▒						▒			
Removal of indications												▒						▒	

Table 7.1. Amphora properties cited in the respective publications.

archaeologists tend to link particular contents with specific amphoras – which is sometimes convincingly demonstrated, as for certain African types (Bonifay 2007). Hellenists, though, are more inclined to the *multi-use view*, which is "supported by the presence of pitch lining amphora shapes traditionally associated with oil [and] both by the rarity of multiple shapes from a single production area despite textual and other evidence for diverse crop production [...] and by descriptions of primary-use contents from Hellenistic papyri" (Lawall 2011a, 43). Probably neither of these positions is adequate on their own. Precise reconstruction of the contents, however, is anything but easy. Physical remains might give some indications, for instance, olive pits or nuts, even though these solid elements have a greater chance of being preserved and might be misleading as reflecting a numerical bias. Further clues are how the amphora has been treated, such as a resin or pitch coating applied on the inner side of wine and fish containers to make them impermeable to water (e.g. Jackson 2008 [1994], 4) and the marks applied, in combination with knowledge drawn from ancient written sources (Lund 2004, 212). In the absence of physical residues, however, it is hard to determine whether the amphora surface treatment corresponds to the actual voyage or whether the vessel was reused. In cases of doubt, excavation reports remain hopelessly similar, as shown by a review of 27 journal articles published between 1946 and 2011 referring to 5,549 Greek amphoras dated from the 5th to 3rd c. BC (Foley *et al*. 2012, 391). In 95% of these cases, the authors assumed that the amphoras contained wine, probably because they were repeating a commonly held belief and neither critically observing nor questioning the facts. In recent years, however, molecular methods have been developed that can detect ancient DNA enclosed in the clay of jars preserved under water, thus revealing the former contents of empty vessels (Hansson and Foley 2008). The presence of multiple substances can be attested within the same containers, which is interpreted either as proof of the transport of products made from several ingredients, and/or an indication of the reuse of these amphoras for the consecutive carriage of different goods.

It is much easier to recognize a reused amphora by marks due to use-wear: altered rims and handles, as well as surface abrasions testify to intensive manipulation, an impression confirmed when sharp edges prove to have been deliberately smoothed. Definitive proof is provided when scratch marks on the inside of amphora necks indicate stopper removal.

Precious clues are also given by amphora surface treatment, like coating of the inside, which strikes one in some instances as unnecessary, as shown by the lined pitch-carrying amphoras recovered from the Giglio wreck. Further indications are marks referring to previous marketing activity and *graffiti* and *tituli picti* attesting to a previous owner, the contents or an earlier storage situation. After studying *dipinti* on amphoras recovered from Pompeii, Elizabeth Lyding Will (2001) suggested that these were applied only in the case of amphora reuse. Indeed, she assumes that amphora contents were standardized and are normally deducible from the vessel type; exceptions therefore have to be pointed out (ibid.).The presence of marks should nonetheless draw our attention to possible reuse. Most obvious cases show multiple indications testifying to repeated amphora manipulation and different goods being carried. In the same way, the removal or invalidation of applied indications may indicate that a vessel has been reused. This is seen when a stamp has been erased, as in Maïre A, or *graffiti* scratched out and overwritten, as in the case of the Yassıada amphoras.

A further valid indicator, within the amphora cargo, is the wide heterogeneity of types, fabrics, stamps, provenances, proportions, capacities and dates, above all when a similar content is attested. In recent years, the importance of stopovers has won growing recognition, establishing the idea that amphoras might pass through several harbours and that a merchant's cargoes might therefore consist of many different items. However, particularly heterogeneous cargoes, above all with amphoras differing in dates and those showing several of the characteristics mentioned above, are likely to contain reused vessels.

Similarly traces of repair might indicate a secondary context, as was shown in the case of the mended amphoras recovered at Coltellazzo, Dor and Serçe Limanı. This is particularly interesting because flawed containers – for example, those holed to take out the content (e.g. Bonifay 2004, 467–468; Adan-Bayewitz 1986, 92, 98) – were thought to have been considered less useful and more likely to be hacked to pieces and employed for building or other purposes than maritime trade. Nevertheless, repair might be a marginal phenomenon occurring in specific regions or at times of material scarcity.

Equally obvious is the replacement of original stoppers. These amphora closures were quite standardized and are almost exclusively known from underwater contexts, as amphoras lost at sea often had their closures preserved. In the Roman world, for instance, most stoppers were made of cork and recovered with chalk, on which a stamp was sometimes impressed (Hesnard and Gianfrotta 1989). Improvised stoppers, however, were often made of locally available material, like sherds of broken amphoras, as can be observed at Maïre A, Grado, Culip IV and Yassıada. These sherds were roughly carved into round shapes and therefore loose-fitting, the gaps sometimes being filled with plaster. Probably can we deduce similar phenomena for the stoppers improvised on ships, though the absence of pozzolana or chalk stressed by the excavators of Culip IV might be an exception. Thomas and Tomber (2006) list diverse stopper types with particular reference to Egypt and the reuse of amphoras in Berenike.

If all the points previously cited also apply to a limited number of amphoras possibly reused by a ship's crew, the quantity of relevant items is determinant in inferring a whole cargo and therefore a commercial or exchange background.

When the reuse situation is clearly demonstrated, further items found on the shipwreck can help the interpretation, among them the goods being carried and the historical background. Indeed, a general awareness of material use-value is to be expected on a ship loaded with other recyclable or processable items, for instance, raw glass as found on the wrecks at Uluburun and Serçe Limanı. The historical or economic background, on the other hand, might help us understand extreme forms of reuse, as mentioned for the ships at Yassıada and Serçe Limanı, which in the one case is thought to have been at sea engaged in a military supply operation and in the other case engaged in small-scale commerce (van Doorninck 2002), in which sometimes severely damaged vessels continued to be employed.

The industry of reused amphoras: Conditions and motivation

Why were amphoras reused, and how was this achieved in practice? In fact, amphoras, when reused on a grand scale, could not simply be gathered up and refilled: their reuse involved a complex organization and the availability of a sufficient quantity of containers. Also labour was necessary to collect, clean and refill the vessels, as well as working and storage areas. Such places have probably been identified in Pompeian houses, where several amphoras were found stacked or leaning against walls in inverted, upright positions, probably for drying after being cleaned (Curtis 1979; Jashemsky 1967). Furthermore, amphoras were not necessarily in possession of the person using them: one cannot exclude the possibility that they were rented as is related in the Procheiros Nomos, a text issued 907 AD (Gofas 2002, 1101) and which penalises that one who rents flawed and leaky wine jars (Procheiros Nomos chapter 17, paragraph 14; Freshfield 1928, 99).

Regarding the shipwrecks mentioned above, the motivation for reusing amphoras was probably practical and/or financial. Often locally processed goods, for example, the fish conserves in Grado, were put into amphoras available in the vicinity that had probably formerly been imported into the area: maybe was there no specific amphora production, or collecting and refilling were considered cheaper or easier. A further reason could be that the local clay did not allow the production of high-quality containers, in particular in Egypt. In the case of institutions, as van Doorninck suggested for the church, a single owner and circuit could appear as a plausible explanation for reuse. In addition, historical events, like wars or other times of crisis, might reduce amphora production and force merchants to reuse old vessels. Custom, finally, should not be forgotten – at some periods, use of amphoras might have decreased in favour of other containers, such as barrels or animal skins, making amphoras and potters less available.

It is very difficult to estimate the frequency of amphora reuse, which must be specific to periods and regions. It might, however, have taken place much more often than we suppose. The Pompeian workshops cited above provide clear evidence of a region and period for which amphora reuse had been largely excluded on the basis of the high degree of commercial activity and production.

Conclusion

All these examples demonstrate that empty amphoras were regarded as valuable. The flawed containers repaired with plugs and those which were simply reused in spite of missing parts are most appealing. At that moment, only bare functionality was important, and it was acceptable to reuse an old vessel rather than obtain a new one. Moreover, a possible sign of value could be seen in the owner *graffiti* and *tituli picti* stamped on the amphoras when their commercial circulation was temporarily interrupted; however, this might rather relate to the goods contained in the amphora rather than the amphora itself. In addition, with regard to the Dor D shipwreck it has been suggested that empty amphoras were subject to trade. Thus is there always an initial content to look for? In the ongoing debate, Katzev raised an interesting point by demonstrating by experimental means that empty amphoras do not rest on the seabed but always rise to the surface (see Lawall 2011a, 44).

The significance of amphoras in particular is seen in their retention for multiple journeys. Itineraries are recorded in commercial signs or toll marks, which mostly refer to the contents. It should not be forgotten, however, that travelling amphoras and objects in general were not necessarily linked with commerce: gift exchange or institutional transfers still remain options. When tending towards a commercial interpretation, however, an amphora reused in shipping is a commodity according to Kopytoff's definition: "a thing that has use value and that can be exchanged in a discrete transaction for a counterpart, the very fact of exchange indicating that the counterpart has, in the immediate context, an equivalent value" (Kopytoff 1986, 68). Most of the time involving amphoras and their contents, this equivalent had to compensate for these two values combined. Shipwrecks directly attest to the moment of actual exchange, in this case revealing complex and multilayered amphora itineraries: amphoras crossed not only geographical space but also time. They changed owners and contents, deteriorated, were repaired and modified. In the end, this also meant undergoing certain transformations. These are all aspects we have to keep in mind when recovering amphoras, whether from shipwrecks or land excavations. Linear and simplistic interpretations certainly do not do justice to such multifaceted objects.

It is essential to look carefully at objects retrieved from underwater contexts. The systematic listing of observations made about the reused amphoras cited in this article (see Table 7.1) reveals that the most often reported element is the unusual content, followed by the heterogeneity of amphora types, use-wear and applied marks and indications. The combination of two or more features allows one to argue strongly for a reuse situation. Furthermore, negligence may also have concealed additional examples of reused amphoras. The systematic reconsideration of previously recovered jars could probably yield more evidence, as van Doorninck suggested with regard to the Bodrum museum. A larger amount of data could help determine recurrent features to demonstrate the increased reuse of certain amphora types at specific places or periods, for the transport of given goods or on restricted categories of ships. Only in this way will it be possible to determine to what extent amphora reuse was a more general practice, or, on the contrary, a truly marginal phenomenon. As a first step, however, preconceived interpretations must be set aside because, before intensive reflection can take place, an unlimited number of possibilities can apply to the jars recovered from a shipwreck. A crucial point, for instance, is the contents. Very often, only a few items of each amphora type are recovered from a site, similar contents and properties being deduced for all the others. This problem has to be addressed by, for example, introducing systematic sampling. In the same way, we should not be influenced by other cultures and spheres. The possibly rare reuse of amphoras in Imperial Italy does not signify that reuse was rare in Late Antique Italy, Classical Greece or Bronze Age Egypt: archaeologists might tend to generalise too much. This is not only valid for amphoras – presented here as particularly appealing cases – but for every other kind of cargo, and even the ships themselves, which in the past have attributed vague concepts such as *identity*. Already begun, the deconstruction of these meanings, which make no sense in maritime archaeology, must be continued in the future.

Acknowledgements

I wish to acknowledge the precious help and constructive suggestions provided by John Lund. I am also grateful to Rita Auriemma, Franca Cibecchini, Florence Richez, André Tchernia and Diana Twede for their valuable comments, as well as to Christoph Bachhuber, Jeremy Rutter and especially Mark Lawall and Fred van Doorninck for their kind assistance.

Note

1   Peña (2007) also mentions some shipwrecks containing reused material in his exhaustive publication on Roman pottery. This list is here extended and completed.

References

Adan-Bayewitz, D. (1986) The pottery from the Late Byzantine building (Stratum 4) and its implications. In L. I. Levine and E. Netzer (eds) *Excavations at Caesarea Maritima 1975, 1976, 1797: Final report. Qedem*, 21, 90–129. Jerusalem, The Hebrew University of Jerusalem, Institute of Archaeology.

Amyx, D. A. (1958) The Attic Stelai: Part III: Vases and other containers. *Hesperia* 27 (3), 163–254.

Auriemma, R. (2000) Le anfore del relitto di Grado e il loro contenuto. *Mélanges d'archéologie et d'histoire de l'École française de Rome, Antiquité* 112 (1), 27–51.

Bachhuber, C. (2006) Aegean interest on the Uluburun ship. *American Journal of Archaeology* 110 (3), 345–363.

Bass, G. F. and van Doorninck, Jr., F. H. (1982) *Yassi Ada: Volume I: A seventh-century Byzantine shipwreck*. College Station, Texas A & M University Press.

Bass, G. F.; Brill, R. H.; Lledó, B. and Matthews, S. D. (2009) *Serçe Limanı: Volume II: The glass of an eleventh-century shipwreck*. College Station, Texas A & M University Press.

Benoît, M. (1956) Épaves de la côte de Provence. Typologie des amphores. *Gallia* 14 (1), 23–34.

Ben-Shlomo, D.; Nodarou, E. and Rutter, J. B. (2011) Transport stirrup jars from the southern Levant: New light on commodity exchange in the eastern Mediterranean. *American Journal of Archaeology* 115 (3), 329–353.

Bernal Casasola, D. (1999) Transporte de envases vacíos en época romana. A propósito de dos talleres anfóricos béticos de época alto (El Rinconcillo, Algeciras, Cádiz) y bajoimperial (Los Matagallares, Salobreña, Granada). In R. de Balbín Behrmann and P. Bueno Ramírez (eds) *II Congreso de arqueología peninsular. Zamora, del 24 al 27 de septiembre de 1996. Tomo IV. Arqueología romana y medieval*, 359–364. Zamora, Fundación Rei Afonso Henriques.

Bonifay, M. (2004) *Études sur la céramique romaine tardive d'Afrique* (= British Archaeological Reports, International Series, 1301). Oxford, Archaeopress.

Bonifay, M. (2007) Que transportaient donc les amphores africaines? In E. Papi (ed.) *Supplying Rome and the Empire* (= Journal of Roman Archaeology Supplements, 69), 8–32. Portsmouth, Rhode Island, Journal of Roman Archaeology.

Bost, J.-P.; Campo, M.; Colls, D.; Guerrero, V. and Mayot, F. (1992) *L'épave Cabrera III (Majorque). Échanges commerciaux et circuits monétaires au milieu du IIIe siècle après Jésus-Christ*. Paris, de Boccard.

Bound, M. (1991) *The Giglio wreck: A wreck of the Archaic period (c. 600 BC) off the Tuscan island of Giglio* (= Enalia Supplement, 1) Athens, Hellenic Institute of Marine Archaeology.

Briant, P. and Descat, R. (1998) Un registre douanier de la satrapie d'Égypte à l'époque achéménide. In N. Grimal and B. Menu (eds) *Le commerce en Égypte ancienne*. Bibliothèque d'Étude, 121, 59–104. Le Caire, Institut Français d'Archéologie Orientale.

Bruni, S. (ed.) (2000) *Le navi antiche di Pisa*. Florence, Polistampa.

Callender, M. (1965) *Roman amphorae: With an index of stamps*. London, Oxford University Press.

Carlson, D. (2003) The classical Greek shipwreck at Tektaş Burnu, Turkey. *American Journal of Archaeology* 107 (4), 581–600.

Curtis, R. (1979) The Garum shop of Pompeii (I. 12. 8). *Cronache Pompeiane* 5, 5–23.

Day, P. M.; Quinn, P. S.; Rutter, J. B. and Kilikoglou, V. (2011) A world of goods: Transport jars and commodity exchange at the Late Bronze Age harbor of Kommos, Crete. *Hesperia* 80 (4), 511–558.

Etienne, R. (2006) Le vin des Baléares. In F. Mayet (ed.) *Itineraria hispanica. Recueil d'articles de Robert Étienne*, 519–525. Pessac, Ausonius.

Foley, B. P.; Hansson, M. C.; Kourkoumelis, D. P. and Theodoulou, T. A. (2012) Aspects of ancient Greek trade re-evaluated with amphora DNA evidence. *Journal of Archaeological Science* 39 (2), 389–398.

Fraser, P. M. (1972) *Ptolemaic Alexandria: Voulme 1: Text*. Oxford, Clarendon Press.

Freshfield, E. (1928) *A manual of Eastern Roman law: The Procheiros Nomos published by the Emperor Basil I at Constantinople between 867 and 879 AD*. Cambridge, Cambridge University Press.

Gibbins, D. J. L. and Parker, A. J. (1986) The Roman wreck of *c.* AD 200 at Plemmirio, near Siracusa (Sicily): Interim report. *International Journal of Nautical Archaeology* 15 (4), 267–304.

Gofas, D. (2002) The Byzantine law of interest. In A. E. Laiou (ed.) The economic history of Byzantium from the seventh through the fifteenth century. Dumbarton Oaks Studies, 39, 1099–1102. Washington, DC, Dumbarton Oaks Research Library and Collection.

Hansson, M. C. and Foley, B. P. (2008) Ancient DNA fragments inside classical Greek amphoras reveal cargo of 2400-year-old shipwreck. *Journal of Archaeological Science* 35 (5), 1169–1176.

Haskell, H. W. (1981) Coarse-ware stirrup-jars at Mycenae. *The Annual of the British School at Athens* 76, 225–238.

Hesnard, A. and Gianfrotta, P. (1989) Les bouchons d'amphores en pouzzolane. In L'Ecole française de Rome (ed.) *Amphores romaines et histoire économique. Dix ans de recherches. Actes du colloque de Sienne (22-24 mai 1986)*. Collection de l'Ecole française de Rome, 114, 393–441. Rome, Ecole française de Rome and Paris, Diffusion de Boccard.

Hirschfeld, N. (1993) Incised marks (post-firing) on Aegean wares. In C. W. Zerner (ed.) *Wace and Blegen: Pottery as evidence for trade in the Aegean Bronze Age, 1939–1989: Proceedings of the international conference held at the American School of Classical Studies at Athens, Athens, December 2–3, 1989*, 311–318. Amsterdam, Gieben.

Hirschfeld, N. (2001) Cypriots to the West? The evidence of their potmarks. In L. Bonfante and V. Karageorghis (eds) *Italy and Cyprus in Antiquity: 1500–450 BC*, 121–130. Nicosia, The Costakis and Leto Severis Foundation.

Jackson, R. S. (2008 [1994]) *Wine science: Principles and applications*. Burlington, Elsevier.

Jashemski, W. F. (1967) A Pompeian vinarius. *The Classical Journal* 62 (5), 193–204.

Kingsley, S. A. (2003a) The Dor D Shipwreck and Holy Land wine trade. *International Journal of Nautical Archaeology* 32 (1), 85–90.

Kingsley, S. A. (2003b) Late Antique trade: Research methodologies and field practices. In L. Lavan and W. Bowden (eds) *Theory and practice in Late Antique archaeology*, 113–138. Leiden and Boston, Brill.

Kopytoff, I. (1986) The cultural biography of things: Commoditization as process. In A. Appadurai (ed.) *The social life of things: Commodities in cultural perspective*, 64–91. Cambridge, Cambridge University Press.

Kruit, N. and Worp, K. (2000) Geographical jar names: Towards a multi-disciplinary approach. *Archiv für Papyrusforschung und verwandte Gebiete* 46 (1), 65–146.

Lawall, M. L. (2000) Graffiti, wine selling and the reuse of amphoras in the Athenian Agora, ca. 430 to 400 BC. *Hesperia* 69 (1), 3–90.

Lawall, M. L. (2011a) Greek amphorae in the archaeological record. In M. L. Lawall and J. Lund, (eds) *Pottery in the archaeological record: Greece and beyond*, 38–50. Aarhus, Aarhus University Press.

Lawall, M. L. (2011b) Socio-economic conditions and the contents of amphorae. In C. Tzochev, T. Stoyanov and A. Bozkova (eds) *PATABS II: Production and trade of amphorae in the Black Sea: Acts of the international round table held in Kiten, Nessebar and Sredetz, September 26–30, 2007, Sofia,* 23–33. Sofia, Bulgarian Academy of Sciences.

Long, L. and Delauze, H.-G. (1996) *L'épave Sud-Caveaux 1. Une nouvelle expérience en matière d'archéologie profonde* (= Bilan Scientifique du DRASSM, 86). Marseille, DRASSM.

Lund, J. (2004) Oil on the waters? Reflections on the contents of Hellenistic transport amphorae from the Aegean. In J. Eiring and J. Lund (eds) *Transport amphorae and trade in the eastern Mediterranean: Acts of the international colloquium at the Danish Institute at Athens, September 26–29, 2002.* Monographs of the Danish Institute at Athens, 5, 211–216. Aarhus, Aarhus University Press.

Lyding Will, E. (2001) The 102nd Annual Meeting of the Archaeological Institute of America: Truth in Roman labeling? *American Journal of Archaeology* 105 (2), 263.

Mallowan, M. (1939) Phoenician carrying trade: Syria (Plate V). *Antiquity* 13, 86–87.

Negueruela Martínez, I.; Gonzáles Gallero, R.; San Claudio Santa Cruz, M.; Méndez Sanmartín, A.; Presa, M. and Marín, C. M. (2004) Mazarrón-2. El barco fenicio del siglo VII a. C. Campaña de noviembre 1999/marzo 2000. In A. González Blanco, G. Matilla Séiquer and A. Egea Vivancos (eds) *El mundo púnico. Religión, antropología y cultura material. Actas del II Congresso Internacional del Mundo Púnico (Cartagena, 6–9 de abril de 2000),* 453–483. Murcia, Universidad de Murcia, Instituto del Próximo Oriente Antiguo, Área de Historia Antigua.

Nieto Prieto, F. J. *et al.* (1989) *Excavacions arqueològiques subaquàtiques a Cala Culip 1.* Girona, Centre d'Investigacions Arqueològiques de Girona.

Parker, A. J. (1992) *Ancient shipwrecks of the Mediterranean and the Roman provinces.* BAR International Series 580. Oxford, Tempus Reparatum.

Peña, J. T. (2007) *Roman pottery in the archaeological record.* Cambridge, Cambridge University Press.

Pulak, C. (2010) Uluburun shipwreck. In E. H. Cline (ed.) *The Oxford handbook of the Bronze Age Aegean (c. 3000–1000 BC),* 862–876. Oxford, Oxford University Press.

Swiny, H. W. and Katzev, M. L. (1973) The Kyrenia shipwreck: A fourth-century B. C. Greek merchant ship. In D. J. Blackman (ed.) *Marine archaeology: Proceedings of the twenty-third symposium of the Colston Research Society held in the University of Bristol, April 4th to 8th, 1971.* Colston Papers, 23, 339–359. London, Butterworths.

Thomas, R. and Tomber, R. (2006) Vessel stoppers. In R. Tomber, K. Knowles, D. Bailey and R. Thomas (eds) *Survey and excavation: Mons Claudianus 1987–1993. Volume III: Ceramic vessels and related objects.* FIFAO, 54, 237–258. Cairo, Institut Français d'Archéologie Orientale.

Twede, D. (2002) The packaging technology and science of ancient transport amphoras. *Packaging Technology and Science* 15 (4), 181–195.

van Doorninck, Jr., F. H. (1989) The cargo amphoras on the seventh-century Yassi Ada and the eleventh-century Serçe Limani shipwrecks: Two examples of a reuse of Byzantine amphoras as transport jars. In V. Déroche and J.-M. Spieser (eds) *Recherches sur la céramique Byzantine.* Supplément au Bulletin de Correspondance Hellénique, 18, 247–257. Paris, Diffusion de Boccard.

van Doorninck, Jr., F. H. (2002) The Byzantine ship at Serçe Limanı: An example of small-scale maritime commerce with Fatimid Syria in the early eleventh century. In R. J. Macrides (ed.) *Travel in the Byzantine world: Papers from the thirty-fourth Spring Symposium of Byzantine Studies, Birmingham, April 2000,* 137–148. Aldershot, Ashgate.

van Doorninck, Jr., F. H. (in press) The seventh-century Byzantine ship at Yassıada and her final voyage: Present thoughts. In D. Carlson *et al.* (eds) *Tradition and transition.* College Station, Texas A & M University Press.

Yardeni, A. (1994) Maritime trade and royal accountancy in an erased customs account from 475 BCE in the Ahiqar Scroll from Elephantine. *Bulletin of the American Schools of Oriental Research* 293, 67–78.

Zecchini, M. (1982) *Relitti romani dell'isola d'Elba.* Lucca, M. P. Fazzi.

Chapter 8

A secondary use of Roman coins? Possibilities and limitations of object biography

Gordana Ciric

Introduction

This chapter presents some preliminary ideas and observations on the secondary use of Roman coins in medieval cemeteries from the territory of Serbia. Although noted by many Serbian medieval archaeologists, these coins have never been discussed as a distinctive topic. I will therefore try to shed some new light on this phenomenon from the perspective of object biography. Since these coins were used in more diverse ways than their primary purpose, lasting a long period of time in which significant social changes took place, the object biography paradigm is a highly suitable approach to the topic. However, in this chapter I would like to explore in greater detail what this concept actually contributes to the understanding of two specific case studies and where it fails to provide a meaningful interpretation.

Apart from Serbian archaeology, studies of reuses of Roman coins and other objects from the Roman period are not uncommon. Such cases occur in many Anglo-Saxon contexts, including graves and settlements (Coock and Dacre 1985; Down and Welch 1990). Here the question is how objects that do not belong to the usual material culture of one group are socially incorporated into the usage. A new aspect to this inquiry comes from the fact that the objects were not exchanged between contemporary societies, but were rather discarded and then rediscovered and reused. Eckardt and Williams (2003) made noteworthy contributions to this phenomenon by examining two main understandings of it, one emphasises the *practical* reasoning (such as recycling) of the new users, while the other seeks for belief in the supposedly magical qualities of these objects.

In the area of present-day Serbia, similar finds have been discovered in several excavations of medieval necropolises from the fifth to fifteenth centuries, such as Aradac (Nađ 1959, 67), Mirijevo (Bajalović-Birtašević 1960, 33), Mačvanska Mitrovica (Ercegović-Pavlović 1980, 65), Trnjane (Marjanović-Vujović 1984, 35, 51–52) and Konopljara (Berić 2001, 110, 113). Usually these coins were understood as just ancient coins with secondary uses without further inquiry. I argue that this derives from, among other things, an *inventory methodology* in exploring necropolises. Putting artefacts from the necropolis into pre-ordained categories, these particular coins tend to *lose* their place in the supposed scheme. Sometimes the coins are reused as pendants on a necklace, so they can be classified as both coins and jewellery. In contrast to their multiple categorizations, these coins are also generally featureless. Another problem in the analysis of coins in general is the division between the numismatic and archaeological approaches (for more on the position of numismatics today, see Kemmers and Myrberg 2011). In traditional numismatic analysis, the coin is usually the primary source of data. Its shape, weight, material, inscription and depiction are of the utmost importance, while little attention is given to the context of a coin's discovery. "Apart from its immediate physical characteristics, a coin's most easily distinguishable features are its types – designs and inscriptions" (Brooke *et al*. 1983, xxvii–xxviii). On the other hand, archaeologists commonly use coin finds as a means of dating a site or smaller units within it. These two approaches, where a coin is self-sufficient or just a dating device, hinder the development of broader insights, since it is clear that they do not suffice in providing a more profound understanding of Roman coins in medieval graves. Numismatic identification of the coins is just a starting point allowing us to notice that there has been some kind of reuse or perhaps a continuation of use. For dating purposes, these coins are useless.

Therefore, in this research coins are analysed as part of a wider social context. They allow us to explore how the same object has alternative meanings and how these meanings vary with the social norms of the community in question, as well as with the social positions of the individuals who use them. For all these reasons it seems that the concept of object biography might help us grasp the wide range of meanings and values of these coins.

The object biography concept in archaeology

The idea of object biography has become very significant in archaeological theory recently, generating major debates. I would like to review briefly how object biography is used in the interpretation of material culture. I will do this by distinguishing between anthropological and archaeological approaches.

In social and economic anthropology, Kopytoff (1986) introduced the idea of object biography to provide new perspectives on the circulation of commodities, focusing more on commodities themselves than on the form or purpose of exchange. Kopytoff (1986, 64) questions the economists' point of view that commodities just exist, stressing that they "must be not only produced materially as things, but also culturally marked as being a certain kind of thing." He uses the biography of a slave to show how something might be treated as a commodity at one point in time but not at another, depending on the social context. He introduces biography as a metaphor suitable even for the *life* of objects. Objects can be categorized as commodities through the notions of the singular and the common (ibid., 68).

In archaeology, object biography has been present for a very long time, although it may not be phrased exactly like that. The investigation of formative processes is an important field in archaeology. Studies of how archaeological sites are created are inseparable from the interpretation of the remains they yield. In research into formation processes, archaeologists try to establish and reconstruct the sequence of events that preceded and affected the creation of an archaeological find, whether a single artefact or an entire site. In other words, archaeologists try to determine the history of the production, use and discarding of material culture. The most important studies in this vein were conducted by Schiffer (1972; 1996 [1987]), with his flow models of artefacts' life-cycles.

The future archaeological context is influenced by both cultural and natural factors (Schiffer 1996 [1987], 7). Cultural factors consist of any human activity or intervention in one's physical surroundings. These include tool-making or settlement, the exploitation of natural resources, the dumping of waste, etc. Natural factors consist of all biophysical occurrences that have an impact on a site after its abandonment. Even though Kopytoff's comprehension of object biography can be considered a cultural factor, processes of cultural formation direct attention towards linking given behaviours to a certain pattern in the archaeological record. Ethnoarchaeological research, especially on the ritual deposition of objects, took these assumptions seriously.

More recently, archaeological discussions on object biography have tended to refer to Kopytoff. Archaeologists who have worked within this framework include Holtorf (2002), Shanks (1998), Gosden and Marshall (1999), to name but a few. This concept has recently been recognized in numismatics as well (von Kaenel 2009; Krmnicek 2009).

Coins from the classical period found in medieval grave offerings, sometimes shaped like a pendant, indicate that these coins have gone through various stages of understanding, evaluation and handling in the course of their *lives*, passing in and out of different social spheres. This resonates with Kopytoff's conception of object biography. Yet the transformation here is not from object to commodity, whether we perceive coins as money, that is, as the ultimate commodity, or only as a means of exchange. Still, the principle of common and singular pertains to this case. In the original context, where coins were used according to their purpose, the common aspect applied. The coins could only be understood in relation to other objects, either coins of different denominations or commodities whose value they expressed. Then coins always had to share some properties with other factors in the exchange. In the secondary context, the coins are singular. Their exclusiveness is not achieved by temporal distance alone. Rather, ultimate *singularization* occurs with the coins' intentional and final deposition in the grave. Also, since the value of the coin is formed, confirmed and modified through the manner of its usage, the challenge is to reconstruct all of the different backgrounds in which it circulated. For this part, a more archaeological or formative approach to object biography is valuable.

The potential of object biography for secondarily used coins

In both approaches to object biography, each class of things is determined by one idealized version of the object's life-cycle or biography. This ideal biography could be shaped either by the social norms of one culture (Kopytoff, 1986), or by the pure usefulness of an object for some specific purpose (Schiffer 1972). In reality, however, multiple factors come into play, and therefore the final biographies often vary significantly from the ideal model. This leads us to question what might be considered the ideal biography for objects such as coins and how this biography varies in the cases included in this study.

Since we are now speaking about an ideal object biography, I will first consider coins

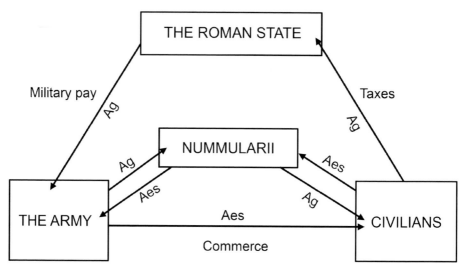

Figure 8.1. A traditional model of coin circulation in the Roman Empire (after Kemmers 2009, 139, fig. 1).

in their ideal sense, focusing more on their economic aspect. Models of the circulation of Roman coins have been heatedly debated in ancient numismatics. Numerous attempts were made during these years of research to compile data and map coin use in the Roman period (starting with Howgego 1994). Although it is impossible to define one single model which could incorporate all of the possibilities of coin circulation, Kemmers (2009, 139) implies that "current ideas on coin supply and circulation can be summarized in one basic model" (Fig. 8.1).

> "In this model, the state supplied the army with precious metal coins. Through daily commerce, coins were disseminated into the civilian sphere, after the soldiers had changed their *denarii* into small change at *nummularii*. Civilians then paid their taxes to the state in precious metal for which they first had to change their bronze coinage back into silver at the same *nummularii*. The state could then melt or reuse the silver coins to pay the army, and so on and so forth. Several additions to this model have been made, allowing for provincial treasuries as intermediaries, payments to civil servants, deposition and hoarding of coins, etc. but in its essence the concept remains the same"

> (Kemmers 2009, 139).

In other words, we could say that the ideal object biography for coins is for them to circulate and be recycled endlessly, without ever leaving the pool and reaching our hands as a final destination. If we were to express it in Schiffer's terminology, coins, as durable elements, would always be somewhere between the phases of manufacture and discard (Fig. 8.2).

Even though the model presented here corresponds more closely to the possible mode of coin circulation before the changes in Late Antiquity, one can say that the basic idea of endless circulation is also present in the monetary policy of the fourth century. However,

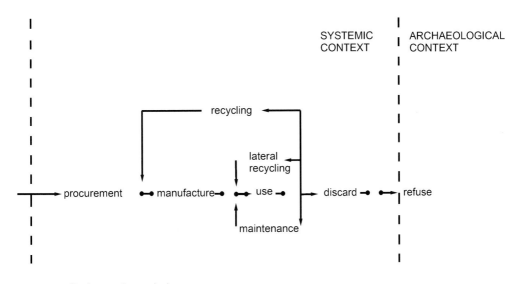

Figure 8.2. A flow model for viewing the life cycle of durable elements (after Schiffer 1972, 159, fig. 2).

we know that this is not the case, and very often the archaeological record, and even our contemporary everyday experience, suggest many other possibilities. Coinage ends up in many different contexts: hoards, lost finds, grave offerings, etc. But what would I like to consider here is evaluation as a key factor for these oscillations with respect to the ideal prototype. From the coin's issuing until its final use, it is primarily the value ascribed to the coin that determines its life-cycle. Divergences in the object biographies of coins can occur in various stages of their life-cycles. Beginning with their minting and identifying the principles on which they would operate further, value, both as concept and as quality, is what drives these changes. It is certainly questionable what makes this value. Usually, the debate is over whether the coin's value consists in the metal content or is purely nominal. The dispute is most intensive in cases of precious metal coinage, while for the base metal denominations, scholars agree that their value is more nominal. There is not the space here to discuss this significant issue (on this debate, see, for example, Strobel 2004, 207–216), but as the system of values is established, it creates a complex network of relationships between different denominations (or between the coins themselves) and creates bonds with various other things (material and immaterial), based on the notion of equivalence. After a coin enters circulation, the stability of its value ensures its *perfect* biography. As soon as some change occurs in its value, an opportunity for different trajectories arises. If, for example, the value of a coin rises, the chances of that coin being temporarily withdrawn from circulation and selected for hoarding grow. Alternatively, if its value decreases, the coin will re-enter circulation in an attempt to exchange it for a coin of greater value. A coin of a smaller denomination (or of lower value) tends to be lost more often because it changes hands more frequently (Collis 1974, 192). Also, once isolated from other coins, its limited purchasing power would no doubt discourage efforts to find it. Finally, with the breakdown of the entire system, and in the interval without a new system in which they can be of use, coins become valueless and are likely to be discarded, hence the occurrence of secondary use as an option.

So far the relevance of object biography for the investigation of coinage has been observed through the peculiarities of coins as a category of monetary objects. To examine the connection between value transformation and possible shifts in the life-cycle, I shall continue by discussing two specific examples from case studies included in my research. While both case studies share the context of a grave and the Roman coins found in it, they differ significantly in their characteristics. One example comes from the necropolis of Singidunum IV, dated to the mid-fifth century (Ivanišević and Kazanski 2007). This necropolis is interpreted as a cemetery of warriors, probably of some Germanic tribe, many of whom migrated into the middle Danube by the end of the fourth and into the fifth centuries. The other example comes from the necropolis of Brestovik-Visoka Ravan, dated to the twelfth and thirteenth century (Ćorović-Ljubinković 1956; 1958). This necropolis is interpreted as the village cemetery of a medieval Serbian population (Ćorović-Ljubinković 1956, 131; 1958, 326).

Singidunum IV

This necropolis is situated beneath the western part of the Belgrade fortress. In close proximity, about 100 metres to the south-west, is another early medieval necropolis, Singidunum I (Bjelajac and Ivanišević 1991). Singidunum IV is a small burial site consisting of only three graves. It was probably a cemetery of warriors buried there around the first half of the fifth century (Ivanišević and Kazanski 2007, 113, 128). Four Roman coins, one *denarius* of Marcus Aurelius (139–161), one AE3 of Valens (364–378) and two non-readable AE4's, also from the fourth century, were found in one grave (no. 2/2006) (Fig. 8.3), having been buried between 420 and 450 (ibid., 117, 128).

In addition to coin finds, there are numerous other significant grave goods. The inventory consists of 49 objects which can be divided into three groups: objects of the deceased (16), offerings (30), and parts of the wooden coffin (3). Interestingly, the Roman coins were found near the right hip, together with two flints where the remains of a buckle were also found. Other objects of the deceased included parts of the dress (fibula, buckles etc.). Offerings mainly consisted of broken weapons (sword, bow and spear), arrowheads and a glass cup (ibid., 116–118).

Brestovik-Visoka Ravan

This necropolis is located in the village of Brestovik, about 40 kilometres south of Belgrade on the banks of Danube. Since the results of the excavations have not yet been fully published, the available data about this necropolis are limited. However, through the courtesy of curator S. Fidanovski of the National Museum in Belgrade, I obtained significant information and access to Roman coins from this necropolis. The number of

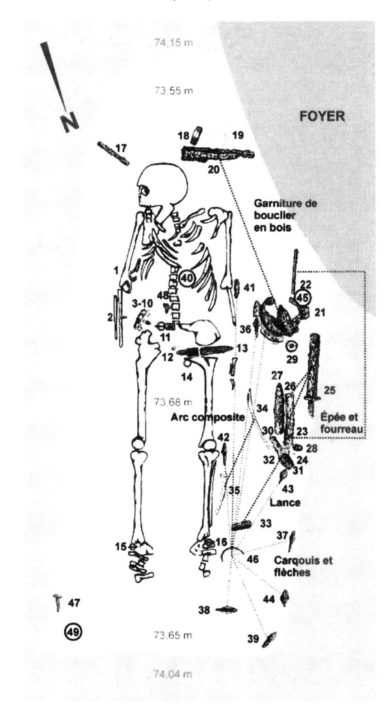

Figure 8.3. g. 2/2006, Singidunum IV, around 450 AD (after Ivanišević and Kazanski, 2007, 117, fig. 4).

Figure 8.4. Necklace from g. 65, Brestovik, twelfth and thirteenth century (after Marjanović-Vujović 1986, 195, fig. 11).

graves excavated so far is 887 (Marjanović-Vujović 1986, 195). All the graves are arranged in regular rows and oriented mainly along an east-west axis (head to the West), with some smaller deviations towards the North and South (Ćorović-Ljubinković 1958, 326). Two layers of burials could be distinguished. The older graves are shallow, the newer burials much deeper. These new burials often disturb the older graves, and usually these bones were then relocated and buried in a new grave nearby. In the earlier phase the deceased was just placed in a pit in the ground, and very rarely the body was covered with or laid on top of a wooden board. Later the deceased was covered with two wooden boards forming a roof on two sides, but burials without a construction are also found. The skeletons were in a supine position with arms placed differently – beside the body, or on the stomach, pelvis or chest (ibid., 326–327). Grave goods are very rare (130 graves), and most of the burials had no offerings. Usually finds included jewellery and pieces of garment. A stylistic analysis of finds indicates that the necropolis is to be dated to the twelfth or thirteenth century (Ćorović-Ljubinković 1956, 136–137; 1958, 329).

Roman coins (20) were found as necklace pendants in four graves of females (no. 41, 65, 68 and 297) (Fig. 8.4).

The majority of coins are base metal denominations from the fourth century (16), two are illegible *antoniniani* from the third century, one is an *as* from the second century, and one is an AE4 from the early fifth century (*Concordia Avg* type). Among the fourth-century coins the majority are actually very worn and illegible (8), but four could be attributed to *Gloria Exercitvs* with two standard types (330–335), one of the type with a wolf and twins with two stars (324–341), one of the *Providentiae Avgg* type, one of the *Iovi Conservatori* type (317–324), and one perhaps an AE3 of Valens (364–378). Necklaces are made of ceramic and glass paste beads of various shapes, fragments of metal and cowry shells. Beside the necklaces, other jewellery was uncovered, namely bracelets, earrings and rings. Some medieval coins were also found, one in a child burial, one, a pendant together with Roman coins, in grave no. 297, while in grave no. 848 a medieval silver coin was found placed in the mouth of the deceased (Ljubinković 1959, 154).

Observing examples from these two necropolises, it is obvious that the object biographies of these particular coins diverged from the assumed ideal version for this category of object. In an attempt to account for this, examining how these coins came to be reused could provide constructive insights. Here I briefly set out the data that are crucial to understanding their object biographies:

- the time difference between the coin's issuance and its deposition in the grave
- the association of coins with other finds in a single grave and the position of the grave in the necropolis as a whole
- the wider sociocultural and historical background of the necropolis and its relation to the remains of Roman towns, fortifications and necropolises.

In the example from the Singidunum IV necropolis, the time difference between the coins' date of issue and their deposition varies. The *denarius* of Marcus Aurelius was deposited about 300 years after its issue, and the copper coins were placed in this grave some 50 to 70 years after they were minted. As we see, there is a significant time span between the issue dates of the coins themselves (more than 200 years). All the coins were found very close to each other, with indications that they were in a purse that was probably hanging from the right side of the waist. As already mentioned, other finds show that the male buried in this cemetery was a warrior of significant social status. Warrior graves are rare and represent a novelty in the territory of Moesia I in the first half of the fifth century. At that time the practice of the Roman Empire of recruiting barbarian mercenaries to defend the boundaries of the Empire became more common. Barbarian soldiers acquired the status of *foederatii* and grew into an important new social group in the Late Roman Empire. After the Hunic invasion of 441 and the collapse of the Roman *limes*, this area became even more open to different barbarian populations, mostly Germanic tribes. This intensive contact between the Roman and *barbarian* worlds involved many transactions in which coins played a major role, from payments to tributes. If we place our warrior from the Singidunum IV necropolis against this background, the coins found in his purse raise several questions. Could these coins in grave no. 2/2006 have ended up there as a consequence of some of these transactions? Are these coins part of some payment or tribute?

If we take this possibility into account, then the question of the circulation period of a coin is of crucial interest. The challenge of determining the disappearance of some coin type from circulation is probably the most difficult one in numismatics. One of the main obstacles is establishing to what extent the dynamics of the circulation was a process of *natural* wastage and to what extent it was affected by the deliberate removal of an older coinage. In his investigations into these matters, Duncan-Jones (1994, 193–206) found that, when it comes to second-century silver coinage, defining the periods of circulation is very complicated, and *denarii* disappear much faster than their wastage rate due to their deliberate withdrawal. His calculations showed that Trajanic and Hadrianic *denarii* stayed in the pool for about 40 to 50 years after they were minted (ibid., 202). However, in some cases this period is much longer. The legionary (republican) *denarii* of Antony were still circulating in the early third century, some 240 or 250 years after they entered circulation (ibid., 205). Could a *denarius* from the Singidunum IV necropolis have stayed in the pool equally long? The context of its deposition and that of another three copper coins from a much later period (fourth century) could support this. In addition, the problem of silver coinage in late antiquity, i.e. its lack, gives us an opportunity to suggest a different appreciation of the *old denarius*. Especially if the parties to which the Roman Empire had obligations of this nature had been fond of certain materials, all the available resources could have been exploited. The other three small copper denominations are in the final phase in terms of circulation period and the general usage of coinage in this area. According to Duncan (1993, 167):

> "On the Danubian limes, the supply of new copper coinage tapered off after 375 and then, in the last decade of the fourth century with SALVS REI PUBLICAE of the western mints or in the first decades of the fifth century with GLORIA ROMANORVM of the eastern mints, practically ceased. Copper coinage ceased altogether to be used along the most of the Danube during the fifth century, in many areas perhaps in the 440s as a result of the devastation caused by the Huns."

As we can see, our warrior's coins were deposited at a crucial moment for Roman coinage, a period of change. In the following centuries, the principles on which Roman coinage was based broke down, and the monetary system of medieval Western Europe and Byzantine Empire became considerably different.

In the second example, the situation is quite different. The time difference is much greater between the coins' date of issue and the period in which they were buried, in some cases as much as a millennium. All these Roman coins were pierced and used as pendants on a necklace. They were found in graves in a village cemetery that was in use for a lengthy period of time. Funerary customs practised in this necropolis show that the deceased was very rarely buried with offerings. The majority of the graves had no objects in them, making our coin necklaces even more exceptional. Also, this was a time when Christianity had been accepted as a religion (Ostrogorsky 1980, 218, 236, 431). However, the offerings were in conflict with Christian funerary customs, indicating the presence of other traditions too. Politically, the twelfth and thirteenth centuries were a period of constant battles between the Hungarian Kingdom and Byzantine Empire on one side, and a newly formed Serbian medieval state on the other (Čubrilović 1974, 131–140). Being in the environs of Belgrade, this necropolis was in an area where political authorities and administrative borders changed very rapidly. With many rulers probably came many different currencies. But what is noticeable in this necropolis is that the number of contemporary medieval coins was much smaller than the number of older Roman coins. Here the question of the availability of both coinages, as well as of the selection process, is important. Most probably, Roman coins were found in the ruins of Roman towns and forts. In the vicinity of Brestovik was a significant Roman fort and settlement, *Castra Tricornia* (Ritopek) (Kondić 1957). Parts of Roman necropolises and monumental tombs are also found in Brestovik (Stričević 1958). One hoard of more than 1,000 bronze coins from the fourth and early fifth centuries, kept in the National Museum in Belgrade, originates from Brestovik (Bendžarević 2005, 568). Is it possible that old Roman coinage was more readily available than the contemporary coinage, or that the process of acquiring Roman coins, discovering them in the ground, created a special affection for them? In his monumental work *Life and customs of the Serbian people* (my translation), V. Karadžić (1867, 238–239), among others, mentioned the practice of digging for money. There was a common popular belief in various supernatural forces that protected the money (coins) that was dug in the ground and prevented people from extracting it. One could dig out the treasure only after sacrificing the appropriate animal. Bearing this in mind, we should not exclude the possibility that certain rules were also applied in the case of Brestovik and that the coins' presence and availability are not enough to explain their reuse. We should also question whether their monetary aspects were even recognized, or whether they had merely become decorative objects. Another reason for their popularity could have been their possible apotropaic functions. The use of pierced coins as amulets in the Early Byzantine period is matter for debate. One example of a *follis* of Justinian I (527–565) with the inscription *Lord, protect the wearer* no doubt testifies to this function of coinage (Fulghum 2001) and therefore should be taken into account in the Brestovik case. Either way I would say that, in the case of Brestovik, Roman coins became a deeply personal possession in the form of valuables.

Concluding remarks

The question raised in the title of this chapter was aimed at initiating a rethink of the concept of object biography in the case of secondarily used Roman coins. In that sense, I hope that the examples presented have raised again some of the important concerns about the subject. However, also I hope that some of the following conclusions will help overcome these concerns.

The study of coinage within a strict framework of numismatics limits the interpretation of these finds. In the traditional numismatic analysis, the coin is observed in isolation from other finds and contexts. The shortcomings of this approach are most observable in cases where coins have been used differently from what is expected. The examples of Roman coins in medieval graves demonstrate the necessity for (a) observing them as part of a wide corpus of material culture, and (b) directing attention to the coin's context. The object biography paradigm seems highly adequate in overcoming these difficulties. Through object biography, it is possible to perceive at the same time the general and particular aspects of these coins. However, object biography is ultimately insufficient on its own and leaves many dilemmas unresolved. As presented in the case studies, in researching the object biographies of Roman coins, many questions require greater consideration.

In the case of the Singidunum IV necropolis, an important issue is the expiry date of a particular coin type and its period of use as an official means of payment. This is crucial in establishing whether it is even possible to say that we are dealing with a secondary use at all. Four coins from our warrior showed us how fuzzy these categories are. Object biography, for all its descriptive advantages, falls short of providing an explanatory model. If we take seriously the possibility that the coins ended up in the grave as a consequence of transactions between the Romans and the barbarians, all theories of exchange should be addressed. These transactions are always social interactions, in this case the establishment of new positions by the Roman Empire towards the barbarians. The coinage involved had most certainly therefore possessed symbolic power and was not just a means of payment. It probably confirmed the new positions of both the barbarians with respect to the Romans, and of the barbarians among themselves.

The much later necropolis at Brestovik provides evidence for the incorporation of coins into the usual material culture of the South Slavic medieval population after their discard. This raises the question of how people in the past perceived the remains of older civilizations, such as the Roman civilization, which they encountered and had even adjusted to their own cultures. The ruins of Roman forts and towns probably dominated the landscape for many centuries after they were deserted because the greatest devastation of Roman sites only started with the modernization of these areas in the late nineteenth and early twentieth centuries. It is uncertain whether the previous cultural meanings imbued in these objects and coins played any role in the creation of the new meaning, or whether they were totally irrelevant. Again, object biography provides a wider framework for the vast field of complex relationships between people and things in this case, but it falls short of clarifying them.

Even if object biography is not sufficient to answer many of our questions, it is nevertheless a very good starting point for further developing our interpretations of material culture.

References

Bajalović-Birtašević, M. (1960) *Srednjevekovna nekropola u Mirijevu*. Beograd, Muzej Grada.

Bendžarević, T. (2005) Ostave bronzanog novca IV veka sa teritorije Srbije. *Zbornik Narodnog muzeja – serija: Arheologija* 18 (1), 553–580.

Berić, N. (2001) Srednjovekovna nekropola na lokalitetu Konopljara. In N. Tasić and E. Radulović (eds) *Arheološka nalazišta Kruševca i okoline*, 109–115. Kruševac and Beograd, Narodni Muzej.

Bjelajac, Lj. and Ivanišević, V. (1991) *Les témoignages archéologiques des Grandes Invasions à Singidunum. Starinar* 42, 123–139.

Brooke, C. N. L.; Stewart, B. H. I. H.; Pollard, J. G. and Volk, T. R. (1983) Introduction. In C. N. L. Brooke, B. H. I. H. Stewart, J. G. Pollard and T. R. Volk (eds) *Studies in numismatic method: Presented to Philip Grierson*, xxvi–xxx. Cambridge, Cambridge University Press.

Collis, J. (1974) Data for dating. In J. Casey and R. Reece (eds) *Coins and the archaeologist*. BAR 4, 189–200, Oxford, Archaeopress.

Coock, A. and Dacre, M. (1985) *Excavations at Portway, Andover 1973–1975: Anglo-Saxon cemetery, Bronze Age and linear barrow ditch*. Archaeology Monographs, 4. Oxford, Oxford University, School of Archaeology.

Ćorović-Ljubinković, M. (1956) La nécropole slave de Brestovik. Rapport préliminaire des fouilles en 1953–1954. *Archaeologia Jugoslavica* 2, 131–137.

Ćorović-Ljubinković, M. (1958) Dosadašnja iskopavanja na lokalitetu Visoka Ravan u Brestoviku. *Zbornik radova Narodnog muzeja* 1, 325–333.

Čubrilović, V. (ed.) (1974) *Istorija Beograda. I Stari, srednji i novi vek*. Beograd, Prosveta.

Down, A. and Welch, M. (1990) *Chichester excavations VII: Apple Down and the Mardens*. Chichester, Chichester District Council.

Duncan, G. L. (1993) *Coin circulation in the Danubian and Balkan provinces of the Roman Empire AD 294–578*. Royal Numismatic Society, Special Publications, 26. London, Royal Numismatic Society.

Duncan-Jones, R. (1994) *Money and government in the Roman Empire*. Cambridge, Cambridge University Press.

Eckardt, H. and Williams, H. (2003) Objects without a past? The use of Roman objects in early Anglo-Saxon graves. In Williams, H. (ed.) *Archaeologies of remembrance: Death and memory in past societies*, 141–170. New York, Kluwer.

Ercegović-Pavlović, S. (1980) *Les nécropoles romaines et médiévales de Mačvanska Mitrovica.* Sirmium, 12. Beograd, Institut Archéologique de Beograd.

Fulghum, M. M. (2001) Coins used as amulets in late antiquity. In S. R. Asirvatham, C. O. Pache and J. Watrous (eds) *Between magic and religion: Interdisciplinary studies in ancient Mediterranean religion and society*, 139–147. Oxford, Rowman and Littlefield.

Gosden, C. and Marshall, Y. (1999) The cultural biography of objects. *World Archaeology* 31 (2), 169–178.

Holtorf, C. (2002) Notes on the life history of a potsherd. *Journal of Material Culture* 7 (1), 49–71.

Howgego, C. (1994) Coin circulation and the integration of the Roman economy. *Journal Roman Archaeology* 7, 15–21.

Ivanišević, V. and Kazanski, M. (2007) Nouvelle nécropole des Grandes Migrations de Singidunum. *Starinar* 57, 113–135.

Karadžić, V. S. (1867) *Život i običaji naroda srpskog.* Vienna.

Kemmers, F. (2009) Sender or receiver? Contexts of coin supply and coin use. In H. M. von Kaenel and F. Kemmers (eds) *Coins in context I: New perspectives for the interpretation of coin finds. Colloquium Frankfurt a.M., October 25–27, 2007.* Studien zu Fundmünzen der Antike, 23, 137–156. Mainz, Philipp von Zabern.

Kemmers, F. and Myrberg, N. (2011) Rethinking numismatics: The archaeology of coins. *Archaeological Dialogues* 18 (1), 87–108.

Kondić, V. (1957) Antički Ritopek. *Godišnjak Muzeja Grada Beograda* 4, 35–46.

Kopytoff, I. (1986) The cultural biography of things: Commoditization as process. In A. Appadurai (ed.) *The social life of things: Commodities in cultural perspective*, 64–91. Cambridge, Cambridge University Press.

Krmnicek, S. (2009) Das Konzept der Objektbiographie in der antiken Numismatik. In H. M. von Kaenel and F. Kemmers (eds) *Coins in context I: New perspectives for the interpretation of coin finds. Colloquium Frankfurt a.M., October 25–27, 2007.* Studien zu Fundmünzen der Antike, 23, 47–59. Mainz, Philipp von Zabern.

Ljubinković, M. (1959) Brestovik, Visoka Ravan. *Arheološki Pregled* 1, 153–156.

Marjanović-Vujović, G. (1984) *Trnjane. Srpska nekropola (kraj XI – početak XIII veka).* Beograd, Narodni Muzej.

Marjanović-Vujović, G. (1986) Srednjovekovne nekropole u Srbiji evidentirane kroz arheološka iskopavanja (I). *Starinar* 37, 191–207.

Nađ, Š. (1959) Nekropola kod Aradca iz ranog srednjeg veka. *Rad Vojvođanskih Muzeja* 8, 45–102.

Ostrogorsky, G. (1980) *History of the Byzantine state.* Oxford, Oxford University Press.

Shanks, M. (1998) Life of an artifact. *Fennoscandia Archaeologica* 15, 15–42.

Schiffer, M. B. (1972) Archaeological context and systematic context. *American Antiquity* 37 (2), 156–165.

Schiffer, M. B. (1996 [1987]) *Formation processes of the archaeological record.* Salt Lake City, University of Utah Press.

Stričević, Đ. (1958) Brestovik rimska grobnica. *Starinar* 7–8, 411–413.

Strobel, K. (2004) Der Geldwesen des Imperium Romanum im Spiegel der papyrologischen Zeugnisse. In K. Strobel (ed.) *Forschungen zur Monetarisierung und ökonomischen Funktionalisierung von Geld in den nordwestlichen Provinzen des Imperium Romanum. Die Entstehung eines europäischen Wirtschaftsraumes. Akten des 2. Trierer Symposiums zur antiken Wirtschaftsgeschichte.* Trierer historische Forschungen, 49, 207–221. Trier, Kliomedia.

von Kaenel, H. M. (2009) Coins in context: A personal approach. In H. M. von Kaenel and F. Kemmers (eds) *Coins in context I: New perspectives for the interpretation of coin finds. Colloquium Frankfurt a.M., October 25–27, 2007.* Studien zu Fundmünzen der Antike, 23, 9–24. Mainz, Philipp von Zabern.

Chapter 9

The role of flint in mediating identities:
The microscopic evidence

Annelou van Gijn and Karsten Wentink

The biographical approach in artefact studies

Material objects have always played an important role in the lives of human beings. Objects are used as tools to reach certain ends, as gifts to negotiate, establish or prolong social relations or as animated subjects that represented or even embody non-human entities such as spirits, gods or ancestors. In many cases, however, objects do not have a single fixed meaning or function, but rather are continually ascribed different meanings and functions. New Guinea stone axes, for example, started life as convenient tools, were exchanged between wedding partners to seal the relationship between the two parties, and after the death of the owner or user could be used to house the spirit of the deceased and were treated as an object of sacred power (Hampton 1999; White and Modjeska 1978). This latter stage, however, only obtained as long as the proper rituals were being performed and repeated, otherwise the ancestor would leave his stone housing to roam the earth, and the axe returned to its former state of being a tool.

The idea of objects having different meanings in different stages of their use lives is not new. Like human beings, objects go through different stages of life and are attributed different meanings, functions and statuses as they pass from one stage to another. Although anthropology and historical archaeology have provided us with numerous examples of this principle, the matter becomes more problematic when dealing with prehistoric artefacts for which no written records survive. One way of obtaining greater insight into the possible meanings, functions and statuses of objects is by studying them from a biographical perspective (Kopytoff 1986). By doing detailed empirical studies involving the selection of raw materials, techniques of production, traces of wear and residue, and the contexts in which objects were deposited, we are able to trace at least some of the choices made by our prehistoric agents. Each stage in the life trajectory of material objects can be studied by means of relatively recently developed analytical techniques in archaeology (Van Gijn 2010, chapter 2).

Although we are fully aware that we are generally not able to reconstruct all the details of the actual use life of things, we can often compile their overall biographies, revealing much of what has previously been invisible. One of the primary tools we have at our disposal is microscopic use wear and residue analysis. As objects are used for various tasks or are involved in certain activities, these will result in wear and tear such as edge rounding, striations, and polish and edge removals (Van Gijn

1990). Although frequently not visible to the naked eye, these traces of wear are made apparent by using various microscopic techniques. Key to understanding the different traces that are observed on archaeological materials are the thousands of experiments that have been performed at the Leiden Laboratory for Artefact Studies in the last 30 or so years. By comparing experimentally used tools with archaeological finds, we are able to interpret the activities these prehistoric tools were used for. Apart from traces of wear, we also study archaeological residues: bits and pieces of materials that have remained stuck to the surfaces of the objects we study.

Flint: A telling material

One of the materials for which the biographical approach has proved most profitable is the study of flint objects (Van Gijn 2010). Flint is often referred to as the metal of the Stone Age because it is an extremely versatile raw material that could be used to make many domestic tools, such as knives, scrapers and borers. Usually many of these tools are not regarded as particularly special. However, flint has several inherent properties that cause it to be less insignificant than we tend to think. First of all, it can appeal to our senses: it usually has a distinctive colour, and sometimes a mottled appearance of contrasting hues. Colour is a feature that many archaeologists tend to overlook, shaped as we are by black and white photographs and line drawings (Hurcombe 2008; Jones and MacGregor 2002). Flint has a texture that can be felt and experienced. The translucency of flint is also likely to have added to its attractiveness. Flint may even have appealed to our auditory senses: it produces a nice ringing sound when knapped, and everybody who ever attended a 'knap-in' (Whittaker 2004, 1) knows the characteristic sound of flakes dropping on top of each other. It can well be imagined that such knapping sessions were undertaken not only for the production of usable end products or to learn how to knap, but for the very experience of knapping in a ritual or ceremonial context (Van Gijn 2010, 183). Another physical property of flint is its capacity to make fire when flakes of flint are struck against pyrite or iron: flint is thus linked to an element that is highly significant in both domestic and ritual contexts (Larsson 2002).

Flint also signals its origin. Because of its characteristic colours and textures, it is often clear to any knowledgeable observer where the material comes from. As a consequence, flint artefacts can constitute, as Bradley and Edmonds (1993) call it, *pieces of places*. Although some archaeologists see the use of cortical flakes as a sign of raw material shortages, fragments of cortex (the outer layer of flint nodules) may well have been left intentionally on flint objects. The reason for this is that the presence of cortex may also contribute information about the origin of the piece of flint. For example, Rijckholt flint with a chalky cortex simply *had* to originate from the flint mines in the southeast Netherlands and could not have been obtained from the gravel beds or terraces along the rivers, as then the cortex would be rolled and hard. Exotic flint can thus make reference to places far removed from the daily sphere of interaction. This may also include contacts with far-away exchange partners or even allusions to the world of mythical ancestors or spirits, a realm that is just as unreachable (and thus threatening) as places that are spatially remote (Helms 1988). The same pertains to flint objects in which much knowledge and expertise is invested: the know-how of a skilled craftsperson is often perceived as being bestowed with special – ancestral – knowledge (Helms 1993; Wentink 2008). Flint objects in which a lot of skills are invested and which are made of foreign raw material are thus likely to have a special meaning extending beyond the daily domestic sphere of local communities (Apel and Knutsson 2006). Such objects are often easily recognizable by a wider public and can be considered inalienable goods materializing collective values.

Two more aspects contribute to the suitability of flint as a symbolic marker: its portability and its longevity (Boivin and Owoc 2004; Cooney 2008). Large flint nodules destined to be reduced to a series of domestic tools are heavy to transport, but individual flakes are not. They can thus easily be moved across vast distances. Stone has a permanency few raw materials can equal as it is less likely to deteriorate than most other materials such as plant fibres and bone. It can thus be inscribed with symbolic information, linking the past and the present and the present to the future. To conclude, as inalienable things, flint objects can have a life of their own and can play a role in negotiating social relationships and processes of change. Flint is more than a simple raw material from which to make weapons and utensils.

Objectives

In this chapter we want to show how microscopic analysis of flint objects can reveal information about their life histories that is not otherwise obtainable, yet provides key information about their past significance. Microscopic examination of flint surfaces has revealed evidence of a special biography of certain flint items, evidence that was hitherto unavailable. Clearly, every archaeologist would be ready to acknowledge the special significance of the oversized axes from the Middle Neolithic Funnel-beaker culture: they are big, display extensive craftsmanship and are commonly found in groups in the peat (hoards). And indeed, microscopic examination has revealed positive evidence of the special treatment of these axes, as will be discussed below. However, it is not only the *usual suspects* like the oversized axes and the Grand Pressigny daggers of the Late Neolithic that have produced such evidence. Use wear and residue analysis of settlement flint has shown that some simple flint items have had a special biographical trajectory as well. We will illustrate this with a few examples in which the cultural biography of flint artefacts, as deduced from a technological and functional analysis, is closely linked to the representation and negotiation of identity.

The usual suspects: Axes and sickles

Over large parts of Northern Europe we find the Funnel-beaker culture, a distinct cultural group that originates from southern Scandinavia and is characterized amongst other things by the first adoption of agriculture in these areas, the burial of the dead in megalithic tombs and a highly characteristic type of pottery known as the funnel beaker (Midgley 1992). In the northern part of the present-day Netherlands remnants of the West-group of the Funnel-beaker culture can be found, dated to 3400–2900 BC (Bakker

1979). As part of the Funnel-beaker *cultural package* we also find extremely large flint axes that have been intentionally deposited, perhaps in sacrifices, in the peat bogs of the northern Netherlands (Ter Wal 1996; Wentink 2006). What is so remarkable about these objects is that they are magnifications of normal flint axes, that is, exaggerations too large to be used as their extreme size makes them highly impractical and susceptible to breakage. Wear trace analysis indeed indicates that these objects had never been used, and in fact many of them were never even polished, so strictly speaking they were not even finished (Wentink 2006; Wentink and Van Gijn 2008). Instead we found wear traces distributed over the entire body of the axe that were most likely caused by the axes having been repeatedly wrapped and unwrapped. In addition they were found

Figure 9.1. Ochre seen on a rectangular axe from the deposition of Een 1898 (orig. magnif. 10×) (after Wentink 2006).

to display traces of red ochre, indicating that they had at least partially been painted red (Fig. 9.1).

What is even more surprising is that these objects, found in the northern Netherlands, were actually produced in southern Scandinavia, an inference based on the raw material used and the absence of the distinctive production waste within the distribution of the West-group of the Funnel-beaker culture. Their use lives must therefore have involved transport and exchange over a distance of at least 200 to 400 kilometres. As they are too large to be used in a utilitarian way, we suggest that they were specifically produced to fulfil a different purpose, one that involved their being painted red, exchanged over vast distances, unwrapped probably to be displayed and wrapped up again, and ultimately ending their lives by being deposited in peat bogs, away from habitations of both the dead and the living. Clearly, these exceptional objects were held in esteem by all the communities *en route*, everyone involved being aware of the rules surrounding them. This indicates that they united people across vast distances through a common identity: that of the Funnel-beaker complex (Wentink *et al.* 2011).

Another type of conspicuous flint item is yet another import from southern Scandinavia: crescent-shaped, bifacially flaked flint sickles dated to the Late Bronze Age or Early Iron Age (Fig. 9.2). The implements were traded to the northern part of the present-day Netherlands as finished products. On the basis of their crescent shape and extensive gloss, they were commonly classified as and referred to as sickles (implicitly related to harvesting cereals). In fact, in southern Scandinavia they do indeed show traces of having been used to harvest cereals (H. Juel Jensen, personal communication). However, it was found that the traces of wear evident on the Dutch finds did not suggest cutting cereals. They were far too blunt for this purpose, and the distribution of the gloss across the entire surface of the object did not match our experimental findings (Van Gijn 1992). It was found that the traces seen on the Dutch finds most closely matched those resulting from experiments done with turf-cutting. Especially in the Dutch wetlands, turf would not only have been an important source of fuel, but would also have provided building materials for dwellings and burial mounds, as wood and stone are largely lacking in the wetlands. Most of the Dutch *sickles* were found outside settlements, either as single finds or in groups as hoards. One such hoard, at Heiloo in West-Friesland, is especially noteworthy: here four flint sickles and a bronze one were placed upright in the soil, suggesting an intentional deposition (Brunsting 1962; Van Gijn 2010, fig. 8.5). Even though these *sickles* were made and used as cereal-cutting implements in southern Scandinavia, in the area of the northern Netherlands they were assigned a different function. They were re-interpreted and, to some extent, *changed identity*.

Figure 9.2. Sickle from Andijk, West-Friesland (Photo by J. Pauptit, Leiden).

Domestic flint in the Rhine/ Meuse delta: Negotiating a new, Neolithic identity

Extensive use wear studies of Neolithic flint assemblages from the area of the Lower Rhine Basin have shown that domestic items may also reflect the identities of their makers and users (Van Gijn 2010, Chapter 6). One telling example will be presented, related to the issue of how, why and when the hunter-gatherers of the Mesolithic period turned to farming. This is a process that started in the Near East around 9000 BC, but it is not until *c*. 5300 BC that the first farmers settled in the southeastern part of the present-day Netherlands. It took another 1,000 years before we find the first evidence of agricultural practices in the northern and western wetlands of the Netherlands (Louwe Kooijmans 2007; Raemaekers 1999). The presence of several flint items of southern origin such as a pre-core of Rijckholt flint and the LBK point at the late Mesolithic site of Hardinxveld-Polderweg (located near the present-day city of Rotterdam) suggests that both groups must have been aware of each others' existence, at least (Van Gijn *et al.* 2001). How these objects got to the wetlands, by down-the-line exchange or through the actual mobility patterns of Mesolithic hunter-gatherers, is difficult to determine. In any case, use wear analysis has shown that these early imported tools do not bear traces of use. Through the early Neolithic, the increase of imported stone items of southern origin in the northern and western parts of the present-day Netherlands indicates that contacts between farmers and hunter-gatherers intensified (Van Gijn and Louwe Kooijmans 2005, fig. 15.5; Verhart 2000). It is not until 4200 cal BC that the neolithisation process in the Rhine/Meuse delta really takes shape. Under the influence of the southern farmers of the Michelsberg culture, the inhabitants of the wetlands gradually change their life-style, but fishing and gathering continue to be very important in their subsistence patterns, and their technology continues to display features typical of the old hunter-gatherer life-style (see various articles in Louwe Kooijmans and Jongste 2006). Imported flint items of southern origin are a regular occurrence. However, it will be shown that it is not merely the relative frequency of imported flint objects, but also the way the receiving society treated these foreign items, that sheds light on the question of shifting identities. This will be demonstrated by comparing the results of the use wear analysis of the flint from three Neolithic sites in the Rhine/Meuse delta of the western Netherlands: Brandwijk (situated to the east of the present-day city of Rotterdam) and Ypenburg and Schipluiden, both located in the vicinity of The Hague. Brandwijk has produced a series of strata, the earliest of which, Layer 30, dated to 4610–4450 cal BC (the Early Neolithic B). However, most finds derive from Layer 50, dated to 4220–3940 cal BC (Swifterbant culture, Middle Neolithic A) (Raemaekers 1999; Van Gijn and Verbruggen 1992). The later sites of Ypenburg and Schipluiden date to the second half of the Middle Neolithic A and are attributed to the Hazendonk group (3750–3400 cal BC) (Louwe Kooijmans and Jongste 2006).

Brandwijk

The site of Brandwijk is situated to the east of Rotterdam in an old riverine landscape (Raemaekers 1999; Van Gijn and Verbruggen 1992). This is a period for which we assume a subsistence pattern that has been called *extended broad spectrum*: hunting, fishing and gathering, and domesticated animals with only very limited access to cereals. The flint industry of Layer 50 is characterized by the use of water-rolled flint pebbles. It involved a flake technology, which also produced the incidental blade-like flake. Most likely the flint nodules were available relatively close by, but the source is unknown. Many of the flakes still display cortex, indicating that the nodules were of limited size. Use wear analysis of these implements shows that many flakes were used for domestic tasks like plant processing. The bone awls, which were also studied microscopically, were used on plants as well, most likely grasses or reeds We can therefore conclude that the occupants of this location spent time making baskets and doing wickerwork. Local flint was also employed in the manufacture of bone implements from metapodia.

In addition to the implements made of local flint, a number of tools were produced on non-local Rijckholt flint. The chalky cortex indicates that this is most likely mined flint. It concerns typical macrolithic Michelsberg tools, such as large pointed blades, end-scrapers and triangular points (Van Gijn 2010, fig. 6.4; Fig. 9.3a).

As production waste of these imported flint types was absent, we conclude that the

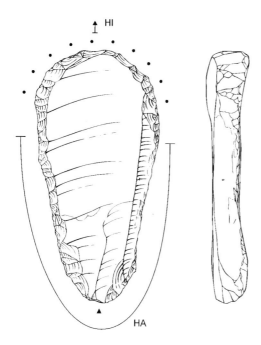

Figure 9.3a (left). Macrolithic end-scraper typical for the Michelsberg culture, found in the wetland site of Brandwijk, displaying traces from working hide.

Figure 9.3b (above). Exotic use wear traces seen on the same tool (orig. magnif. 200×).

tools must have been brought to the site as finished products. Use wear research has shown that these imported tools displayed traces of use that are normally only found on tools of the Early Neolithic farming communities in the southeastern loess zones (Van Gijn 2008a). This includes *polish 10*, a type of polish that displays traces also associated with hide- and plant-working. This type of polish was first reported for the Michelsberg site of Maastricht-Klinkers (Schreurs 1992), but has occasionally been found on Early Neolithic artefacts of the Bandkeramik culture as well (Verbaas and Van Gijn 2007). Other imported tools display heavily developed traces of hide working of a kind to suggest the very time-consuming softening and thinning stage of the hide-working process, something we normally do not see in coastal assemblages (Van Gijn 2010) (Fig. 9.3b).

It is noteworthy that the wetland inhabitants did not use these imported tools, even though they constituted perfectly usable implements of better quality than the locally produced implements. There are no signs of any re-sharpening of the imported items. Instead they were kept exactly in the state in which they were received, as finished items already used by farmers to the south or southeast.

The question is why the inhabitants of the wetlands of Brandwijk did not make use of these perfectly made flint items for their own purposes. We would argue that these tools of Michelsberg signature were imported not as used tools to *use*, but to *keep* (Van Gijn 2008a, 197). The imported items had therefore already acquired a history that was relevant to the inhabitants of Brandwijk: they link the recipients in the wetlands (broad-spectrum hunter-gatherers) with the users of these tools in the uplands (farmers).

Ypenburg and Schipluiden

Around 3750 BC the wetlands were settled by people of the Hazendonk group (Louwe Kooijmans 2005). We find a number of their sites in the micro-region of Delfland, situated close to the present-day city of The Hague. Here three sites have been extensively excavated: Ypenburg, Wateringen 4 and Schipluiden (Koot and Van der Have 2001; Louwe Kooijmans and Jongste 2006; Raemaekers *et al.* 1997). The sites have provided the earliest undisputed evidence of crop cultivation in the western coastal zones.

The flint assemblage of these sites shows a similar pattern to the material from the earlier site of Brandwijk: the majority of the flint artefacts were made on relatively small pebbles of local origin, and they were used for a variety of domestic tasks, including wood working and plant cutting. In addition to the local technology, tools of southern flint with a Michelsberg signature are present. The presence of waste flakes and an incidental core of imported flint indicate that the flint was locally knapped (Van Gijn *et al.* 2006). These imported tools are all heavily used and frequently display traces of rejuvenation. Remarkably enough, they were almost exclusively selected for carrying out *special activities*: for the production of amber and jet ornaments, reaping cereals and making fire. Ornament making can be considered *special* because beads and pendants constituted the predominant burial gift at the cemetery of Ypenburg (Koot and Van der Have 2001; Van Gijn 2008b). Cereal harvesting can be regarded as *special* because it concerns the first crop to be grown in this area. All the implements with traces of use for reaping cereals are large imported tools, which, after use, seem to have been intentionally destroyed: they were burned and their functional edges were damaged by intentional flaking (Fig. 9.4). Lastly, the edges of some sickles were rubbed with an unknown red substance, possibly a pigment. The intentional fracturing of objects usually has a ritual significance and

Figure 9.4. Large flake used to reap cereals, from the Middle Neolithic site of Ypenburg, burnt and broken after use (Photo by Q. Bourgeois, Leiden).

may be related to the wish to *kill* an object that is considered ambiguous or dangerous. Possibly farming was still considered dangerous to these first agriculturalists in the wetlands, as it involved the destruction of the natural surroundings that still provided many of the food sources and raw materials needed to survive, and which may also have been the residence of ancestral spirits. Returning these harvesting tools to nature by ritually killing them may be seen as a way of appeasing the ancestral spirits. The third *special activity* in which the imported flint was involved was fire making. A large number of strike-a-lights were discovered at Schipluiden, many of which were made of southern flint. The special significance of this type of tool is indicated by their presence in a remarkable grave found within the settlement area of Schipluiden. It contained the skeleton of a middle-aged man, buried on his side with his legs flexed tightly to his body. In his hands, which were positioned in front of his face, he was holding three strike-a-lights and a nodule of pyrite, evoking the image of someone blowing a spark (Louwe Kooijmans and Smits 2006; Van Gijn and Houkes 2006; Van Gijn *et al.* 2006).

The Hazendonk inhabitants of the wetlands thus selected the large imported tools of *Michelsberg signature* for specific tasks. It has been argued that these tasks were not just ordinary ones, employed in domestic tasks like wood or plant working, but tasks with a special importance like cereal harvesting, fire making and manufacturing amber and jet ornaments (Van Gijn 2008a; 2010). These tools were used intensively and show evidence of re-sharpening and curation. However, unlike the imported tools found at the earlier wetland site of Brandwijk, they did not show traces typical of the inland *Michelsberg* activities. Rather than *being kept* as valued items of exchange, these tools were *incorporated* into the technological system of the Hazendonk inhabitants of the wetlands (Van Gijn 2008a).

Import flint and changing identity

The period discussed in this part of our chapter, the Middle Neolithic A (4200–3400 BC), is the time during which the inhabitants of the wetlands gradually adopted a *Neolithic lifestyle* (Louwe Kooijmans 2005). During this entire period, large retouched blades and other typical Michelsberg macrolithic tools found their way to the wetlands, either through exchange or the actual mobility of people. There is, however, a crucial difference in the way these imported tools were treated during the early part of this period, represented by the site of Brandwijk, and the later period, exemplified by the Hazendonk sites of Schipluiden and Ypenburg. In the early period the Michelsberg tools were imported as *used* tools: they displayed the typical traces of wear normally found only on the implements of the farmers living to the southeast and south. Strangely enough, even though these imported tools were highly usable due to their size and high-quality flint, they were not subsequently used by their recipients. Instead they were left unaltered in the state in which they were received, as gifts from the distant *others* (see Mauss 1990 [1923/1924]), and were kept separate from the local technological system.

The later Hazendonk people continued to import macrolithic Michelsberg tools from the South, but these implements no longer constituted a gift or token that could not be altered. Instead, they were incorporated into the technological system of the wetland people of the Hazendonk group and thus, in a way, *appropriated*. It is highly significant that they used these foreign tools for a very new activity like cereal harvesting and for other, arguably special activities. These imported tools evidently had a special status, yet very much formed part of the local technological system. This indicates a change in attitude towards the Michelsberg farmers in the southeast and may be seen as reflecting a change in identity, from an affiliation with the Neolithic farmers in the South to the gradual appropriation of a new identity. It is therefore in the way this rather inconspicuous material was treated by its recipients that we can see the shift in mentality. Flint tools, even settlement material, played a role in the negotiation, construction and expression of a new, Neolithic identity.

Conclusion

The case studies presented above all show the importance of a detailed, biographical study of artefacts when studying the implications of imported flint objects, especially regarding the representation and negotiation of identity. It was shown that there is substantial variation in the biography of flint objects and that a study focussing merely on the presence or absence of imported flint – or other materials for that matter – is not enough to shed light on the possible meaning(s) these objects had for past societies. Such a biographical study requires different analytical techniques. The conception of the flint tool is represented by the selection of raw materials, determined by sourcing and raw material identification. The birth of the tool is the manufacturing stage, studied by means of technological analysis and experimental replication. The life of the object can be assessed by means of use wear and residue studies. Last, the deaths of objects can be interpreted by examining the context of deposition and their associations with other objects.

Rather than just mapping and categorizing objects, the focus of this approach is on what people were actually doing. By carefully analysing the different details about how people dealt with the things that surround them, we can at least acquire a glimpse of how prehistoric people interacted with their material world: how different objects played various roles, not only as tools used for everyday activities, but also as items of exchange, as gifts from far-away affines, as tokens of identity or personhood, or as sacred objects playing roles in various religious or ritual activities. In short, especially for prehistoric societies, this approach can help us shed light on what is otherwise obscured.

Acknowledgements

The authors would like to thank the organizers of the conference 'Itineraries of Material Culture' for an inspiring event.

References

Apel, J. and Knutsson, K. (eds) (2006) *Skilled production and social reproduction: Aspects of traditional stone-tool technologies: Proceedings of a symposium in Uppsala, August 20–24, 2003*. SAU Stone Studies, 2. Uppsala, Societas Archaeologica Upsaliensis.

Bakker, J. A. (1979) *The TRB West Group: Studies in the chronology and geography of the makers of the hunebeds and Tiefstich pottery*. PhD thesis, University of Amsterdam, (Reprint (2009) *The TRB West Group*. Leiden, Sidestone Press).

Boivin, N. and Owoc, M. A. (eds) (2004) *Soils, stones and symbols: Cultural perceptions of the mineral world*. London, UCL Press.

Bradley, R. and Edmonds, M. R. (1993) *Interpreting the axe trade: Production and exchange in Neolithic Britain*. New Studies in Archaeology. Cambridge and New York, Cambridge University Press.

Brunsting, H. (1962) De sikkels van Heiloo. *Oudheidkundige Mededelingen uit het Rijksmuseum van Oudheden te Leiden* 43, 107–115.

Cooney, G. (2008) Engaging with stone: Making the Neolithic in Ireland and Western Britain. In H. Fokkens, B. J. Coles, A. L. Van Gijn, J. P. Kleijne, H. H. Ponjee and C. G. Slappendel (eds) *Between foraging and farming: An extended broad spectrum of papers presented to Leendert Louwe Kooijmans. Analecta Praehistorica Leidensia*, 40, 203–214. Leiden, Faculty of Archaeology, Leiden University.

Hampton, O. W. (1999) *Culture of stone: Sacred and profane uses of stone among the Dani*. College Station, Texas A and M University Press.

Helms, M. W. (1988) *Ulysses' Sail: An ethnographic Odyssey of power, knowledge, and geographical distance*. Princeton, Princeton University Press.

Helms, M. W. (1993) *Craft and the kingly ideal: Art, trade and power*. Austin, University of Texas Press.

Hurcombe, L. (2008) A sense of materials and sensory perception in concepts of materiality. *World Archaeology* 39 (4), 532–545.

Jones, A. and MacGregor, G. (eds) (2002) *Colouring the past: The significance of colour in archaeological research*. Oxford and New York, Berg.

Koot, H. and Van der Have, B. (2001) *Graven in Rijswijk. De steentijdmensen van Ypenburg*. Rijswijk, Stichting Rijswijkse Historische Projecten en Gemeente Rijswijk.

Kopytoff, I. (1986) The cultural biography of things: Commoditization as process. In A. Appadurai (ed.) *The social life of things: Commodities in cultural perspective*, 64–91. Cambridge, Cambridge University Press.

Larsson, L. (2002) Fire as a means of ritual transformation during the prehistory of southern Scandinavia. In D. Gheorghiu (ed.) *Fire in archaeology: Papers from a session held at the European Association of Archaeologists 6th Annual Meeting in Lisbon 2000*. BAR International Series, 1089, 35–44. Oxford, Archaeopress.

Louwe Kooijmans, L. P. (2005) Hunters become farmers: Early Neolithic B and Middle Neolithic A. In L. P. Louwe Kooijmans, P. W. Van den Broeke, H. Fokkens and A. L. Van Gijn (eds) *The prehistory of the Netherlands*, 249–272. Amsterdam, Amsterdam University Press.

Louwe Kooijmans, L. P. (2007) The gradual transition to farming in the Lower Rhine Basin. In A. Whittle and V. Cummings (eds) *Going over: The Mesolithic-Neolithic transition in north-west Europe*. Proceedings of the British Academy, 144, 287–309. Oxford, Oxford University Press.

Louwe Kooijmans, L. P. and Jongste, P. F. B. (eds) (2006) *Schipluiden: A Neolithic settlement on the Dutch North Sea coast c. 3500 cal BC. Analecta Praehistorica Leidensia*, 37/38. Leiden, Faculty of Archaeology, Leiden University.

Louwe Kooijmans, L. P. and Smits, L. (2006) Graves and human remains. In L. P. Louwe Kooijmans and P. F. B. Jongste (eds) *Schipluiden: A Neolithic settlement on the Dutch North Sea coast c. 3500 cal BC. Analecta Praehistorica Leidensia*, 37/38, 91–112. Leiden, Faculty of Archaeology, Leiden University.

Mauss, M. (1990 [1923/1924]) *The gift: The form and reason for exchange in archaic societies*. London, Routledge, [First published in French: (1923/1924) Essai sur le don. Forme et raison de l'échange dans les sociétés archaïques. *L'Année Sociologique*, N. S., (1), 30–186].

Midgley, M. S. (1992) *TRB culture: The first farmers of the North European plain*. Edinburgh, Edinburgh University Press.

Raemaekers, D. C. M. (1999) *The articulation of a 'New Neolithic': The meaning of the Swifterbant culture for the process of neolithisation in the western part of the North European plain (4900–3400 BC.)*. PhD thesis, University of Leiden. Archaeological Studies, 3. Leiden, Faculty of Archaeology, University of Leiden.

Raemaekers, D. C. M.; Bakels, C. C.; Beerenhout, B.; Van Gijn, A. L.; Hänninen, K.; Molenaar, S.; Paalman, D.; Verbruggen, M. and Vermeeren, C. (1997) Wateringen 4: A settlement of the Middle Neolithic Hazendonk 3 Group in the Dutch coastal area. *Analecta Praehistorica Leidensia* 29, 143–192.

Schreurs, J. (1992) The Michelsberg site Maastricht-Klinkers: A functional interpretation. *Analecta Praehistorica Leidensia* 25, 129–171.

Ter Wal, A. (1996) Een onderzoek naar de depositie van vuurstenen bijlen. *Palaeohistoria* 37/38, 127–159.

Van Gijn, A. L. (1990) *The wear and tear of flint: Principles of functional analysis applied to Dutch Neolithic assemblages*. PhD thesis, University of Leiden. *Analecta Praehistorica Leidensia*, 22. Leiden, Faculty of Archaeology, Leiden University.

Van Gijn, A. L. (1992) The interpretation of 'sickles': A cautionary tale. In P. C. Anderson (ed.) *Préhistoire de l'agriculture. Nouvelles approches expérimentales et ethnographiques*, 363–372. Paris, CNRS.

Van Gijn, A. L. (2008a) Exotic flint and the negotiation of a new identity in the 'margins' of the agricultural world: The case of the Rhine-Meuse delta. In H. Fokkens, B. J. Coles, A. L. Van Gijn, J. P. Kleijne, H. H. Ponjee and C. G. Slappendel (eds) *Between foraging and farming: An extended broad spectrum of papers presented to Leendert Louwe Kooijmans. Analecta Praehistorica Leidensia*, 40, 193–202. Leiden, Faculty of Archaeology, Leiden University.

Van Gijn, A. L. (2008b) De ornamenten van Ypenburg. In J. M. Koot, L. Bruning and R. A. Houkes (eds) *Ypenburg-locatie 4. Een nederzetting met grafveld uit het Midden-Neolithicum in het West-Nederlandse kustgebied*, 277–288. Leiden, Station Drukwerk.

Van Gijn, A. L. (2010) *Flint in focus: Lithic biographies in the Neolithic and Bronze Age*. Leiden, Sidestone Press.

Van Gijn, A. L.; Beugnier, V. and Lammers, Y. (2001) Vuursteen. In L. P. Louwe Kooijmans (ed.) *Hardinxveld-Giessendam Polderweg. Een mesolithisch jachtkamp in het rivierengebied (5500–5000 v. Chr.)*. Rapportages Archeologische Monumentenzorg, 83, 119–161. Amersfoort, Rijksdienst voor het Oudheidkundig Bodemonderzoek.

Van Gijn, A. L. and Houkes, R. (2006) Stone: Procurement and use. In L. P. Louwe Kooijmans and P. F. B. Jongste (eds) *Schipluiden: A Neolithic settlement on the Dutch North Sea coast c. 3500 cal BC. Analecta Praehistorica Leidensia*, 37/38, 167–194. Leiden, Faculty of Archaeology, Leiden University.

Van Gijn, A. L. and Louwe Kooijmans, L. P. (2005) The first farmers: Synthesis. In L. P. Louwe Kooijmans, P. W. Van den Broeke, H. Fokkens and A. L. Van Gijn (eds) *The prehistory of the Netherlands*, 337–355. Amsterdam, Amsterdam University Press.

Van Gijn, A. L.; Van Betuw, V.; Verbaas, A. and Wentink, K. (2006) Flint: Procurement and use. In L. P. Louwe Kooijmans and P. F. B. Jongste (eds) *Schipluiden: A Neolithic settlement on the*

Dutch North Sea coast c. 3500 cal BC. Analecta Praehistorica Leidensia, 37/38, 129–166. Leiden, Faculty of Archaeology, Leiden University.

Van Gijn, A. L. and Verbruggen, M. (1992) Brandwijk – het kerkhof. In J.-K. A. Hagers and W. A. M. Hessing (eds) *Archeologische kroniek van Holland 1992*, 349–352. Amersfoort, Rijksdienst voor het Oudheidkundig Bodemonderzoek.

Verbaas, A. and Van Gijn, A. L. (2007) Use wear analysis of the flint tools from Geleen-Janskamperveld. In P. Van de Velde (ed.) *Excavations at Geleen-Janskamperveld 1990/1991. Analecta Praehistorica Leidensia*, 39, 173–184. Leiden, Faculty of Archaeology, Leiden University.

Verhart, L. B. M. (2000) *Times fade away: The neolithization of the southern Netherlands in an anthropological and geographical perspective.* PhD thesis, University of Leiden. Archaeological Studies, 6. Leiden, Faculty of Archaeology, University of Leiden.

Wentink, K. (2006) *Ceci n'est pas une hache. Neolithic depositions in the northern Netherlands.* RMA thesis, University of Leiden. Leiden, Sidestone Press.

Wentink, K. (2008) Crafting axes, producing meaning: Neolithic axe deposition in the northern Netherlands. *Archaeological Dialogues* 15 (2), 151–173.

Wentink, K. and Van Gijn, A. L. (2008) Neolithic depositions in the northern Netherlands. In C. Hamon and B. Quilliec (eds) *Hoards from the Neolithic to the metal ages: Technical and codified practices. Session of the XIth annual meeting of the European Association of Archaeologists.* BAR International Series, 1758, 29–43. Oxford, Archaeopress.

Wentink, K.; Van Gijn, A. L. and Fontijn, D. R. (2011) Changing contexts, changing meanings: Flint axes in Middle and Late Neolithic communities in the northern Netherlands. In V. Davis and M. R. Edmonds (eds) *Stone axe studies III*, 399–408. Oxford, Oxbow.

White, J. P. and Modjeska, N. (1978) Acquirers, users, finders, losers: The use axe blades make of the Duna. *Mankind* 11, 276–287.

Whittaker, J. C. (2004) *American flintknappers.* Austin, University of Texas Press.

Chapter 10

Wampum as Maussian *objet social totalitaire*

Mario Schmidt

> *"Now I don't love no material things*
> *but I'm in love with the feelings they bring"*
> (J. Cole – It cost me a lot)

Introduction

Descriptions of the daily life of the Narragansett and neighbouring Indian groups at the beginning of the seventeenth century are replete with seemingly irresolvable paradoxes, as told in the following account of the status of an indigenous political leader (*sachem*). This was drawn up by Roger Williams (1936 [1643], 142), the founder of Rhode Island and ethnographer *avant la lettre* and describes political decision-making as based on consensus of the whole group *and* the direct authority of the *sachem* simultaneously: "The Sachims, although they have an absolute Monarchie over the people; yet they will not conclude of ought that concernes all, either Lawes, or Subsidies, or warres, unto which the People are averse" (for a similar description, see Mayhew 1695, 13 ff.).

How should we read such a passage? The most straightforward solution is to take the biographical and cultural background of the observer into account and to evaluate Indian society as either highly egalitarian or highly unequal. But I do not want to understand this and similar examples as reflecting inconsistency of description. On the contrary, I think that the contradictions we observe were part of a contradictory reality and can be resolved at a meta-level that was inaccessible to Williams and his contemporaries. I will show that wampum, small black and purple beads made out of two different shells, served to obscure these contradictions in the society because of their itineraries, which took them between different spheres of value-generation. In what follows I will argue that, while on the level of everyday life wampum was one main sign of the Coastal Algonquian 'hypergood' (Taylor 1989),[1] the actual recognition of being someone imbued with value had specific prerequisites, namely belonging to the male gender and/or being a descendant of a former *sachem*. Thus the generation of value derived from domestic and political power was structured by notions of kinship and gender, and hence beyond the reach of both ordinary individuals and women. Nevertheless the sphere of everyday life in reality strengthened the position of political leaders through the massive circulation of wampum beads as the main materialized index of the *hypergood*. While *sachem*s wore signs of their power in the form of highly unique belts (*máchequoce*) sometimes made out of thousands of individual wampum beads, the same wampum passed through the hands of Indians in almost every transaction in daily life in either its strung (*enomphósachick*) or generic (*sawhóog*) form. Its circulation added value to individual persons, while at the same time restricting their political agency with respect to that of the *sachem*s, who used wampum in political negotiations to bolster their political influence. As both archaeological and textual evidence suggests that wampum beads did not play any important role in pre-contact societies (Ceci 1988; Bradford 1981), I understand the massive explosion of their distribution to have been a means of stabilizing hierarchical political relations,[2] which were questioned by the newly developing colonial situation and further contested following several smallpox epidemics in 1617–1618 and 1633. Wampum thus emerged to close the gap between the traditional hierarchy and newly enabled processes of individual relocation.[3]

To support my argument, I would like to introduce a structurally similar problem in the interpretation of one of anthropology's most discussed works: Marcel Mauss's 'Essai sur le don' (Mauss 1923/1924).[4] Recent discussions among the *Mouvement anti-utilitariste en sciences sociales (M.A.U.S.S.)* revolve around the question: "What rule of *legality* and *self-interest*, in societies of a backward or archaic type, compels the gift that has been received to be obligatorily reciprocated?" (Mauss 2000 [1923/1924], 3); in other words, how can the paradoxical nature of gifts as 'voluntary-obligatory' (Mauss 2007 [1923/1924], 102, my translation) be resolved?[5] The way to answer this question is to give Mauss's notion of *fait social total* a new twist. Here I will read Mauss's gift as a fetishized object, that is, one that reproduces a social totality by "effacing the traces of its own impossibility" (Zizek 2008 [1989], 50). In the present case, wampum determines individual self-completion as a quest that reproduces a repressive political economy. By mediating supra-personal relations through personal-emotional responses, wampum obscures inequality and injustice. The critical power of Mauss's theory of the gift can help resolve the paradox that Williams encountered.

Thus, after explaining in detail what the *hypergood* of Coastal Algonquian culture consists of, I will discuss the role that wampum plays in its mediation. I will show that, by circulating through every important part of society, wampum constructs a totality and enforces belief in the availability of an equal share of value for everyone. To explain how this can be achieved despite the system being openly non-egalitarian, I use a new interpretation of Mauss's notion of the *fait social total* which enables me to understand why Coastal Algonquian are able to disregard the oppressive structure of their society.

Transformation, autonomy and *uniqueness* as *hypergoods* of the coastal Algonquian ethos

Contemporary sources present Coastal Algonquian culture as almost obsessed with transformative processes as a way to achieve the status of a unique, complete character.[6] Its members attain value, in the sense of distinction, by overcoming physical and mental changes. They speak of gaining *manitou*, an evaluative term marking uniqueness

(Williams 1936 [1643]; Haefeli 2007), by enduring transformational processes – for whose enactment they themselves are fully responsible – that take place in quotidian activities such as eating,[7] talking (see Bragdon 1987), preparing and pursuing warfare (see Malone 2000 [1991]) or cosmological myths.[8] For the sake of brevity, I will focus on three examples: (1) rituals such as name-giving, vision quests and *powwows*; (2) economic transactions such as gambling; and (3) bodily decoration. Once the *hypergood* of the Coastal Algonquian has been unpacked, the specific role that wampum plays in its mediation can be better understood.

1. In contrast to Iroquoian name-giving, in which the names were eternal and individuals exchangeable (Graeber 2001, 120–121), in Coastal Algonquian cultures names were given "according to […] deeds or dispositions" (Winslow 1996 [1624], 64). They have therefore been "significant and variable" (ibid.) acoustic reminders of the individuality of their bearers and were changed several times during a lifetime (Occom 2006 [1761], 49). Persons without character were left nameless: "meane persons amongst them have no names" (Williams 1936 [1643], 5). Individuality through transformation is likewise visible in the initiation rites of young males, who were sent into the woods to undertake a so-called *vision quest*. Visions were summoned by hard and enduring physical transformations of one's relation to the world. These practices included sleep deprivation, repeated vomiting until it "seem[s] to be all blood" (Winslow 1996 [1624], 61) and severe physical punishments. The body was thereby opened up, turned inside out and emptied to receive spiritual strength (Mayhew 1695, 17–18). The same process occurred in the *pésoponck* or sweat-house. As a Fox told William Jones (1905, 184): "Often one will cut one's self over the arms and legs, slitting one's self only through the skin. It is done to open up many passages for the manitou to pass into the body. […]. It comes out in the steam, and in the steam it enters the body wherever it finds entrance."

Contrary to the enduring hardships of young initiates, a *powwow* was surprised by a vision that introduced him into the world of shamanistic practices. Through transformative actions such as ecstatic dancing, drumming, tobacco-smoking,[9] "horrible outcries, hollow bleatings, painful wrestlings, and smiting their own bodies" (Eliot and Mayhew 1653, B5), shamans were able to release powers to heal or to predict the future. A shaman acquired the power to affect transformations such as turning water into ice "in the heat of all summer" (Morton 2000 [1632], 29) or the ability to "make the water burn, the rocks move, the trees dance, [and] metamorphose himself into a flaming man" (Wood 1977 [1634], 100–101). Shamans thus personified the Coastal Algonquian *hypergood*.

2. The description of Indian economic behaviour is at least as paradoxical as that of their political system. On the one hand they are portrayed as paragons of generosity, on the other as competitive hagglers. While Williams (1936 [1643], 163) observes that they "are so marvailous subtle in their Bargaines to save a penny: And very suspicious that *English* men labour to deceive them: Therefore they will beate all markets and try all places, and runne twenty thirty, yea forty mile, and more, and lodge in the Woods, to save six pence", he is also impressed by their sheer generosity, which he describes in the context of two feasts. One occurred during the harvest season:

> "But their chiefest Idoll of all for sport and game, is (if their land be at peace) toward Harvest, when they set up a long house […], sometimes an hundred, sometimes two

hundred foot long, upon a plaine neer the Court [...] where many thousands, men and women meet, where he that goes in danceth in the sight of all the rest; and is prepared with money, coats, small breeches, knifes, or what hee is able to reach to, and gives these things away to the poore, who yet must particularly beg and say, Cowequetummous, that is, I beseech you: which word (although there is not one common beggar amongst them) yet they will often use when their richest amongst them would fain obtain ought by gift"

(ibid., 180).

The other is a feast called *Nickommo*:

"He or she that makes this Nickommo Feast or Dance, besides the Feasting of sometimes twenty, fifty, and hundredth, yea I have seene neere a thousand persons at one of these Feasts: they give I say a great quantity of money, and all sort of their goods (according to and sometimes beyond their Estate) in severall small parcells of goods, or money, to the value of eighteen pence, two Shillings, or thereabouts to one person"

(ibid., 128–129).

Both feasts are accompanied by massive physical transformations and corresponding material translocations. They enable their participants to achieve value by acting according to the *hypergood*. The same pattern is visible in the Coastal Algonquian gambling games, in which they spend "half their days" (Wood 1977 [1634], 103), although they "will lose sometimes all they have" (ibid., 104). These games can be viewed as symbolic translocations of wealth, which signal the importance of the person's status. Both Wood and also Williams thus miss the central point that it does not matter if you lose or win as long as it is everything or at least a substantial part of one's wealth. It is the enactment of huge translocations of wealth, whether negative or positive, which enables one to achieve the valued character of being distinct through transformation.[10]

3. While most scholarly explanations of bodily decorations among the Coastal Algonquian suggest their role in marking belonging to specific groups, whether social, gender or age-groups, most contemporary observers are eager to express the individuality of different *styles* and their arbitrariness. Williams (1936 [1643], 121, 157), for example, describes the appearance of Native Americans using words like "varietie" and "curiously" and Morton (2000 [1632], 25, my emphasis) observes that they decorate their mantles with "works of *several fashions* very curious, according to the *several fantasies* of the workmen, wherein they strive to *excel one another*"; a depiction, which shows both the importance of individuality and the competitive character of its acquisition. The salience of tattooing and scarification could similarly mark former transformative actions (Wood 1977 [1634], 85) and are consequently materializations of the Coastal Algonquian *hypergood*, as are personal names and the generous redistributions of personal wealth: all of these actions materialize the belief in the possibility of reaching the status of a distinct and thus valuable part of society autonomously.

Wampum as an iconic sign of the *hypergood*

In all the spheres I have mentioned, wampum circulated in enormous amounts. In daily transactions with the Europeans, beads stringed on cords of diverse lengths

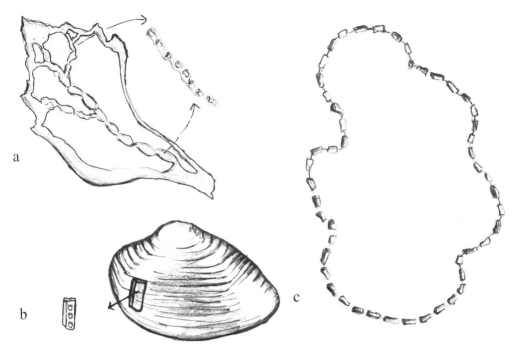

Figure 10.1. Construction of individual wampum beads from Busycotypus canaliculatus *(a) and* Mercenaria mercenaria *(b) and finished fathom of wampum (c).*

were used as a means of payment and exchange. They were wrought into ornaments, serving as icons of completeness and individuality, and *powwows* were paid for their services in wampum beads (Wilson 1865 [1647], 27; Williams 1936 [1643], 169). Following Weiss's discussion of cowrie bundles and the importance of their material shape (Weiss 2003, 53–59) and Graeber's insights into the unique ability of beads to mediate inter-cultural transactions (Graeber 1996), I would like to argue for the political relevance of the relationship between wholes and parts and the actions of stringing, unstringing and restringing wampum beads into generic or concrete forms. I will start with a reconstruction of the production process of a single bead (Fig. 10.1).

While single cowries and coins are frequently charged with meaning in different cultures[11], single wampum beads were apparently useless.[12] The two means of producing wampum beads, namely using the hard clam or quahog (*Mercenaria mercenaria)* and the channelled whelk (*Busycotypus canaliculatus*), were likely to have been charged with value by virtue of their transformative powers. As gastropods, they existed between water and land, fish and mammal, and each shell had a unique form. To produce the white beads, one had to destroy the outer shell of the channelled whelk and uncouple the centre column; for the black beads one had to quarry out parts of the hard clam's shell. After drilling the beads, they were deliberately polished to achieve a uniform appearance. In other words, the production of wampum beads entailed the destruction of uniqueness in favour of generality. It could thus be interpreted as an inversion of the *hypergood* (Munn

1986).[13] This process was reversed in the process of stringing generic beads together to make unique ornaments, which could be perceived as a visible manifestation of completeness and personhood. Hence it should come as no surprise that they were "as particular about the stringing and sorting as we can be here about pearls" (de Rasieres 1909 [1628], 106) and that they were eager to assure the identicalness of single beads "so cunningly that neither Jew nor Devil can counterfeit" (Josselyn 1865 [1675], 110).

Wampum was further used in the form of strung beads in liquidating transactions and in the form of single beads put into baskets or passed by hand in non-liquidating transactions (Znoj 1998). The spatial boundedness of strung beads is an iconic sign of the ending of a relationship after an economic transaction, for example, in separating a wife from her kinsmen through a bridewealth payment (Williams 1936 [1643], 147–148), or in the "fixed fine of sewan"[14] (de Rasieres 1909 [1628], 109) as reconciliation following a blood feud. The tough bargaining described by Williams and others could be seen as a way of establishing a liquidating transaction by performatively fixing exact exchange rates.[15] Unstrung wampum beads, in turn, are iconic of the ongoing character of transactions that establish ongoing relationships of mutual intra- or intercultural dependence. Sources suggest that during feasts beads were not redistributed in the form of strings or belts, but as generic beads (Winslow 1996 [1624], 60; for Powhatan Indians, see Spelman 1872 [1609], 49). Williams gives an amount of 18 to 24 pence, which hints at the distribution of single beads, since the unit of one fathom, which was an arm's length string of wampum beads, was worth ten shillings at the time that Williams observed the *nickommo*. In his letters we find several accounts of the exchange of baskets of beads as *presents*:

> "I cannot learn of him that there are above twenty men, beside women and children; that they live on ground nuts, andc., and deer; that Aawaysewaukit is their Sachem; and twelve days ago, he sent his son, Wunnawmeneeskat to Uncas, with a present of a basket or two of wampum"
> (Williams [1676], cited after Bartlett 1874, 385; for other examples, see ibid., 68, 80, 382; see Dunn *et al.* 1996, 74)

Much has been written about the significance of burials, the enormous quantities of ornaments in children's graves, and the difference between *sachem* and non-*sachem* graves (Brenner 1988; Rubertone 2001; Crosby 1988). But the variety in the shape of wampum in graves can also illuminate the influence of the Coastal Algonquian *hypergood* in burial practices. Textual evidence does not usually differentiate between strung and unstrung beads, belts and other ornaments, but the archaeological record does preserve these distinctions. The most important burial sites are West Ferry, located close to the modern town of Jamestown, RI (Simmons 1976), and RI-1000, situated near North Kingstown, RI (Turnbaugh 1984). Both necropolises have the following in common:

1. Wampum in its generic form is almost never found in the graves of women.
2. Wampum ornaments are rarely found in the graves of adult men. What we find instead are single beads.
3. Children are often buried with strings or ornaments of wampum.

This evidence should be combined with a comment on the burial practices by Edward Winslow (1996 [1624], 63):[16]

"When they bury the dead, they sow [sew] up the corpse in a mat, and so put it in the earth. If the party be a sachem, they cover him with many curious mats, and bury all his riches with him, and enclose the grave with a pale [pole]. If it be a child, the father will also put his own most special jewels and ornaments in the earth with it".

The corpses of adult commoners were apparently *bounded* by wrapping them in a mat, to prevent their dissolving and causing their incompleteness to reappear. This same incompleteness, which inverts the general structure of attaining value, is marked by breaking up strings and ornaments of wampum and placing indistinguishable, i.e. valueless beads into a grave. A comparable loss of completeness is experienced with the unforeseen death of a child or wife. The sacrifice of intact wampum ornaments might therefore be described as a way of dealing with the emotional break experienced upon the passing away of a loved one, as in the transfer of the autonomy and uniqueness materialized in the ornaments to the vulnerable child. The *sachem*'s engagement with the world is signalled by the spatial extension of the corpse. Mats are placed upon it with a pole on top that mirrors the ongoing influential position of the deceased. The burying of intact belts and ornaments reflects his eternal authority: as an ancestor, he will ascribe the role of *sachem* to its biological successors.

The marking of the construction and deconstruction of value by the threading, unthreading and rethreading of wampum beads appears on four different levels, which link the whole society in its totality through the circulation of wampum between men and women, commoners and *sachem*, the dead and the living:

1. The production process of individual wampum beads.
2. The stringing of wampum beads for transactions instead of leaving them in their generic form, to activate their liquidating character. Strung wampum signals boundedness.
3. The beads' ornamental function, as iconic signs of constructed and self-inscribed uniqueness (character).
4. In the form of belts, they function as status symbols for *sachem*s.

The contradiction between the different spheres of value-generation, that is, through individual effort on the one hand and kinship affiliations and gender belonging on the other, is obscured by the fact that wampum is not only an icon of the *hypergood* on the four levels separately, it also functions as a crystallized amplifier of the overarching totality by means of its encompassing itineraries between the spheres of achieved and ascribed status. Although one becomes a *valuable* man and a *valuable sachem* through one's own efforts, one becomes a valuable *man* and a valuable *sachem* by the coincidence of birth.

The omnipresence of wampum nevertheless suggests universal accessibility of value. I propose that every act of stringing as a form of reaching completeness through transformation creates a fetishized totality by reifying the *hypergood* in ornaments or cords of wampum, which, through their circulation, enable the oppressed to forget about their inferior status and to continue believing in the (native) American Dream. In order to explain how that belief in an equal share of value can be sustained, even though it seems that a glance at real social relations would immediately reveal an unjust allocation of value, I turn to consider the aforementioned paradox in Mauss's theory of the gift, that is his assertion that gifts are both *voluntary* and *obligatory* at the same time.

Mauss's *fait social total* as *objet social totalitaire*

Mauss's *The Gift* is generally interpreted as analysing exchange relations that differ significantly from the monetary transactions of capitalistic societies. This approach gives rise to a common misreading, whereby pre-monetary societies have not yet outsourced the establishment of social bonds to the juridical system and therefore reproduce themselves through so-called *faits sociaux totaux*, i.e. undifferentiated economic, religious, aesthetic, juridical and morphological phenomena.

Yet this approach comes into conflict with Mauss's implied intentions. We can begin to observe this in Mauss's explanation of *totaux*:

> "The facts that we have studied are all, if we may be allowed the expression, *total [totaux]* social facts, or, if one wishes – although we do not like the word – general [*generaux*] ones. That is to say, in certain cases they set in motion [*mettent en branle*] the totality of society and its institutions"
>
> (Mauss 2007 [1923/1924], 241, my translation).

Here Mauss defends his use of the term *totaux* rather than *generaux*, which would have been far more in line with the usual misreading. Elements in a general whole have only a contingent relation to one another, while elements in a totality possess a necessary relation to one another. Due to a well-grounded suspicion of any kind of systemic holism in anthropology, most interpretations avoid ascribing such a totalizing approach to Mauss. Yet how can exchange between two parties reproduce entire social systems? Mauss (2000 [1923/1924], 6) addresses this question in the following paragraph: "There is total service [*prestation*] in the sense that it is indeed the whole clan that contracts on behalf of all, for all that it possesses and for all that it does, through the person of its chief."

This passage seems to suggest that this reproduction is performed by moments of implosion of the whole with the aid of the chief. The question remains how this contraction is achieved and legitimated. I suggest that *faits sociaux totaux* reproduce social systems through the feelings of intensity and obligation they evoke in individual persons as they implode in specific objects. These *objets sociaux totalitaires* mediate suprapersonal relations through personal-emotional responses, which in turn obscure inequalities and injustice.[17]

All of Mauss's objects share an obligatory circulation and the blurring of boundaries between persons and objects. Those who view Mauss as primarily interested in exchange relations overlook his concern with object-revelation and different forms of circulation.[18] While supposedly preoccupied with the separate actions of giving, receiving and reciprocating, *The Gift* brims over with phrases reminiscent of eternal circulation, culminating in the circle par excellence: the *kula* ring. This obligatory circulation is often attributed to the object's *force*, its *vertu*. Mauss repeatedly talks about the ability of objects to provoke emotions, actions and responses. Those who possess or would like to possess them are described as captives of the object's *hau*, and each object has "its individuality, its names, its qualities" (Mauss 2000 [1923/1924], 45) and even its "productive power" (ibid.). Indeed, Mauss regularly attributes anthropomorphic features to objects. It is therefore fascinating – but due to Mauss's own rejection of the term *fetish* (Mauss 1969

[1906/1907], 244) understandable[19] – that there has been no serious scholarly attempt to connect his observations with theories of fetishism.[20]

One probable explanation for this oversight is that Mauss avoids the negative associations of his model in favour of a positive evaluation. One might even say that, whereas most scholars talk about fetishistic objects, Mauss makes them. He does this by virtue of his confidence in having solved the problem posed by Durkheim in his discussion of the moral erosion of modern society, namely: What could be the moral glue holding society together? Nevertheless, a formal equivalence between Freudian,[21] Marxian and Maussian fetish objects can be found in their schizophrenic nature: they are saturated and over-determined with meaning through social processes, while perceived as individualized and devoid of cultural meaning due to their corporality. All three scholars explore the ability of fetishized objects to obscure crisis or to postpone the fulfilment of desires. Because a state of crisis cannot be revealed without threat of personal dissolution (sexual fetish) or unearthing an oppressive socio-economic system (commodity fetishism), the fetish becomes both sign of the fulfilment and cause of the desire and is thus able to maintain a placating totality and to obscure an oppressive one. As fetishes, the paradox of gifts is hence resolved: they are both *voluntary* and *obligatory* because their role in maintaining oppressive systems demands this of them. Instead of placing the Hegelian notion of recognition at the centre of the interpretation of Mauss (Henaff 2002; Moebius and Quadflieg 2009), his theory of the gift can be interpreted as contributing towards explaining the establishment and perpetuation of "universal contexts of delusion" (Horkheimer and Adorno 2002 [1947]). But moving beyond the formal and temporal structure of the exchange relationship (Bourdieu 1980; Derrida 1991),[22] scholars should begin to focus on the materiality of the circulating objects and how *they* enable the *illusio* that affects and chains society as a whole to be maintained.

What is true of Mauss's gifts can now be asserted of wampum. On the one hand, wampum beads circulate obligatorily to systemically sustain the illusion of self-determination among Indian commoners. On the other hand, they circulate voluntarily because they signal the possibility of self-determination. The flow of wampum can be described as an auto-poetic system amplifying a cultural chasm. Collective blindness towards the oppressive situation stems from the fact that the objects, as fetishes,

> "are real, *imperative* precepts, which imply a positive belief in the objectivity of the chain of ideas which they form. As far as the mind of an individual is concerned, there is nothing which requires it to associate [...] words, actions or instruments with the desired effects, unless it be *experience*"
>
> (Mauss 2001 [1902/1903], 154, my emphasis).

Hence the strength of Mauss's approach with respect to oppressive totalities, wherein members are removed from the sources of value-generation via the circulation of objects, which leaves people in good faith of partaking in the redistribution of *value*. Some objects function in this way because they are "condensed treasuries" (Mauss 2007 [1923/1924], 109, my translation), reifications of society at large evoking feelings which block realization of the repressive status quo. Stringing, re-stringing, producing, exchanging and displaying wampum entangles every individual in the feeling of being able to transform him- or herself into a valuable person, who actually only experiences a miserable rip-off. With Zizek, one could say that they no longer partake in the *hypergood*, but wampum itself partakes for them.[23] Real value is distributed between elite families and influential shamans. As a fetish, wampum enables and neglects the hierarchical structure of coastal Algonquian culture at the same time.

Even though it is difficult ultimately to determine whether the importance of the *hypergood* and its obscuring real processes of value-distribution are a result of contact with Europeans and the consequently increased possibilities of locational rearrangement,[24] I suggest that such actions as decorating women and children with ornaments,[25] redistributing beads to poor members of society and paying bridewealth in the form of fathoms of beads blur the difference between ascribed and achieved status and stabilize what is a hierarchical society. The circulation of wampum between men and women, *sachems* and ordinary people is emically perceived as an index of not only the *hypergood* but also of the society as a whole: wampum is appropriated as an object embodying a social totality that appears as fairness and justice. Yet these movements could also be described as itineraries bridging harsh social divides which are made invisible through the territorial and spatial totality of that object and its movements. Coastal Algonquian are thus in the paradoxical situation of enthusiastically pursuing paths towards value promoted by their *hypergood*, while at the same time their pursuit of value obstructs their ambitions and reproduces inequality.

Notes

1   The term 'hypergood' (Taylor 1989) refers to unquestioned concepts of ethical and moral consequence. All actions, objects and human beings that partake in this *hypergood* are perceived as valuable. Nevertheless the concept is here enhanced by the assumption that there are always requirements to fulfil in accessing the *hypergood* which lie outside of the actual *hypergood*. Thus I differentiate between values that lie inside the notion of the *hypergood* and those outside of it.

2   Contrary to the above-quoted passage by Williams, Giovanni da Verrazano (1905 [1524]), the Italian explorer and first visitor to Long Island Sound, leaves no doubt regarding the strict hierarchical constitution and status marking among the Coastal Algonquian.

3   See Gupta and Ferguson (2002) for a discussion of the term *location*.

4   When quoting Mauss (1923/1924) I will use the W. D. Hall's translation (Mauss 2000 [1923/1924]), while amending it at certain points with my own translation.

5   M.A.U.S.S. was founded with the establishment of the interdisciplinary *Revue du Mauss* in 1981. Its aim is to establish a third paradigm between methodological individualism and holism (Caillé 1996). Alain Caillé, one of the founders, has tirelessly announced the discovery of an appropriate solution to Mauss's apparently contradictory remarks. One of his most recent statements nevertheless shows that he is not able to resist a non-dialectical resolution of the contradiction. He writes that "the anti-utilitarian gift simply *subordinated* the moment of utility, calculation and self-interest to the imperatives of a primal disinterestedness and unconditionality" (Caillé 2010, 181, my emphasis). The main problem with Caillé's undertaking is its indecisiveness over whether it is a moral critique of modern society or a new theory of action. What it is definitely not is a close reading of Mauss's own examples.

6   An apt parallel is the Ancient Greek *kharaktēr*, which carries the meaning of being marked by engravings, brandings, scratched, cut or embossed (see also Ancient Greek *kharassō, I engrave*).

7   "At home they will eat till their bellies stand forth, ready to split with fullness, it being their fashion to eat all at some times and sometimes nothing at all in two or three days" (Wood 1977 [1634], 87). The same pattern is visible in the use of alcohol among the Coastal Algonquian; see Trenk (2001).

8   The theme of transformation and the power inherent in it is, for example, clearly visible in the "Pequot-Mohegan witchcraft tale", collected by Speck (1903).

9   The *Nicotiana rustica* used by Coastal Algonquian had an almost ten times higher content of nicotine than the nowadays common *Nicotiana tabacum* and consequently his intake led to more *intense* consequences.

10   Having described the appearance and demeanour of a *sachem* as equal to King Charles, Wood (1977 [1634], 85, my emphasis) adds that "this Pompey can endure no equal till one day's adverse lottery at their game (called puim) metamorphose him into a Codrus, robbing him of his conceited wealth, leaving him in mind and riches equal with his naked attendants, *till a new taxation furnish him with a fresh supply*". This quote shows the contradiction *and* amalgamation between real political power and ascribed value.

11   See Weiss (2003) for cowries in Tanzania, Ciric, this volume, for coins in medieval Serbian graves, Ritzenthaler (1978) for the cowrie shell among the Chippewa.

12   As well as single coins, compare this observation of Megapolensis (1909 [1644], 176, my italics): "I once showed one of their chiefs *a* rix-dollar; he asked how much it was worth among the Christians; and when I told him, he laughed exceedingly at us, saying we were fools to value *a* piece of iron so highly; and if he had such money, he would throw it into the river."

13   Due to the shortage of information on the production process, one might cautiously assume that the wampum beads could be produced by anybody.

14   *Sewan* is the Dutch word for wampum.

15   This difference was probably reflected semantically in the dichotomy between *Nanówwe*, translated by Williams (1848 [1652], 217) as 'Giving their Commodities freely', and *Anaqúshento*, translated as 'Trading'. In his 'A key into the languages of America', Williams (1936 [1643]) gives us a very different translation: 'they adde *Nanoūe*, give me this or that, a disease which they are generally infected with" (ibid., 164). I think this ambivalence in translation emanates from a cultural misunderstanding. *Nanoue* is the semantic envelope of enforcing the liabilities which incur in debt relations, which are due to their status as mediating both personal relations and the past and future. As such they can easily slip from *sanctioned* to *unsanctioned* and back again (Roitman 2003).

16   My discussion of the burial practices of the Coastal Algonquian draws heavily on the insights of Turner (2006).

17   Joel Robbins (2003) discusses the problem of the non-existence of anthropological contributions to the emotional structure of gift exchanges.

18   A notable exception is the so far neglected article of Foster (1993), and of course Lévi-Strauss's suggestion that we view the three obligations as parts of one, that is, of exchange (Lévi-Strauss 1950).

19   The fact that he wants to replace it with *mana* seems to suggest that his abandonment of it was solely politically inspired.

20   Lojkine (1989) and Taussig (1993) are exceptions in so far as the first tries to establish a "fétichisme non marchand" (Lojkine 1989, 153) and states that "réciprocité n'est pas transparence" (ibid.). Taussig (1993), on the other hand, is trying to identify a fetishistic core to Durkheim's theory of religion. For a general overview of the theory of fetishism, see Böhme (2006).

21   I am referring to Freud's later theory of fetishism as presented in Freud (1927).

22   "[L]'intervalle de temps qui sépare le don et le contre-don est ce qui permet de percevoir comme *irréversible* une relation d'échange toujours menace d'apparaitre et de s'apparaitre comme réversible, c'est-à-dire comme à la fois *obligée* et *intéressée*" (Bourdieu 1980, 179 f., Bourdieu's emphasis).

23   Compare with Zizek's discussion of commodity fetishism: "They no longer believe, *but the things themselves believe for them*" (Zizek, 2008 [1989], 34, Zizek's emphasis).

24   The most promising relocation for Coastal Algonquian was to convert to Christianity, which went hand in hand with a complete discarding of their old *hypergood*. It is no wonder that Indians like Hiacoomes, "*the first* Christian Indian, *and* Minister *on the Island of* Martha's Vineyard" (Mayhew 1695, 96), who were "therefore by the *Indian Sachims,* and others of their principal Men, looked on as but a mean Person, scarce worthy of their Notice or Regard" (ibid.) became the first embracers of the new religion. This is elucidated by the prohibition of alcohol, *powwows*, gambling and long hair (Shepard 1865 [1648], 5–7).

25   While women wear ornaments of wampum, they are actually given to them by men: "They hang these strings of money about their necks and wrists; as also upon […] the necks and wrists of their wives and children" (Williams 1936 [1643], 157). Compare this with Mauss (2000 [1923/1924], 102): "It seems

that in the Trobriand Islands the women, like the princesses in the American Northwest, together with a few other persons, serve to some extent [en quelque sorte] as a means of displaying the objects on show [les objets de parade]".

References

Bartlett, J. R. (ed.) (1874) *The letters of Roger Williams 1632–1682: Now first collected*. Providence, Printed for the Narragansett Club.

Böhme, H. (2006) *Fetischismus und Kultur. Eine andere Theorie der Moderne*. Reinbek bei Hamburg, Rowohlt.

Bourdieu, P. (1980) *Le sens pratique*. Paris, Minuit.

Bradford, W. (1981) *Of Plymouth plantation 1620–1647. Edited with an introduction and notes by Samuel Eliot Morison*. New York, Random House.

Bragdon, K. J. (1987) 'Emphatical speech and great action': An analysis of seventeenth-century native speech events described in early sources. *Man in the Northeast* 33, 101–111.

Brenner, E. M. (1988) Sociopolitical implications of mortuary ritual remains in 17th-century native southern New England. In M. P. Leone and P. B. Potter (eds) *The recovery of meaning: Historical archaeology in the eastern United States*, 147–181. Washington, DC, Smithsonian Institution Press.

Caillé, A. (1996) Ni holisme ni individualisme méthodologiques. Marcel Mauss et le paradigme du don. *Revue Européenne des Sciences Sociales* 34 (105), 181–224.

Caillé, A. (2010) Gift. In K. Hart, J.-L. Laville and A. D. Cattani (eds) *The human economy: A citizen's guide*, 180–186. Cambridge, Polity Press.

Ceci, L. (1988) Tracing wampum's origins: Shell bead evidence from archaeological sites in western and coastal New York. In C. F. Hayes III and C. Lynn (eds) *Proceedings of the 1986 shell bead conference: Selected paper*. Research Records, 20, 63–80. Rochester, Rochester Museum and Science Center.

Crosby, C. A. (1988) From myth to history, or why King Philip's ghost walks abroad. In M. P. Leone and P. B. Potter (eds) *The recovery of meaning: Historical archaeology in the eastern United States*, 183–209. Washington, DC, Smithsonian Institution Press.

da Verrazano, G. (1905 [1524]) Narragansett Bay (1524). In G. P. Winship (ed.) *Sailor's narratives of voyages along the New England coast 1524–1624*, 1–24. Boston, Houghton, Mifflin and Company.

de Rasieres, I. (1909 [1628]) Letter of Isaack de Rasieres to Samuel Blommaert, 1628 (?). In J. F. Jameson (ed.) *Narratives of New Netherland, 1609–1664*, 97–115. New York, Charles Scribner's Sons.

Derrida, J. (1991) *Donner le temps 1. La fausse monnaie*. Paris, Galilée.

Dunn, R. S.; Savage, J. and Yeandle, L. (eds) (1996) *The journal of John Winthrop, 1630–1649*. Cambridge and London, The Belknap Press of Harvard University Press.

Eliot, J. and Mayhew, T. (1653) *Tears of repentance, or, a further narrative of the progress of the gospel amongst the Indians in New-England*. London, Peter Cole.

Foster, R. J. (1993) Dangerous circulation and revelatory display: Exchange practices in a New Ireland society. In J. Fajans (ed.) *Exchanging products: Producing exchange*, (= Oceania Monographs, 4), 15–31. Sydney, Sydney University Press.

Freud, S. (1927) Fetischismus. In A. J. Storfer (ed.) *Almanach der Psychoanalyse 1928*, 17–24. Wien, Internationaler Psychoanalytischer Verlag.

Graeber, D. (1996) Beads and money: Notes toward a theory of wealth and power. *American Ethnologist* 23 (1), 4–24.

Graeber, D. (2001) *Toward an anthropological theory of value: The false coin of our own dreams*. New York, Palgrave.

Gupta, A. and Ferguson, J. (2002) Discipline and practice: The 'field' as side, method, and location in anthropology. In A. Gupta and J. Ferguson (eds) *Anthropological locations: Boundaries and grounds of a field science*, 1–46. Berkeley and Los Angeles, University of California Press.

Haefeli, E. (2007) On first contact and apotheosis: Manitou and men in North America. *Ethnohistory* 54 (3), 407–443.

Hénaff, M. (2002) *Le prix de la vérité. Le don, l'argent, la philosophie*. Paris, Seuil.

Horkheimer, M. and Adorno, T. W. (2002 [1947]) *Dialectic of enlightenment*. Stanford, Stanford University Press, [First published in German: (1947) *Dialektik der Aufklärung*. Amsterdam, Querido].

Jones, W. (1905) The Algonkin Manitou. *Journal of American Folklore* 18 (70), 183–190.

Josselyn, J. (1865 [1675]) *An account of two voyages to New-England: Made during the years 1638, 1663*. Boston, William Veazie.

Lévi-Strauss, C. (1950) Introduction à l'œuvre de Marcel Mauss. In M. Mauss (1950) *Sociologie et anthropologie précédé d'une introduction à l'œuvre de Marcel Mauss par Claude Lévi-Strauss*, IX–LII. Paris, PUF.

Lojkine, J. (1989) Mauss et l''Essai sur le don'. Portée contemporaine d'une étude anthropologique sur une économie non marchande. *Cahiers Internationaux de Sociologie* 86, 141–158.

Malone, P. M. (2000 [1991]) *The skulking way of war: Technology and tactics among the New England Indians*. Lanham, Madison Books.

Mauss, M. (1923/1924) Essai sur le don. Forme et raison de l'échange dans les sociétés archaïques. *L'Année Sociologique*, N. S., (1), 30–186.

Mauss, M. (1969 [1906/1907]) Résumé de cours (1906–1907). In M. Mauss *Œuvres. Présentation de Victor Karady. II: Représentations collectives et diversité des civilisations*, 244–245. Paris, Minuit.

Mauss, M. (2000 [1923/1924]) *The gift: The form and reason for exchange in archaic societies*. London, Routledge, [First published in French: (1923/1924) Essai sur le don. Forme et raison de l'échange dans les sociétés archaïques. *L'Année Sociologique*, N. S., (1), 30–186].

Mauss, M. (2001 [1902/1903]) *A general theory of magic*. London and New York, Routledge, [First published in French: Hubert, H. and Mauss, M. (1902/1903) Esquisse d'une théorie générale de la magie. *L'Année Sociologique* (7), 1–146].

Mauss, M. (2007 [1923/1924]) *Essai sur le don. Introduction de Florence Weber*. Paris, PUF.

Mayhew, M. (1695) *The conquests and triumphs of grace: Being a brief narrative of the success which the gospel hath had among the Indians of Martha's Vineyard (and the places adjacent) in New-England* [...]. London, Printed for Nath. Hiller.

Megapolensis, J. (1909 [1644]) A short account of the Mohawk Indians (1644). In J. F. Jameson (ed.) *Narratives of New Netherland, 1609–1664*, 163–180. New York, Charles Scribner's Sons.

Moebius, S. and Quadflieg, D. (2009) Negativität und Selbsttransendenz. Hegel und Mauss als Denker einer dreirelationalen Anerkennung. *Journal Phänomenologie* 31, 44–57.

Morton, T. (2000 [1632]) *New English Canaan*. Stoneham, Digital Scanning.

Munn, N. D. (1986) *The fame of Gawa: A symbolic study of value transformation in a Massim (Papua New Guinea) society*. Cambridge, Cambridge University Press.

Occom, S. (2006 [1761]) Account of the Montauk Indians, on Long Island (1761). In J. Brooks (ed.) *The collected writings of Samson Occom, Mohegan: Leadership and literature in eighteenth-century native America*, 47–51. Oxford, Oxford University Press.

Ritzenthaler, R. E. (1978) Southwestern Chippewa. In B. G. Trigger (ed.) *Handbook of North American Indians, Volume 15: The Northeast*, 743–759. Washington, DC, Smithsonian Institution Press.

Robbins, J. (2003) Given to anger, given to shame: The psychology of the gift among the Urapmin of Papua New Guinea. *Paideuma* 49, 249–261.

Roitman, J. (2003) Unsanctioned wealth; or, the productivity of debt in northern Cameroon. *Public Culture* 15 (2), 211–237.

Rubertone, P. E. (2001) *Grave undertakings: An archaeology of Roger Williams and the Narragansett Indians*. Washington, D.C., Smithsonian Institution Press.

Shepard, T. (1865 [1648]) The clear sunshine of the gospel breaking forth upon the Indians in New-England. New York, Reprinted for Joseph Sabin.

Simmons, W. S. (1976) Southern New England shamanism: An ethnographic reconstruction. In W. Cowan (ed.) *Papers of the Seventh Algonquian Conference*, 217–256. Ottawa, Carleton University.

Speck, F. G. (1903) A Pequot-Mohegan witchcraft tale. *The Journal of American Folklore* 16 (61), 104–106.

Spelman, H. (1872 [1609]) *Relation of Virginia*. London, Chiswick Press.

Taussig, M. (1993) Maleficium: State fetishism. In E. Apter and W. Pietz (eds) *Fetishism as cultural discourse*, 217–250. Ithaca, Cornell University Press.

Taylor, C. (1989) *Sources of the self: The making of the modern identity*. Cambridge, Harvard University Press.

Trenk, M. (2001) *Die Milch des weißen Mannes. Die Indianer Nordamerikas und der Alkohol*. Berlin, Reimer.

Turnbaugh, W. A. (1984) *The material culture of RI-1000: A mid-17th-century Narragansett Indian burial site in north Kingstown, Rhode Island*. Kingston, University of Rhode Island, Department of Sociology and Anthropology.

Turner, T. (2006) *Kayapo values: An application of Marxian value theory to a non-commoditiy based system of production*. Unpublished paper contributed to the panel, 'Values of Value', 100th Annual Meeting of the American Anthropological Association, New Orleans.

Weiss, B. (2003) *Sacred trees, bitter harvests: Globalizing coffee in northwest Tanzania*. Portsmouth, Heinemann.

Williams, R. (1848 [1652]) *The bloody tenent yet more bloody: By Mr Cotton's endevour to wash it white in the blood of the lambe* […]. London, J. Haddon.

Williams, R. (1936 [1643]) *A key into the language of America* […]. Fifth edition. Reprinted with an introduction by Howard M. Chapin. Providence, The Rhode Island and Providence Plantations Tercentenary Committee.

Wilson, J. (1865 [1647]) The day-breaking, if not the sun-rising of the gospell with the Indians in New-England. New York, Reprinted for Joseph Sabin.

Winslow, E. (1996 [1624]) *Good newes from New England: A true relation of things very remarkable at the plantation of Plimoth in New England*. Bedford, Applewood Books.

Wood, W. (1977 [1634]) *New England's prospect*. Amherst, University of Massachusetts Press.

Zizek, S. (2008 [1989]) How did Marx invent the symptom? In S. Zizek *The sublime object of ideology*, 3–55. London, Verso.

Znoj, H. (1998) Hot money and war-debts: Transactional regimes in southwestern Sumatra. *Comparative Studies in Society and History* 40, 193–222.

Chapter 11

Bright as the sun: The appropriation of amber objects in Mycenaean Greece

Joseph Maran

Introduction

The archaeological treatment of intersocietal exchange has suffered from the diffusionist legacy of directing attention to the reconstruction of abstract flows of cultural traits, while neglecting changes in meaning brought about by the agency of the social actors who integrated such traits into local contexts (Spittler 2002; Hahn 2004, 213–225; 2008, 195–200; 2012, 29–38). As a consequence, research has condemned objects of foreign derivation to remain foreign, irrespective of the meaning attached to them in a new cultural environment. It is only recently that awareness has increased in archaeology of the need to study the re-contextualization of foreign cultural traits through acts of appropriation (cf. Cline 2005). This focus, however, requires a methodological approach that combines the macro-contextual framework of the social imaginaries of a society with a micro-contextual analysis using find associations to infer past patterns of practice (Maran 2011, 283–284; 2012a, 62–64). This has to go along with a shift of perspective towards what Bruno Latour (1986, 266–269; 1993 [1991], 10–11) has called *translation*, that is, negotiation of the meanings of cultural traits received from the outside through their integration into social practice and discourses within constantly re-assembled networks comprising human and non-human actants. Due to this fluidity of meaning, generalizing designations as *exotic* or *prestige* objects should be avoided because they suggest a semantic stability which cannot be taken for granted.

Of all foreign substances appearing in Mycenaean Greece, amber is distinctive not only because of its arrival from extremely distant lands, but also because of its extraordinary inherent properties (Ganzelewski 1996; Barfod 1996, 453). Amber has a special shine and is translucent, it has a much warmer feel than other stones, it floats on water, it can be burned, giving off an aromatic scent, and when it is rubbed with cloth it becomes electrostatically charged, which is why, in the early modern period, *electricity* was named after *elektron*, the Greek word for amber. The root of this word must have referred to the capacity of an object to shine (Geerlings 1996, 395), which partially accounts for the strange fact that in Classical Greece it was used for amber as well as a specific kind of gold (Geerlings 1996; see also Hughes-Brock 1985, 260; 1993, 223–224; Bouzek 1993, 141; Whittaker 2011, 142–143).

Amber in Early Mycenaean Greece: Distribution, origin and chronological interrelations

In Greece, amber objects first make their appearance in the seventeenth or sixteenth centuries BCE at the very beginning of the Mycenaean period. While from find contexts dating to MH III only a single amber object is known, namely a bead from Shaft Grave Iota of Grave Circle B (Mylonas 1972/1973, 112; for a chronological assessment of the grave context with further literature, see Maran 2004, 48 with footnote 3), the LH I phase has yielded around 1,560 amber objects and the ensuing LH IIA sub-phase around 630 (Harding and Hughes-Brock 1974, 147–149). These seemingly impressive figures need to be qualified, though: first, because we are dealing with rather small items, mostly beads; and secondly, because the distribution in Greece is highly uneven. In LH I almost all of the numerous amber objects derive from a few of the richest shaft graves of Mycenae, while of the 630 objects dating to LH IIA around 500 alone were found in Tholos Tomb A of Kakovatos in the Western Peloponnese.

Based on the results of scientific analyses, Heinrich Schliemann already had to assume that the amber objects in the shaft graves consist of Baltic amber (Helm 1886; for a critical assessment of Otto Helm's results, see Beck 1966, 191–197). Only much later did it become evident that the amber objects had not reached Greece from the Baltic, but, mostly as finished products, from the area of the Wessex culture of southern England. The crucial evidence for this is provided by rectangular amber spacer plates with a particular complex-bored pattern (Sandars 1959, 293) that only appear in funerary contexts in three regions of Europe, namely the Wessex culture, the Tumulus Burial culture in Central Europe and the Early Mycenaean culture in the Peloponnese (Milojčić 1955; Hachmann 1957; Gerloff 1975, 215–222; 1993, 74–80; 2010, 628–630; du Gardin 2003; Verschueren 2009/2010, 24–25, 124–125). The transmission of amber objects from the Wessex culture to Greece during the LH I phase predates the earliest appearance of components of amber necklaces, including spacer plates, in graves of the Tumulus Burial culture. Thus, in the latter culture the first grave contexts with such objects date to the Reinecke Bz B2 sub-phase, which cannot have started earlier than roughly 1500 BCE.[1] Prior to that, occasional finds of probable Wessex origin in settlements like Koblach-Kadel, Zürich-Mozartstraße and the Padnal[2] attest to a circulation of amber objects during the advanced stage of the younger Early Bronze Age (Reinecke Bz A2c) and the incipient Middle Bronze Age (Reinecke Bz B1). At that time, however, such amber components do not yet seem to have been deposited in graves. It is this period of transition between the central European Early and Middle Bronze Age, in which the main transfer of Wessex amber components to Early Mycenaean Greece seems to have taken place (Gerloff 1993; 2010, 628; Maran 2004, 51 with footnote 8; Stahl 2006, 140–148; for the absolute dating of the Wessex culture, see Needham *et al.* 2010).

There is an amazing similarity between the shaft grave period and the Wessex culture not only in the amber items as such and their close association with gold (Whittaker 2011), but also in the social contexts of the appearance of amber jewellery. As Steven Shennan (1982, 38; 1993, 59–61) has pointed out, while in the Early Bronze Age in the British Isles amber is by no means confined to elite tombs, special forms like crescentic amber necklaces with spacer plates and trapezoid end-pieces remain restricted to the richest Wessex burials (see also Beck and Shennan 1991, 77–98, 133–137). This exactly corresponds to the find situation of amber jewellery with spacer plates in the Early Mycenaean Peloponnese, thus emphasizing that in both regions such special amber objects were confined to the very small group of the most richly furnished burials. If, for instance, the shaft graves of Mycenae had not yet been discovered, we would know next to nothing of the existence of such foreign objects in the LH I phase (Maran 2004, 55).

The routes of transmission of the amber objects between southern England and the Peloponnese are still very difficult to trace. The exchange was probably carried out over several land routes along the river systems of Western or Central Europe. Various routes then branched off towards the Central Alps, as attested by the sites already mentioned like Koblach-Kadel, Zürich-Mozartstraße and the Padnal, with early occurrences of amber objects in contexts predating the time of their first appearance in graves of the Tumulus Burial culture. From there one route went along the Tyrrhenian coast of Italy until it reached trade settlements with strong ties to Early Mycenaean Greece situated on small islands like Vivara in the Gulf of Naples.[3] Deciding on the mechanism of transmission depends on the range and volume of goods and materials exchanged between the distant partners. If the long-distance exchange concerned only the amber, all objects of that material found in Early Mycenaean Greece could have easily been transferred in a single journey (Harding and Hughes-Brock 1974, 159; Harding 1984, 80). However, I find this unlikely and fully agree with James Muhly (1973, 249–253, 275–335) that amber is likely to have reached Greece as a concomitant of the trade in tin with the North, just as, in the middle of the third millennium BCE, Mesopotamia received lapis lazuli from Afghanistan through exchange networks that were established above all to obtain tin from Central Asian sources (Maran 2004, 58). By the shaft grave period bronze had finally prevailed over copper, but since sources of tin existed only in Wessex and Brittany, the Erzgebirge of Central Europe or in Central Asia, Mycenaean bronze-working was, one way or another, dependent on tin from distant regions. For this reason, as Muhly (1973, 287, 343–350) already stated, Atlantic Europe remains a likely supply region for the tin used in Early Mycenaean Greece (see also Gerloff 1993, 85–86; 2010, 633; Hughes-Brock 1998, 254–255; Bachhuber 2003, 15–17; Ruppenstein 2010, 649). It seems doubtful whether a flourishing bronze industry could have relied on tin from occasional long-distance visits. Therefore, the amber objects probably arrived in Greece in the course of regular long-distance trade carried out by specialists (Maran 2004, 58).

Let me be clear here that I am not reviving the old idea of Mycenaean merchants travelling to southern England and bringing back tin and amber. On the contrary, I am suggesting indirect exchange made possible through the existence of a chain of interlocking networks, in which the direct Mycenaean presence need not have extended further than the Central Mediterranean. Furthermore, it is probable that exchange partners in the vast expanse between Atlantic Europe and Greece were not guided by the same motives and attitudes, so that a combination of different ways of exchange is likely (Maran 2004, 58–60). Still, the rarity of indications of the circulation of special amber objects in Western and Central Europe at the time of the shaft graves of Mycenae remains just as enigmatic as the marked concentration at both end-points of the distribution: Wessex and Mycenae. This means that, whatever the exact exchange mechanisms were, one thing seems certain: the trade must have been directional to some degree in order to ensure that specific objects reached the aspiring Mycenaean elite in considerable numbers (Harding 1984, 82; Beck and Shennan 1991, 135; Maran 2004, 58).

Early Mycenaean amber: The unaddressed issue of appropriation

Hitherto, discussions of Early Mycenaean amber objects have revolved mainly around issues such as their morphological differentiation, chronological attributions and routes of dispersal, while the forms of appropriation have not yet been sufficiently investigated. Since the amber components were shown to be conceived for use as necklaces, somehow research seems to have assumed that they were necessarily worn as such. When in 1988, on the occasion of a major exhibition, amber jewellery from Shaft Grave Omicron was arranged as a crescentic Wessex necklace, it seemed like the final proof of an exact correspondence in the way such jewellery was worn in the two distant areas (Demakopoulou 1988, 256 no. 280; Hughes-Brock 1993, 219; Gerloff 2010, 628; but see the cautionary remarks by Hughes-Brock 2005, 301). Indeed, it is likely that crescentic amber necklaces of this particular type had reached the Peloponnese by the beginning of the Mycenaean period. The still valid argument for this interpretation, first presented by Rolf Hachmann (1957, 10–11), is that it is only in Wessex and the Peloponnese that we encounter, in addition to the rectangular spacers, trapezoid plates with converging perforations needed as end-pieces in such crescentic necklaces (Harding and Hughes-Brock 1974, 161–162; du Gardin 2003; Verschueren 2009/2010, 32, 60). But research has made the mistake of equating the arrival of the foreign form of the crescentic amber necklace with an unaltered manner of usage, thereby disregarding the indications of pronounced differences between Mycenae and Wessex in how these objects were perceived and worn. Not only are some of the shapes of Early Mycenaean amber objects unknown in Wessex and other regions of Europe (Harding and Hughes-Brock 1974, 155), but, in contrast to the British Isles, prior to the Mycenaean period there also existed no local tradition of wearing crescentic necklaces in Greece (Maran 2004, 54). Even in Early Mycenaean Greece amber end-pieces are extremely rare, and of the two such objects each from Kakovatos Tholos Tomb A (Müller 1909, 280–281; Beck *et al.* 1970, 18; Verschueren 2009/2010, 32, 60, 125) and Pylos, Tholos Tomb IV (Blegen *et al.* 1973, 128; Beck and Beck 1995, 124–125; Verschueren 2009/2010, 60), only the examples from Pylos – one entirely preserved, the other fragmentary – could theoretically have constituted a pair of end-pieces of equal size and with the same number of converging perforations required for them to form parts of one and the same crescentic necklace. Finally, while in the Wessex culture crescentic amber necklaces seem to be found exclusively in assemblages attributed to female burials (Gerloff 1975, 198–203; 2010, 628; Hughes-Brock 1998, 254; 2005, 306), in Greece components of such necklaces appear with female individuals as well as in some of the richest warrior burials of the shaft grave period (Karo 1930a, 179–180, 183; Mylonas 1972/1973, 350; Matthäus 1980, 20; Kilian-Dirlmeier 1986, 176–190; Cavanagh and Mee 1998, 50). Until now, the appearance of components of necklaces of amber and semi-precious stones in Early Mycenaean warrior burials has been explained either by pointing to the function of enhancing the prestige of the person, or by referring to the desire of the warriors to adorn themselves (Kilian-Dirlmeier 1986, 185; 1987, 200; 1988, 164–165). In my opinion, however, such explanations fall short of grasping the whole meaning of the presence of amber objects in Early Mycenaean Greece. I argue that the differences between the Peloponnese and Wessex in the forms of amber objects and the contexts of their appearance reflect a much more creative engagement of Mycenaean Greeks with such foreign materials and objects than has hitherto been realized.

In the following, a contextual analysis will be offered for the small number of LH I and IIA grave assemblages on which any investigation of the crucial problem of how amber was worn and perceived in Early Mycenaean Greece must be based

The contexts of Early Mycenaean amber: Necklaces and cases of unclear usage

Regarding the use of amber objects in Early Mycenaean female burials, Shaft Grave Omicron, dating to LH I (Maran 2004, 48 with footnote 3) and excavated in 1953 by Ioannis Papadimitriou and Georgios E. Mylonas, has yielded the most important clues. The amber objects, consisting of 119 beads, at least three spacer plates (Beck *et al.* 1971, 382–384; Harding und Hughes-Brock 1974, 164) and possibly a D-shaped end-piece (Milojčić 1955, 318, fig. 1:4; Harding and Hughes-Brock 1974, 164; Maran 2004, 54 with footnote 17), accompanied the last interment in the grave, a skeleton lying on its back and deposited in a north-south direction, with the head pointing towards south. The arms of the skeleton were arranged in circular position in relation to the spine, with the underarms of the skeleton bent and directed towards the pelvis (Mylonas 1972/1973, 188). The excavators make slightly different statements regarding the find situation of the amber components. In contrast to Papadimitriou (1953, 236), who stated immediately after the excavation that they were found at the arms and hip of the skeleton, Mylonas writes in the final publication that the amber components were found together with semi-precious stones on the breast of the skeleton, with the amber beads reaching down to the hip. According to Mylonas (1972/1973, 189, 350), the beads of amber and semi-precious stones had belonged to different necklaces, but he does not say what led him to this assessment.[4] Hence, a combination of amber with other stones in one and the same necklace should be definitely considered a possibility.[5] The two descriptions agree that the amber objects were not concentrated on one part of the body, but were found dispersed from the upper body to the hip. Provided that this find situation accurately reflects the original arrangement (for a caveat, see Maran 2004, 52), the amber components seem to have been worn as a long necklace.[6]

To my knowledge, the only unequivocal example of amber components being used as necklaces in Early Mycenaean male grave assemblages comes from the unfortunately still unpublished Tholos Tomb 2 of Myrsinochori-Routsi dating to LH II. According to the description of Spyridon Marinatos (1956, 203–206) two individuals who were identified by their weapons as males were furnished with amber necklaces. The tomb yielded at least seven interments, of which one was encountered on the tomb floor, while the remains of the others were divided between two pits. The skeleton lying in an extended position on the floor was the last interment in the Tholos Tomb. It wore a *voluminous* amber necklace of around 50 amber beads around its neck, and on its right side lay ten swords and knives. In the uppermost part of Pit 2 a skeleton was found of which only the upper body was well preserved. Its neck and breast were covered by an amber necklace of 54 beads (Marinatos 1956, 205; Harding and Hughes-Brock 1974, 166), and in addition the burial was accompanied by a mirror and two daggers richly decorated with gold and silver inlays. No spacer plates or end-pieces seem to have been among the furnishings of these two burials,[7] which suggests that the amber components are unlikely to have been worn as crescentic necklaces (Maran 2004, 53 with footnote 13).

In turning to grave assemblages of male type in the shaft graves of Mycenae, regrettably Schliemann only specified the find position of amber objects in two cases. The first is a group of more than 400 amber beads found next to the skull of the skeleton in the centre of the three interments with their heads oriented towards the East in Shaft Grave IV of the LH I phase (Schliemann 1878, 283). The usual interpretation that this was a necklace deposited next to the head of the deceased (ibid., 245) is far from certain because the deposition by the body rather than on it could also indicate that it was part of a piece of equipment with a different function, possibly a belt (see below). Roughly the same number of amber components was found, again in Shaft Grave IV, with one of the burials with the head pointing towards north, but Schliemann (1878, 283) does not provide any information on their position in relation to the skeleton. It is also unclear how the at least four or five spacer plates in Shaft Grave IV were divided between these two amber concentrations (Harding and Hughes-Brock 1974, 162).

The only other case in which Schliemann left some information on find circumstances is a single amber bead in Shaft Grave V, to the interpretation of which I shall return later.

The contexts of Early Mycenaean amber: The Kakovatos shoulder belt and other objects not worn as necklaces

Of special interest for the meaning attributed to amber in the Early Mycenaean period are the roughly 500 amber objects from Tholos Tomb A of Kakovatos, already mentioned, which are also likely to come from a male burial. Unfortunately, the tomb was encountered in a looted state, with the sole grave shaft empty (Dörpfeld 1908, 306) and the remains of grave furnishings found scattered in a 10–15 cm thick layer above the floor of the chamber. According to the assessment of Sklavounos, a professor of anatomy, cited by Kurt Müller (1909, 325), the human bones from that tomb belonged to only one individual, a young adult about 30 years of age. In spite of the high number of objects and especially decorated palatial jars deriving from the tomb (Kalogeropoulos 1998, 128–135), the range of attested items does not give any reason to doubt that the tomb only held one burial,[8] while the two fragments of a richly decorated blade, probably of a sword, together with more than 40 flint arrowheads and one made of bronze, as well as numerous boar's tusks from a helmet (Müller 1909, 291–293), point to the deceased having been male (Nikolentzos 2003, 628). As Müller (1909, 279–281) had already emphasized, Kakovatos Tholos Tomb A is the Mycenaean amber assemblage not only with the largest beads and spacer plates, but also with by far the greatest wealth of shapes, some of them unknown outside this particular context. Until now, the Kakovatos amber objects have been unanimously interpreted by research as evidence for the occurrence of necklaces as a grave good. That these objects have never been comprehensively published in drawings or photographs is particularly unfortunate in light of the fact that, for unknown reasons, Müller seems to have failed to mention or probably even inspect some of the objects, which evidently were not made available to Anthony Harding and Helen Hughes-Brock either in the course of their ground-breaking study on amber in the Mycenaean world. That these unpublished objects must exist is borne out by the most detailed available description provided in 1970 by Curt W. Beck, Constance A. Fellows and Audrey B. Adams (Beck *et al.* 1970), who mention, in addition to the well-known and particularly large examples of a spacer plate and a trapezoid end-piece (Müller 1909, 280–281, figs 3–4), at least five other smaller rectangular spacer plates and an additional trapezoid end-piece of smaller size and with fewer perforations than the example first published by Müller (Beck *et al.* 1970, 18; Verschueren 2009/2010, 125).

Concerning the crucial question of the reconstruction of the original shape and nature of the items, to which the amber components from Kakovatos Tholos Tomb A have belonged, the find circumstances evidently do not provide any information. In addition, the components are so varied and numerous that, although I do not think this is the case, they could have derived from different parts of the equipment of the deceased, and some of them may indeed have been worn around the neck. Nevertheless, to give up on the question of reconstruction in the face of such uncertainties would be mistaken. Instead, all the available information on material, manufacture and morphology has to be used to be able to integrate as many amber components as possible into a coherent set of interrelated parts. Such a procedure, which in this contribution is for the first time attempted for the Kakovatos amber objects shows that some of the objects exhibit morphological traits and signs of manipulation in the course of secondary usage that are not consistent with reconstruction as a necklace and rather point to a different functional context to which originally all the amber items found in the tomb may have belonged.

First, as Hachmann (1957, 10–11) already noted, the published amber spacer plate and the trapezoid end-piece, which both stand out due to their size, show signs of having been reworked by drilling an additional transverse hole into the flat surface (see also Sandars 1959; Woodward 2002, 1046). No such secondary perforations are mentioned by Beck *et al.* (1970) for the unpublished end-piece and spacer plates from the same context. An interpretation of the transverse boring as a means of transforming the two amber plates into pendants (Sandars 1959, 293; Schon 2009, 223) is not particularly convincing because it would not be clear why such a simple form of reuse would necessitate the risk of drilling an additional hole and possibly breaking a valuable object, instead of using the already existing borings to string the plate as a pendant on to the necklace.[9] In contrast to previous research, I would like to propose that, in their final usage, these two particularly large re-worked amber components were not threaded on to a necklace, but rather were attached to something else. The transverse holes were probably drilled in order to use the two plates as intermediate pieces at the transition between a strap

Figure 11.1. Ring-shaped suspension devices of sheet gold from a Mycenaean sword scabbard found in Shaft Grave Lambda at Mycenae (after Mylonas 1972/1973, pl. 125:β).

and the multiple strings holding amber beads. Second, the two trapezoid amber plates differ significantly in size and number of perforations. Hence, they could not have served as end-pieces of the same necklace (Beck *et al.* 1970, 18) which means that also in Kakovatos Tholos Tomb A there is no evidence for a crescentic amber necklace as a grave offering. Third, the different sized ring-shaped amber objects, of which three are said to be entirely preserved[10] and at least five were encountered in a fragmentary state (Müller 1909, 279; Beck *et al.* 1970, 9–11; Harding and Hughes-Brock 1974, 162), have been interpreted until now as decorative pendants of necklaces (Beck *et al.* 1970, 8–11; Harding and Hughes-Brock 1970, 155). While I know of no parallels for such decorative pendants in Mycenaean Greece, these amber rings bear the greatest resemblance to the golden ring-shaped suspension devices of Mycenaean sword scabbards from the shaft graves of Mycenae (Fig. 11.1; Mylonas 1972/1973, 142–143, pl. 125:β; Karo 1930a, pl. 45). The importance of ring-shaped suspension or connection devices in Early Mycenaean weaponry is also emphasized by the design of the so-called *Gamaschenhalter* (Fig. 11.5; Mylonas 1972/1973, 330–331, pls. 59:α2, 102:α1–2; Karo 1930a, pls. 67–68) from the shaft graves of Mycenae that Laffineur (1996) interpreted as parts of the scabbard or straps of a sword suspension. These similarities provide an important clue to the use of these most unusual amber components from Kakovatos. Fourth, while almost all of the objects from Kakovatos analysed by Curt W. Beck's group proved to consist of Baltic amber, the ring-shaped pieces gave infrared spectra typical of Baltic amber, as well as of a fossil resin of clearly non-Baltic origin, probably Schraufite either from the Bukovina region of the northeastern Carpathian Mountains or from Lebanon (Beck *et al.* 1970, 9–12; Beck 1986, 59). These analytical results point to local manufacture in Greece[11] by using raw pieces of fossil resins of different origin and adding the ring-shaped objects to components received as finished products like the beads, spacer plates and end-pieces. Fifth, the also unique tongue-shaped amber object with multiple perforations (Müller 1909, pl. 15:21), for which hitherto no convincing explanation has been put forward,[12] should be interpreted as a reinforcement for the end of a strap.

Based on these observations, I would like to suggest that at Kakovatos one or several Wessex crescentic amber necklaces were broken up in order to be rearranged for a different purpose. The components, some of which were reworked, were combined with locally made pieces and attached to a leather band to form an impressive shoulder belt with the largest ring-shaped object serving as a buckle and the smaller ones as devices on which weapons and other items were suspended (Fig. 11.2). It was Schliemann (1878, 322) himself who postulated the existence of such shoulder belts with devices for suspending weapons and other items in the shaft grave assemblages. Indeed, we know of the existence of luxurious sword belts or baldrics both from finds of long gold stripes from Schliemann's shaft graves (Schliemann 1878, 281–282; Karo 1930a, 213; Kilian-Dirlmeier 1993, 136–137; Buchholz 1980, 239–240; Steinhübl 2011, 298) and from images like the shell relief from the Knossos throne room (Fig. 11.3; Kilian-Dirlmeier 1993, 136, pl. 69:16), as well as the fighting scene on the famous gold cushion from Shaft Grave III (Fig. 11.4; Karo 1930a, pl. 24:35; Kilian-Dirlmeier 1993, 136–137). The curious curving double row of small dots connecting a sword scabbard with the upper body of the attacking warrior in that scene may even allude to a shoulder belt comprising beads. How many of the amber objects from Kakovatos Tholos Tomb A should be attributed to the belt remains unclear, and therefore the proposed reconstruction must be taken as an approximation. Due to the reworking of the two large amber plates and the combination with other local forms of spacers, namely of the triple circle and the figure of eight types (Harding and Hughes-Brock 1974, 155) – one of which also exhibits a secondary drilled hole (Müller 1909, 280, pl. 15:20) – it seems likely that in the middle part of the belt (Fig. 11.2B) at least the smaller beads and some of the medium-sized beads were threaded on multiple strands and probably combined with the smaller spacer plates, which are not shown on the reconstruction because they are still unpublished. The reconstruction also assumes that the largest amber beads were sewn on the leather strap (Fig. 11.2A).[13] Indeed, since the parts of the leather strap forming the ends of the belt may have been considerably longer than shown in the reconstruction, there may also have been enough space to attach some or even all of the decorated bone discs from Kakovatos Tholos Tomb A to the same belt (Müller 1909, 282–287). Although the discs, whose function is unclear, do not seem to have a fastening device, in some cases a red colouring was observed on their back, which may derive from a substance used

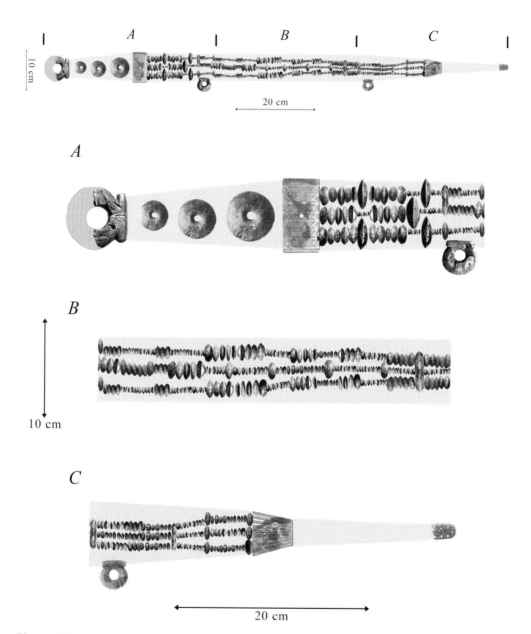

Figure 11.2. Reconstruction of the amber objects from Kakovatos Tholos Tomb A as a shoulder belt (digital reconstruction by M. Kostoula based on a draft drawing by J. Maran; rearranged after Müller 1909, figs 3–4, pl. 15; Harding 1984, fig. 15; Demakopoulou 1988, 258 no. 283).

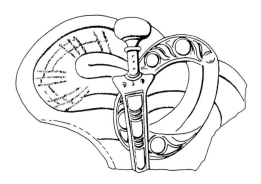

Figure 11.3. Miniature shell relief of a sword belt from the Knossos throne room (after Kilian-Dirlmeier 1993, pl. 69:16).

Figure 11.4. Drawing of a fighting scene on a gold cushion from Shaft Grave III at Mycenae (after Kilian-Dirlmeier 1993, pl. 69:12).

Figure 11.5. Assemblage of swords, a golden Gamaschenhalter, other gold objects and an amber bead in Shaft Grave V at Mycenae (after Schliemann 1878, 347 no. 460).

to glue the discs on to the leather strip (Müller 1909, 283).[14]

To understand the reasons why of all substances amber was chosen to become a frequent part of the equipment of Early Mycenaean warriors, an observation of Heinrich Schliemann (1878, 347 no. 460) concerning the find assemblage in Shaft Grave V of Mycenae, also of LH I date, is of relevance (Fig. 11.5). He was so surprised to encounter a single large amber bead next to two swords that he declared the bead to have been displaced (ibid., 349).[15] In contrast, I have argued that the find association makes sense when we assume the amber object to have served as a sword bead, a magically protective device known from Early Medieval swords (Maran 2004, 59). A possible analogy for this find assemblage in Shaft Grave V may be represented by the rare cases of the appearance of seemingly unworked small lumps of amber attested in Early Mycenaean elite graves of Messenia that were interpreted by the excavators as talismans (Blegen *et al.* 1973, 129, 143, 162, figs 227:5, 231:7; Hughes-Brock 1985, 260). In a secondary deposition of grave goods in Pit 3 of the so-called Grave Circle of Pylos, two such amber lumps were associated with few large amber beads, one amethyst bead, an amber spacer plate, swords and other items (Blegen *et al.* 1973, 143). Although the objects were not found in their primary depositional context, the small number of amber components, together with the association with swords and lumps of probably un-worked amber, again point to amber being used in a different way than as a necklace.

In my opinion, the main motif for equipping warriors with amber whether as a necklace, a shoulder belt, a sword-bead or another form of a talisman consisted in the wish to ensure its bearer the protection and assistance of supernatural powers (Bouzek 1993, 141; Maran 2004, 60). For this reason, a classification of the amber as *jewellery* is misleading, since in the emic perspective the desired effects of amber were rather supposed to resemble a weapon.

The manifold ways of appropriating amber objects in Early Mycenaean Greece: Between adornment and weapon

In summary, the contextual analysis of the appearance of amber objects in Early Mycenaean graves points to a striking variation in how the various components were selected, combined and deposited, thereby contradicting the hitherto predominant notion of a uniform use of such objects as necklaces. In combination with an assessment of their morphological peculiarities, as well as of the manipulations of the amber objects in the course of secondary usage, this leads me to the conclusion that, while some of the amber components were indeed worn as necklaces by men and women, in not a single case are their find circumstances and/or morphological features consistent with reconstruction as a crescentic necklace. In addition, the find situation in Shaft Grave Omicron may exemplify a combination of amber beads with other such materials in the same necklace, which would not come as a surprise in light of the evidence for necklaces made up of different materials in Late Minoan Crete (Effinger 1996, 77–78). Most importantly, some of the male grave assemblages discussed here provide evidence for uses of amber objects in completely different functional contexts than as necklaces, namely as protective devices that were perceived to be charged with supernatural power. Due to the quantity and variety of its amber components, the Kakovatos shoulder belt forms an outstanding work of craftsmanship marking the culmination of the association of amber with the Early Mycenaean warrior elite. While currently the Kakovatos belt seems to constitute a unique and isolated example, the uncertain function of the concentrations of about 400 amber objects, each with two burials of Shaft Grave IV, which almost equal the Kakovatos finds in number, needs to be borne in mind. Although the lack of pieces suitable for suspension in this grave context precludes an unequivocal interpretation as belts, the amber beads and spacer plates could have been sewn on a leather strap which was fastened and worn differently than the one from Kakovatos.

I regard this combination of three closely interrelated factors as crucial for the ascription of a supernatural meaning to amber in Early Mycenaean Greece: The first factor was rooted in the extraordinary properties of amber I have mentioned, which predestined it to be identified as a material with supernatural effects (Hughes-

Brock 1985, 260; Woodward 2002, 1046). The second factor was an already existing acquaintance with systems of the ascription of certain effects to stone materials, which had a long tradition in the ancient Near East and Egypt (Schuster-Brandis 2008) and represent an excellent example of the significance of the perceived agency of non-human actants. It is likely that the influx of objects made of amber, which had been unknown until the beginning of the Mycenaean period, led to an enrichment of these already pre-existing discourses about the efficacy of stones. The highly directional exchange and the choice of exactly those amber objects that were of special significance for the Wessex elite even make it seem possible that, as in the *kula ring* (Campbell 1983, 236–244; Firth 1983, 96; Appadurai 1986, 18–21), specific object biographies revealing their origins, effects and previous owners were transmitted together with the amber necklaces. These biographies are likely to have been modified more or less extensively in the course of the long-distance exchange until they reached the Peloponnese, where they were merged with and adapted to local oral traditions (Hughes-Brock 1993, 224). The third factor was linked to peculiarities in the construction of a religiously based identity by the Early Mycenaean elite (Whittaker 2011, 144–145). It is precisely those shaft graves that have yielded amber objects that also contain an unusual concentration of foreign items, mostly of a religious character, deriving from Crete, but also from Anatolia, Eastern Europe and the West (Heitz 1998, 40–46; 2008, 21–31). Elaborating on an idea of Sue Sherratt, I have argued that, by appropriating special objects from, so to speak, *all corners of the world*, those who buried their dead in the shaft graves placed themselves in the wider cosmos, at the centre of which they probably imagined they stood (Maran 2011, 289). This also explains why amber, as Hélène Whittaker (2011, 144) has correctly observed, gained such importance in the construction of the Mycenaean warrior elite identity.

Amber at the end of the Mycenaean period: The Tiryns sun wheels

Strikingly, in Greece after the Early Mycenaean period special amber items like the spacer plates and end-pieces disappear from the archaeological record (Harding and Hughes-Brock 1993, 147–152; Harding 1984, 82; Hughes-Brock 1985, 259), while, according to Janusz Czebreszuk (2011, 66–68, 108–123), during LH IIIA and IIIB amber objects in general may have been more common than was hitherto thought. Towards the end of the Mycenaean period we encounter beads of the so-called *Tiryns type*, a new kind of amber object, whose routes of transmission and social contexts of appearance, however, seem to have differed from the situation during Early Mycenaean times (Harding and Hughes-Brock 1974, 155–156; Harding 1984, 82–87; Hughes-Brock 1985, 261; Bouzek 1997, 122; Cultraro 2006). The association of amber beads with LH IIIC warrior burials, if it exists at all (Cultraro 2006, 1544–1550), is much more tentative than in Early Mycenaean times. Such objects are not exclusively found in richly furnished graves, nor are they restricted to only a few sites. Nevertheless, we have one remarkable example of the association of amber with supernatural powers as late as the end of the Mycenaean period.

In the so-called *Tiryns Treasure* found in 1915 in the southeastern Lower Town of

Tiryns and dated to the twelfth or early thirteenth centuries BCE (Arvanitopoulos 1915; Karo 1930b; Maran 2006), there appear two unique wheels of woven and wound gold wire with bronze spokes bearing the eponymous amber beads of the *type Tiryns* (Karo 1930b, 127, Beilage XXXA, XXXI; Harding 1984, 82–85, fig. 22). As Reinhard Jung (2007, 234–240, with further literature) has demonstrated, the two wheels were made in the image of the astral symbol of the wheel cross that often appears on contemporary Italian sheet-gold objects (see also already Bouzek 1997, 122). The similarity even extends to the beads on the spokes, which probably correspond to the dots on the wheel cross of the sheet-gold objects (Jung 2007, 234). This, in turn, points to the beads' symbolic rather than merely decorative significance. A linkage to distant areas is also provided by the particular style of gold wirework of the wheels, which finds its closest parallels in a group of golden objects from the Urnfield culture of Bohemia (Marinatos 1960; Bouzek 1985, 172–173; 1997, 122; Plesl 1993; Jung 2007, 234 with footnote 101). Still, the wheels seem to have been made in Tiryns because additional gold wire and amber beads for at least a third wheel were also part of the treasure (Karo 1930b, 128; Jung 2007, 236 with footnote 115), and, moreover, a comparable small basket of albeit much simpler bronze wirework was found in nearby Midea (Ostenso 1998, 158, pl. 112:M8).

The combination of the form with the shining materials of gold and amber suggests the wheels should be interpreted as images of the sun (Hughes-Brock 1993, 221; Dickinson 1994, 255; 2006, 205; Bouzek 1997, 122; Jung 2007, 240), which makes it particularly noteworthy that in the centre of the *sky* above the cult scene on the famous gold signet ring from the same treasure there appears an astral symbol resembling the design of the wheels (Maran 2012b, 124). As I have shown elsewhere, this may not be the only semantic linkage of the image on the signet ring and actual objects of the treasure, since the highly unusual large bronze chalice, in which the signet ring and other jewellery were deposited, bears a resemblance to the chalice held by the goddess (ibid., 123–124). We therefore have to confront the possibility of an *interactive* relationship of objects and images in ritual communication practices, thus connecting realms that are usually treated separately in archaeological research. This means that the perceived meaning of the scenes was integrated into discourses explaining the special significance of certain objects. This contributed significantly to the possibility of providing objects with *biographies*, linking them with religious or mythical beings and displaying such objects on certain occasions. In turn, the ability to *prove* the supernatural character of objects by referring to an image may have facilitated the appropriation of the Central Mediterranean version of the wheel cross, inasmuch as the reference to earlier local forms of religious iconography served to *naturalize* the symbol.

The Tiryns wheels represent ritual objects that were made locally by combining certain foreign traits of material, form and technique. This may be an indication of the producer herself or himself being a person of foreign descent, who may have been regarded as having special religious knowledge. In ritual action the wheels were probably perceived as being charged with celestial energy, while at the same creating a semantic linkage to distant lands through which the ritual community was placed in the wider framework of the cosmos. The wheels also already exemplify the emic perception of amber and gold as twin solar materials (Hughes-Brock 1993, 224; Bouzek 1993, 141), which must lie at the heart of the curious semantic ambivalence of the term *elektron* in classical Greek antiquity.

Amber in Mycenaean Greece: From diffusion to translation

The appearance of amber objects in Mycenaean Greece clearly shows that, in order to understand the appropriation of foreign objects, archaeology has to replace the customary model of diffusion with one of *translation*. As Latour (1986, 266–269) has remarked, the notion of diffusion assigns a decisive role to the initial force triggering the movement of an object, while the people further along the chain are only able to transmit or reject this initial energy. Accordingly in this perspective, the original meaning of an object is accurately transmitted, and the spreading of the object does not need to be explained since, as long as there is no obstacle, it will move in a certain direction. In *translation*, on the contrary, the initial force does not predetermine later steps because agency is attributed to the people in the chain, who, through their actions and discourses, constantly shape and change the meaning of the object. Therefore, in Latour's words: "Instead of the *transmission* of the same token […] you get, in the second model, the continuous *transformation* of the token" (Latour 1986, 268, italics in the original text).

Until now, when dealing with amber objects in Bronze Age Europe, research has followed the model of diffusion, thereby explicitly or implicitly suggesting a uniformity of use in the different regions where such objects have been uncovered. As demonstrated here, a shift to the model of *translation* reveals marked peculiarities in the meanings ascribed to amber objects in the course of Mycenaean culture. Most importantly, by assigning amber objects to the realm of *jewellery*, research has failed to capture the role of objects made of this particular material in the construction of the Early Mycenaean warrior elite identity and of the emic perception of such objects as devices empowering and protecting their bearers. The particular linkage of amber with members of the warrior elite, which finds its most astonishing reflection in the Kakovatos shoulder belt, seems not to have outlasted the Early Mycenaean period. While the perception of amber in Mycenaean palatial times is currently impossible to specify, for the post-palatial period the Tiryns sun wheels indicate a cosmological significance for amber that, in this clarity, is just as much unmatched in the earlier phases of Mycenaean culture as the combination of amber with gold as twin solar materials in objects that were not worn on the body of persons, but rather were integrated as religious paraphernalia in ceremonies.

Acknowledgements

I would like to thank Hans Peter Hahn and Hadas Weiss for inviting me to the exciting conference on which the current volume is based. Special thanks are due to Maria Kostoula for her digital reconstruction of the Kakovatos shoulder belt, as well as for remastering the digital images used in this article. Research for this article was conducted within the framework of the Heidelberg Cluster of Excellence, *Asia and Europe in a Global Context*. Finally, I would like to express my gratitude to an unknown reviewer, whose comments and suggestions have helped to improve this paper.

Notes

1   Du Gardin (2003, 196) postulated a development of amber spacer plates with a complex-bored pattern within the central European Early Bronze Age Únětice culture. This assumption, however, is not supported by actual finds of such spacer plates in Únětice contexts, but rests solely on an extremely late dating of the crescentic necklaces of the Wessex culture to the time of the Tumulus Burial culture, which is contradicted by both archaeological synchronisms (Gerloff 1993; 2010) and radiocarbon dates (Needham *et al.* 2010).

2   Barfield (1991), Gerloff (1993, 85), (2010, 624–629), Maran (2004, 56). Among the central European objects cited by Gerloff, the amber spacer plate and beads from a probable hoard found on the Padnal near Savognin (Graubünden, Switzerland) should probably be disregarded for questions related to the trade during the time of the shaft graves of Mycenae, since the hoard may date to an advanced stage of the Tumulus Burial culture (Rageth 1976, 172–174). For a comprehensive discussion of the find circumstances and dating of the amber objects from Koblach-Kadel, Zürich-Mozartstraße and the Padnal, see Stahl (2006, 140, 147–148.); for the piece from Koblach-Kadel in particular, whose attribution to a context of the late central European Early Bronze Age is well-founded see Hughes-Brock (2005, 303), Maran (2004, 56 with footnote 28). For other signs of Early Bronze Age contacts between Britain and Central Europe, see O'Connor (2010, 597–599).

3   Graziadio (1998, 63–64), (2000, 252–259), Maran (2004, 55–56). Although he did not know about the trade settlements in the area of the Gulf of Naples, Marinatos (1962, 166) already emphasized the importance of the Tyrrhenian side of Italy for the long-distance transfer of amber objects in Early Mycenaean times by pointing to Lipari as an important connecting link. The route of the transmission of amber objects through the Adriatic Sea preferred by other authors (cf. Dickinson 1994, 249; Ruppenstein 2010, 650) seems to me less likely because there are no similar sites with LH I pottery along the coasts of the Adriatic (cf. Jung 2010, 661–665). For the role of Kakovatos in the long-distance trade, see Vermeule (1972, 131), Nikolentzos (2003), Eder (2011, 107–110).

4   Dietz (1991, 130, fig. 44) mentioned only the amber beads found at the hip, which he interprets as belonging to a belt (see also Hughes-Brock 2005, 301), but he disregards the beads found on the upper body that would not be consistent with a belt-like reconstruction.

5   As for the question of whether in Mycenaean times different materials were combined or worn *purely* in the same necklace, it could be that the modern aesthetics of wearing jewellery are unknowingly influencing research. While at the time of the excavation and publication of Grave Circle B it was usual to wear female necklaces consisting of only one material (cf. pearls, turquoise, carnelian, amber etc.), thereby possibly guiding scholarly interpretation, the willingness in more recent research to accept the integration of different materials in one and the same necklace may be just as much a reflection of contemporary fashions for wearing such jewellery as a colourful combination of various materials.

6   The interpretation that these finds were of a long necklace was doubted by Hughes-Brock (1993, 219 with footnote 2). For a rebuttal of her arguments, see Maran (2004, 52 with footnote 11). Hughes-Brock (2005, 301) now accepts that the beads in Shaft Grave Omicron may have been strung as a very long necklace.

7   Marinatos (1962, 167) and Beck and Beck (1995, 122–125) only mention beads as components of the necklaces.

8   Due to the large number and variety of finds from Kakovatos Tholos Tomb A, Dickinson (1977, 93) doubted the attribution to only one burial (see also Kalogeropoulos 1998, 128–129). However, the shaft of the Tholos Tomb of Vapheio also held a bewildering variety and number of different objects, though Kilian-Dirlmeier (1986) has convincingly supported the original view of the excavator, Christos Tsountas, of the existence of only one interment. What is especially striking in the case of Kakovatos Tholos Tomb A is the absence of grave goods that would be clearly consistent with an assemblage of female type, as well as the fact that, with the exception of the palatial jars and amber objects – which, however, all may have belonged to one and the same part of the equipment – the categories of items represented do not seem to repeat themselves. Boyd (2002, 190) has cited the early destruction of Tholos Tombs A and B by an earthquake as a possible reason for the lack of signs of the frequent reuse of the tombs.

9   The famous reconstruction of the amber necklace from Asenkoven Grave E (Bavaria) can be used as

an example of how spacer plates can be reused as pendants without drilling any additional holes, see Hachmann (1957, 17, fig. 5), Harding (1984, 77–78, fig. 18).

10 These are probably to be identified with the three ring-shaped components that are illustrated by photographs in publications. The first such object is large with a maximum width of 64 mm according to Müller (1909, 279) or 61.5 mm according to Beck *et al.* (1970, 9–11). The differences in measurement may be attributed to the fact that at the time of the original publication the object was still complete, while it later broke into separate pieces, so that in the studies undertaken in the 1960s and 1970s only the upper half was available for inspection and measurement (Beck *et al.* 1970, 9–11; Harding 1984, fig. 15 [upper left corner]). The two smaller ring-shaped objects have maximum diameters of 30 mm and 36 mm respectively and are illustrated in Müller (1909, pl. 15:22) and Demakopoulou (1988, 258 no. 283). The latter photograph, in which three objects from Kakovatos Tholos Tomb A are combined with an amber bead of the *type Tiryns* from the chamber tomb necropolis of Tiryns, has unfortunately encouraged the mistaken impression that the objects all come from Kakovatos (Nikolentzos 2003).

11 Beck *et al.* (1970, 12), Harding and Hughes-Brock (1974, 155) and Nikolentzos (2003, 623, footnote 11) have referred in passing to the existence of comparable ring pendants from Early Bronze Age Eastern Europe. It is unfortunate that they have not specified what objects they had in mind because I do not know of any good comparisons for the Kakovatos ring-shaped objects.

12 Müller (1909, 280) thought that the object may have served to hold the fringes of a broad tassel.

13 That the largest amber beads from Kakovatos Tholos Tomb A were strung on a necklace was doubted by Müller (1909, 279).

14 Mylonas (1966, 425–426) interpreted brown stains on the back of gold petals from the shaft graves "and the brownish matter often seen in inlaid work" (ibid., 426) as traces of a substance used for gluing. I would like to thank Kalliope Nikita (Nottingham) for drawing my attention to this reference.

15 This remark of Schliemann's lends additional credibility to his observation.

References

Appadurai, A. (1986) Introduction: Commodities and the politics of value. In A. Appadurai (ed.) *The social life of things: Commodities in cultural perspective*, 3–63. Cambridge, Cambridge University Press.

Arvanitopoulos, A. S. (1915) Ανασκαφαί και έρευναι εν Τιρύνθι. *Πρακτικά της εν Αθήναις Αρχαιολογικής Εταιρείας*, 201–236.

Bachhuber, C. (2003) *Aspects of late Helladic sea trade.* Unpublished MA thesis, Texas A and M University. 22.04.2012, http://anthropology.tamu.edu/papers/Bachhuber-MA2003.pdf

Barfield, L. H. (1991) Wessex with and without Mycenae: New evidence from Switzerland. *Antiquity* 65 (246), 102–107.

Barfod, J. (1996) Bernstein in Volksglauben und Volksmedizin. In M. Ganzelewski and R. Slotta (eds) *Bernstein. Tränen der Götter. Katalog der Ausstellung des Deutschen Bergbau-Museums Bochum in Zusammenarbeit mit dem Ostpreußischen Landesmuseum Lüneburg und dem Siebenbürgischen Museum Gundelsheim.* Veröffentlichungen aus dem Deutschen Bergbau-Museum Bochum, 64, 453–456. Bochum, Deutsches Bergbau-Museum.

Beck, C. W. (1966) Analysis and provenience of Minoan and Mycenaean amber, I. *Greek, Roman and Byzantine Studies* 7 (3), 191–211.

Beck, C. W. (1986) Spectroscopic investigations of amber. *Applied Spectroscopy Reviews* 22 (1), 57–110.

Beck, C. W. and Beck, L. Y. (1995) Analysis and provenience of Minoan and Mycenaean amber, V. Pylos and Messenia. *Greek, Roman and Byzantine Studies* 36 (2), 119–135.

Beck, C. W. and Bouzek, J. (eds) (1993) *Amber in archaeology: Proceedings of the Second International Conference on Amber in Archaeology, Liblice 1990.* Prague, Institute of Archaeology.

Beck, C. W.; Fellows, C. A. and Adams, A. B. (1970) Analysis and provenience of Minoan and Mycenaean amber, III. Kakovatos. *Greek, Roman and Byzantine Studies* 11 (1), 5–22.

Beck, C. W. and Shennan, S. (1991) *Amber in Prehistoric Britain*. Oxbow Monographs, 8. Oxford, Oxbow.

Beck, C. W.; Southard, G. C. and Adams, A. B. (1972) Analysis and provenience of Minoan and Mycenaean amber, IV. Mycenae. *Greek, Roman and Byzantine Studies* 13 (4), 359–385.

Blakolmer, F.; Reinholdt, C.; Weilhartner, J. and Nightingale, G. (eds) (2011) *Österreichische Forschungen zur ägäischen Bronzezeit 2009. Akten der Tagung am Fachbereich Altertumswissenschaften der Paris-London-Universität Salzburg vom 6. bis 7. März 2009*. Wien, Phoibos.

Blegen, C. W.; Rawson, M.; Taylour, L. W. and Donovan, W. P. (1973) *The palace of Nestor at Pylos in Western Messenia. Volume III. Acropolis and lower town. Tholoi, grave circle, and chamber tombs. Discoveries outside the citadel*. Princeton, Princeton University Press.

Bouzek, J. (1985) *The Aegean, Anatolia and Europe: Cultural interrelations in the second millennium BC*. Studies in Mediterranean Archaeology, 29. Göteborg, Åström.

Bouzek, J. (1993) The shifts of the amber route. In C. W. Beck and J. Bouzek (eds) *Amber in archaeology: Proceedings of the Second International Conference on Amber in Archaeology, Liblice 1990*, 141–146. Prague, Institute of Archaeology.

Bouzek, J. (1997) *Greece, Anatolia and Europe: Cultural interrelations during the early Iron Age*. Studies in Mediterranean Archaeology, 122. Göteborg, Åström.

Boyd, M. J. (2002) *Middle Helladic and Early Mycenaean mortuary practices in the Southern and Western Peloponnese*. BAR International Series, 1009. Oxford, Archaeopress.

Buchholz, H.-G. (1980) *Kriegswesen. Teil 2, Angriffswaffen: Schwert, Dolch, Lanze, Speer, Keule*, (= Archaeologia Homerica, IE2). Göttingen, Vandenhoek and Ruprecht.

Campbell, S. F. (1983) Attaining rank: A classification of kula shell valuables. In J. W. Leach and E. Leach (eds) *The kula: New perspectives on Massim exchange*, 229–248. Cambridge, Cambridge University Press.

Cavanagh, W. and Mee, C. (1998) *A private place: Death in prehistoric Greece*. Studies in Mediterranean Archaeology, 125. Jonsered, Åström.

Cline, E. H. (2005) The multivalent nature of imported objects in the ancient Mediterranean world. *Annales d'archéologie égéenne de l'Université de Liège* [Aegaeum], 25, 45–51.

Cultraro, M. (2006) I vaghi di ambra del tipo Tirinto nella protostoria italiana. Nuovi dati dall'area egeo-balcanica. In D. Cocchi Genick (ed.) *Atti della XXXIX Riunione Scientifica 'Materie prime e scambi nella preistoria italiana', Firenze, 25–27 novembre 2004*, 1535–1553. Firenze, Istituto Italiano di Preistoria e Protostoria.

Czebreszuk, J. (2011) *Bursztyn w kulturze mykeńskiej. Zarys problematyki badawczej*. Poznań, Wydawnictwo Poznańskie.

Demakopoulou, K. (ed.) (1988) *Das mykenische Hellas. Heimat der Helden Homers*. Sonderausstellungshalle der staatlichen Museen Preussischer Kulturbesitz, 1. Juni – 19. August 1988. Berlin, Reimer.

Dickinson, O. T. P. K. (1977) *The origins of Mycenaean civilisation*. Studies in Mediterranean Archaeology, 49. Göteborg, Åström.

Dickinson, O. T. P. K. (1994) *The Aegean Bronze Age*. Cambridge World Archaeology. Cambridge, Cambridge University Press.

Dickinson, O. T. P. K. (2006) *The Aegean from Bronze Age to Iron Age: Continuity and change between the twelfth and eighth centuries BC*. London and New York, Routledge.

Dietz, S. (1991) *The Argolid at the transition to the Mycenaean Age: Studies in the chronology and cultural development in the shaft grave period*. Copenhagen, The National Museum of Denmark, Department of Near Eastern and Classical Antiquities.

Dörpfeld, W. (1908) Alt-Pylos. I. Die Kuppelgräber von Kakovatos. *Athenische Mitteilungen* 33, 295–322.

du Gardin, C. (2003) Amber spacer beads in the Neolithic and Bronze Ages in Europe. In C. W.

Beck, I. B. Loze and J. M. Todd (eds) *Amber in archaeology: Proceedings of the Fourth International Conference on Amber in Archaeology, Talsi 2001*, 180–197. Riga, Institute of the History of Latvia.

Eder, B. (2011) Zur historischen Geographie Triphyliens in mykenischer Zeit. In F. Blakolmer, C. Reinholdt, J. Weilhartner and G. Nightingale (eds) *Österreichische Forschungen zur ägäischen Bronzezeit 2009. Akten der Tagung am Fachbereich Altertumswissenschaften der Paris-London-Universität Salzburg vom 6. bis 7. März 2009*, 105–117. Wien, Phoibos.

Effinger, M. (1996) *Minoischer Schmuck*. BAR International Series, 646. Oxford, Archaeopress.

Firth, R. (1983) Magnitudes and values in kula exchange. In J. W. Leach and E. Leach (eds) *The kula: New perspectives on Massim exchange*, 89–102. Cambridge, Cambridge University Press.

Ganzelewski, M. (1996) Aussehen und Eigenschaften von 'Bernstein'. In M. Ganzelewski and R. Slotta (eds) *Bernstein. Tränen der Götter. Katalog der Ausstellung des Deutschen Bergbau-Museums Bochum in Zusammenarbeit mit dem Ostpreußischen Landesmuseum Lüneburg und dem Siebenbürgischen Museum Gundelsheim*. Veröffentlichungen aus dem Deutschen Bergbau-Museum Bochum, 64, 19–29. Bochum, Deutsches Bergbau-Museum.

Ganzelewski, M. and Slotta, R. (eds) (1996) *Bernstein. Tränen der Götter. Katalog der Ausstellung des Deutschen Bergbau-Museums Bochum in Zusammenarbeit mit dem Ostpreußischen Landesmuseum Lüneburg und dem Siebenbürgischen Museum Gundelsheim*. Veröffentlichungen aus dem Deutschen Bergbau-Museum Bochum, 64. Bochum, Deutsches Bergbau-Museum.

Geerlings, W. (1996) Die Tränen der Schwestern des Phaethon. Bernstein im Altertum. In M. Ganzelewski and R. Slotta (eds) *Bernstein. Tränen der Götter. Katalog der Ausstellung des Deutschen Bergbau-Museums Bochum in Zusammenarbeit mit dem Ostpreußischen Landesmuseum Lüneburg und dem Siebenbürgischen Museum Gundelsheim*. Veröffentlichungen aus dem Deutschen Bergbau-Museum Bochum, 64, 395–400. Bochum, Deutsches Bergbau-Museum.

Gerloff, S. (1975) *The Early Bronze Age daggers in Great Britain and a reconsideration of the Wessex culture*. Prähistorische Bronzefunde, Abteilung VI, 2. Band. München, Beck.

Gerloff, S. (1993) Zu Fragen mittelmeerländischer Kontakte und absoluter Chronologie der Frühbronzezeit in Mittel- und Westeuropa. *Prähistorische Zeitschrift* 68 (1), 58–102.

Gerloff, S. (2010) Von Troja an die Saale, von Wessex nach Mykene. Chronologie, Fernverbindungen und Zinnrouten der Frühbronzezeit Mittel- und Westeuropas. In H. Meller and F. Bertemes (eds) *Der Griff nach den Sternen. Wie Europas Eliten zu Macht und Reichtum kamen. Internationales Symposium in Halle (Saale), 16.–21. Februar 2005*. Tagungen des Landesmuseums für Vorgeschichte Halle, 5, 603–639. Halle, Landesmuseum für Vorgeschichte.

Graziadio, G. (1998) Trade circuits and trade-routes in the shaft grave period. *Studi Micenei ed Egeo-Anatolici* 40, 29–76.

Graziadio, G. (2000) L'Egeo e l'Italia nel periodo delle tombe a fossa. In G. Castellana (ed.) *La cultura del Medio Bronzo nell'agrigentino ed i rapporti con il mondo miceneo*, 246–263. Palermo, Agrigent Regione Siciliana, Assessorato Regionale Beni Culturali ed Ambientali e della Pubblica Istruzione.

Hachmann, R. (1957) Bronzezeitliche Bernsteinschieber. *Bayerische Vorgeschichtsblätter* 22, 1–36.

Hahn, H. P. (2004) Global goods and the process of appropriation. In P. Probst and G. Spittler (eds) *Between resistance and expansion: Explorations of local vitality in Africa*. Beiträge zur Afrikaforschung, 18, 211–229. Münster, LIT.

Hahn, H. P. (2008) Diffusionism, appropriation, and globalization: Some remarks on current debates in anthropology. *Anthropos* 103 (1), 191–202.

Hahn, H. P. (2012) Circulating objects and the power of hybridization as a localizing strategy. In P. W. Stockhammer (ed.) *Conceptualizing cultural hybridization: A transdisciplinary approach*, 27–42. Berlin and Heidelberg, Springer.

Harding, A. (1984) *The Mycenaeans and Europe*. London and Orlando, Academic Press.

Harding, A. and Hughes-Brock, H. (1974) Amber in the Mycenaean world. *Annual of the British School at Athens* 69, 145–172.

Heitz, C. (1998) *Burying the palaces? Ideologies in the shaft grave period.* Unpublished M.Phil. thesis, University of Cambridge.

Heitz, C. (2008) *Burying the palaces? Ideologies in the shaft grave period.* Heidelberg, UB Heidelberg, Publikationsplattform Altertumswissenschaften. 28.04.2012, http://archiv.ub.uni-heidelberg.de/propylaeumdok/volltexte/2008/89/

Helm, O. (1886) Anhang. Der mykenische Bernstein. In H. Schliemann (1886) *Tiryns. Der prähistorische Palast der Könige von Tiryns. Ergebnisse der neuesten Ausgrabungen*, 425–432. Leipzig, Brockhaus.

Hughes-Brock, H. (1985) Amber and the Mycenaeans. *Journal of Baltic Studies* 16 (3), 257–267.

Hughes-Brock, H. (1993) Amber in the Aegean in the Late Bronze Age: Some problems and perspectives. In C. W. Beck and J. Bouzek (eds) *Amber in archaeology: Proceedings of the Second International Conference on Amber in Archaeology, Liblice 1990*, 219–229. Prague, Institute of Archaeology.

Hughes-Brock, H. (1998) Greek beads of the Mycenaean period (ca. 1650–1100 BC): The age of the heroines of Greek tradition and mythology. In L. D. Sciama and J. B. Eicher (eds) *Beads and bead makers: Gender, material culture and meaning*, 247–271. Oxford and New York, Berg.

Hughes-Brock, H. (2005) Amber and some other travellers in the Bronze Age Aegean and Europe. In A. Dakouri-Hild and S. Sherratt (eds) *Autochthon: Papers presented to O.T.P.K. Dickinson on the occasion of his retirement.* BAR International Series 1432, 301–316. Oxford, Archaeopress.

Jung, R. (2007) Goldene Vögel und Sonnen. Ideologische Kontakte zwischen Italien und der postpalatialen Ägäis. In E. Alram-Stern and G. Nightingale (eds) *KEIMELION. Elitenbildung und elitärer Konsum von der mykenischen Palastzeit bis zur homerischen Epoche. = The formation of elites and elitist lifestyles from Mycenaean palatial times to the Homeric period. Akten des internationalen Kongresses vom 3. bis 5. Februar 2005 in Salzburg.* Denkschriften der philosophisch-historischen Klasse 350; Veröffentlichungen der Mykenischen Kommission, 27, 219–255. Wien, Verlag der Österreichischen Akademie der Wissenschaften.

Jung, R. (2010) Der Charakter der Nordkontakte der minoischen und mykenischen Zivilisation um 1600 v.u.Z. In H. Meller and F. Bertemes (eds) *Der Griff nach den Sternen. Wie Europas Eliten zu Macht und Reichtum kamen. Internationales Symposium in Halle (Saale), 16.–21. Februar 2005.* Tagungen des Landesmuseums für Vorgeschichte Halle, 5, 657–674. Halle, Landesmuseum für Vorgeschichte.

Kalogeropoulos, K. (1998) *Die frühmykenischen Grabfunde von Analipsis (Südöstliches Arkadien). Mit einem Beitrag zu den palatialen Amphoren des griechischen Festlandes.* Βιβλιοθήκη της εν Αθήναις Αρχαιολογικής Εταιρείας, 175. Athens, Archaeological Society.

Karo, G. (1930a) *Die Schachtgräber von Mykenai.* München, Bruckmann.

Karo, G. (1930b) Schatz von Tiryns. *Mitteilungen des Deutschen Archäologischen Institutes, Athenische Abteilung* 55, 119–140.

Kilian-Dirlmeier, I. (1986) Beobachtungen zu den Schachtgräbern von Mykenai und zu den Schmuckbeigaben mykenischer Männergräber. Untersuchungen zur Sozialstruktur in späthelladischer Zeit. *Jahrbuch des Römisch-Germanischen Zentralmuseums* 33, 159–198.

Kilian-Dirlmeier, I. (1987) Das Kuppelgrab von Vapheio. Die Beigabenausstattung in der Steinkiste. Untersuchungen zur Sozialstruktur in späthelladischer Zeit. *Jahrbuch des Römisch-Germanischen Zentralmuseums* 34, 197–212.

Kilian-Dirlmeier, I. (1988) Jewellery in Mycenaean and Minoan 'warrior graves'. In E. B. French and K. A. Wardle (eds) *Problems in Greek prehistory: Papers presented at the Centenary Conference of the British School of Archaeology at Athens, Manchester April 1986*, 161–171. Bristol, Classical Press.

Kilian-Dirlmeier, I. (1993) *Die Schwerter in Griechenland (außerhalb der Peloponnes), Bulgarien und Albanien.* Prähistorische Bronzefunde, IV, 12. Stuttgart, Steiner.

Laffineur, R. (1996) À propos des 'Gamaschenhalter' des tombes à fosse de Mycènes. In E. de Miro, L. Godart and A. Sacconi (eds) *Atti e memorie del secondo congresso internazionale di micenologia, Roma-Napoli, 14–20 ottobre 1991*, 1229–1238. Rome, Gruppo Editoriale Internazionale.

Latour, B. (1986) The powers of association. In J. Law (ed.) *Power, action and belief: A new sociology of knowledge?.* Sociological Review Monograph, 32, 264–280. London and Boston, Routledge and Kegan Paul.

Latour, B. (1993 [1991]) *We have never been modern.* Cambridge, MA, Harvard University Press, first published in French, 1991, *Nous n'avons jamais été modernes. Essai d'anthropologie symétrique.* Paris, La Découverte.

Leach, J. W. and Leach, E. (ed.) (1983) *The kula: New perspectives on Massim exchange.* Cambridge, Cambridge University Press.

Maran, J. (2004) Wessex und Mykene. Zur Deutung des Bernsteins in der Schachtgräberzeit Südgriechenlands. In B. Hänsel and E. Studeníková (eds) *Zwischen Karpaten und Ägäis. Neolithikum und Ältere Bronzezeit. Gedenkschrift für Viera Němejcová–Pavúková.* Internationale Archäologie, Studia Honoraria, 21, 47–65. Rahden, Leidorf.

Maran, J. (2006) Coming to terms with the past: Ideology and power in Late Helladic IIIC. In S. Deger-Jalkotzy and I. S. Lemos (eds) *Ancient Greece: From the Mycenaean palaces to the age of Homer.* Edinburgh Leventis Studies, 3, 123–150. Edinburgh, Edinburgh University Press.

Maran, J. (2011) Lost in translation: The emergence of Mycenaean culture as a phenomenon of glocalization. In T. C. Wilkinson, S. Sherratt and J. Bennet (eds) *Interweaving worlds: Systemic interactions in Eurasia, 7th to 1st Millennia BC*, 282–294. Oxford, Oxbow.

Maran, J. (2012a) One world is not enough: The transformative potential of intercultural exchange in prehistoric societies. In P. W. Stockhammer (ed.) *Conceptualizing cultural hybridization: A transdisciplinary approach*, 59–66. Berlin and Heidelberg, Springer.

Maran, J. (2012b) Ceremonial feasting equipment: Social space and interculturality in post-palatial Tiryns. In J. Maran and P. W. Stockhammer (eds) *Materiality and social practice: Transformative capacities of intercultural encounters*, 121–136. Oxford, Oxbow.

Marinatos, S. (1956) Ανασκαφαί εν Πύλω. *Πρακτικά της εν Αθήναις Αρχαιολογικής Εταιρείας*, 202–206.

Marinatos, S. (1960) Lausitzer Goldschmuck in Tiryns. In F. Eckstein (ed.) *Theoria. Festschrift für W.-H. Schuchhardt.* Deutsche Beiträge zur Altertumswissenschaft, 12, 151–157. Baden-Baden, Grimm.

Marinatos, S. (1962) The Minoan and Mycenaean civilization and its influence on the Mediterranean and on Europe. In M. Pallottino, L. Cardini and D. Brusadin (eds) *Atti del VI Congresso Internazionale delle scienze Preistoriche e Protostoriche, Roma 1962. Relazioni Generali*, 161–176. Rome, Sansoni.

Matthäus, H. (1980) *Die Bronzegefäße der kretisch-mykenischen Kultur.* Prähistorische Bronzefunde, Abteilung II, 1. Band. München, Beck.

Meller, H. and Bertemes, F. (eds) (2010) *Der Griff nach den Sternen. Wie Europas Eliten zu Macht und Reichtum kamen. Internationales Symposium in Halle (Saale), 16.-21. Februar 2005.* Tagungen des Landesmuseums für Vorgeschichte Halle, 5. Halle, Landesmuseum für Vorgeschichte.

Milojčić, V. (1955) Neue Bernsteinschieber aus Griechenland. *Germania* 33, 316–319.

Müller, K. (1909) Alt Pylos. II. Die Funde aus den Kuppelgräbern von Kakovatos. *Mitteilungen des Deutschen Archäologischen Institutes, Athenische Abteilung* 34, 269–328.

Muhly, J. D. (1973) Copper and tin: The distribution of mineral resources and the nature of the metals trade in the Bronze Age. *Transactions of the Connecticut Academy of Arts and Sciences* 43, 155–535, [to be obtained from: Archon Books, Hamden].

Mylonas, G. E. (1966) The east wing of the palace of Mycenae. *Hesperia* 35 (4), 419–426.

Mylonas, G. E. (1972/1973) *Ο ταφικός Κύκλος B των Μυκηνών*. Βιβλιοθήκη της εν Αθήναις Αρχαιολογικής Εταιρείας, 73. Athens, Archaeological Society.

Needham, S.; Pearson, M. P.; Tyler, A.; Richards, M. and Jay, M. (2010) A first 'Wessex I' date from Wessex. *Antiquity* 84 (324), 363–373.

Nikolentzos, K. (2003) Κακόβατος. Ένας εμπορικός σταθμός εισαγωγής ηλέκτρου στον πρώιμο μυκηναϊκό κόσμο. In A. Vlachopoulos and K. Birtacha (eds) *Αργοναύτης. Τιμητικός τόμος για τον καθηγητή Χρίστο Γ. Ντούμα απο τους μαθητές του στο Πανεπιστήμιο Αθηνών (1980–2000)*, 619–631. Athens, Kathimerini.

O'Connor, B. (2010) From Dorchester to Dieskau: Some aspects of relations between Britain and Central Europe during the Early Bronze Age. In H. Meller and F. Bertemes (eds) (2010) *Der Griff nach den Sternen. Wie Europas Eliten zu Macht und Reichtum kamen. Internationales Symposium in Halle (Saale), 16.-21. Februar 2005*. Tagungen des Landesmuseums für Vorgeschichte Halle, 5, 591–602. Halle, Landesmuseum für Vorgeschichte.

Ostenso, A. (1998) The small finds. In G. Walberg (ed.) *Excavations on the Acropolis of Midea: Results of the Greek-Swedish excavations. Vol. I: 1. The Excavations on the Lower Terraces 1985–1991*, 150–167. Stockholm, Åström.

Papadimitriou, I. (1953) Ανασκαφαί εν Μυκήναις. *Πρακτικά της εν Αθήναις Αρχαιολογικής Εταιρείας*, 205–237.

Plesl, E. (1993) Zur Frage des Bernsteinvorkommens während der Urnenfelderperiode in der Tschechoslowakei. In C. W. Beck and J. Bouzek (eds) *Amber in archaeology: Proceedings of the Second International Conference on Amber in Archaeology, Liblice 1990*, 164–170. Prague, Institute of Archaeology.

Rageth, J. (1976) Die bronzezeitliche Siedlung auf dem Padnal bei Savognin (Oberhalbstein GR). Grabungen 1971 und 1972. *Jahrbuch der Schweizerischen Gesellschaft für Ur- und Frühgeschichte* 59, 123–179.

Ruppenstein F. (2010) Einfache Radnadeln als Indikatoren europaweiter Fernbeziehungen zur Zeit der Deponierung der Himmelsscheibe von Nebra. In H. Meller and F. Bertemes (eds) *Der Griff nach den Sternen. Wie Europas Eliten zu Macht und Reichtum kamen. Internationales Symposium in Halle (Saale), 16.-21. Februar 2005*. Tagungen des Landesmuseums für Vorgeschichte Halle, 5, 641–653. Halle, Landesmuseum für Vorgeschichte.

Sandars, N. K. (1959) Amber spacer-beads again. *Antiquity* 33 (132), 292–295.

Schliemann, H. (1878) *Mykenae. Bericht über meine Forschungen und Entdeckungen in Mykenae und Tiryns*. Leipzig, Brockhaus.

Schon, R. (2009) Think locally, act globally: Mycenaean elites and the Late Bronze Age world-system. In W. A. Parkinson and M. L. Galaty (eds) *Archaic state interaction: The Eastern Mediterranean in the Bronze Age*, 213–236. Santa Fe, School for Advanced Research Press.

Schuster-Brandis, A. (2008) *Steine als Schutz- und Heilmittel. Untersuchung zu ihrer Verwendung in der Beschwörungskunst Mesopotamiens im 1. Jt. V. Chr.* Alter Orient und Altes Testament, 46. Münster, Ugarit-Verlag.

Shennan, S. (1982) Exchange and ranking: The role of Amber in the earlier Bronze Age of Europe. In C. Renfrew and S. Shennan (eds) *Ranking, resource and exchange: Aspects of the archaeology of early European society*, 33–45. Cambridge, Cambridge University Press.

Shennan, S. (1993) Amber and its value in the British Bronze Age. In C. W. Beck and J. Bouzek (eds) *Amber in archaeology: Proceedings of the Second International Conference on Amber in Archaeology, Liblice 1990*, 59–66. Prague, Institute of Archaeology.

Spittler, G. (2002) Globale Waren – Lokale Aneignungen. In B. Hauser-Schäublin and U. Braukämper (eds) *Ethnologie der Globalisierung. Perspektiven kultureller Verflechtungen*, 15–30. Berlin, Reimer.

Stahl, C. (2006) *Mitteleuropäische Bernsteinfunde von der Frühbronze- bis zur Frühlatènezeit. Ihre Verbreitung, Formgebung, Zeitstellung und Herkunft.* Würzburger Studien zur Sprache und Kultur, 9. Dettelbach, Röll.

Steinhübl, R. (2011) Die Ikonographie von Schwert und Schwertkampf im bronze- und früheisenzeitlichen Griechenland. In F. Blakolmer, C. Reinholdt, J. Weilhartner and G. Nightingale (eds) *Österreichische Forschungen zur ägäischen Bronzezeit 2009. Akten der Tagung am Fachbereich Altertumswissenschaften der Paris-London-Universität Salzburg vom 6. bis 7. März 2009,* 295–303. Wien, Phoibos.

Stockhammer, P. W. (ed.) (2012) *Conceptualizing cultural hybridization: A transdisciplinary approach.* Berlin and Heidelberg, Springer.

Vermeule, E. (1972) *Greece in the Bronze Age.* Chicago and London, University of Chicago Press.

Verschueren, K. (2009/2010) *Amber in de Griekse Bronstijd. Hoe amber, specifiek in de vorm van verdeelkralen, nieuw licht kann werpen op Myceense langeafstandscontacten.* Unpublished MA thesis University of Gent. 28.04.2012, http://lib.ugent.be/fulltxt/RUG01/001/457/547/RUG01–001457547_2011_0001_AC.pdf

Whittaker, H. (2011) Exotica in Early Mycenaean burials as evidence for the self-representation of the elite. In A. Vianello (ed.) *Exotica in the prehistoric Mediterranean,* 137–146. Oxford, Oxbow.

Woodward, A. (2002) Beads and beakers: Heirlooms and relics in the British Early Bronze Age. *Antiquity* 76 (294), 1040–1047.

Chapter 12

The materiality of medieval heirlooms:
From biographical to sacred objects

Roberta Gilchrist

Disciplinary legacies: Questions about heirlooms

Archaeologists are instinctively wary of heirlooms. This is because *old things* excavated from stratified contexts possess the power to contaminate site chronologies. Potential heirlooms are usually regarded as taphonomic or methodological problems. These stratigraphic anomalies are often explained as *residual* objects and ultimately dismissed as the *background noise* of archaeological objects, even when stratigraphy permits greater resolution in dating their deposition (Evans and Millett 1992; Lucas 2008). But archaeologists have also recognised the social importance of inter-generational artefacts to past societies and the material practices that surrounded the *curation* of objects. Forty years ago, processual archaeologists proposed the *heirloom hypothesis* to explain why old things are sometimes detected in the archaeological record divorced from their usual temporal context (Binford 1973, 242 f.; Thomas 1976).

More recent archaeological perspectives on heirlooms have shifted from methodological to interpretative concerns. Heirlooms have been reappraised with reference to the framework of object biographies that was pioneered by Arjun Appadurai (1986) and Igor Kopytoff (1986). This approach is based on the premise that the *life history* of an object can be traced to reveal its connections with the social world around it. Archaeologists, especially prehistorians, have focused on the role of heirlooms in forging ancestral memory: it is argued that these objects were conserved and strategically reused in order to sustain connections with previous generations of the same lineage group. Heirlooms are understood as objects which served as repositories for *collective memory*, representing the material emblems of an ancestral past (e.g. Skeates 1995; Lillios 1999; Joyce 2003).

Anthropologists have been more concerned with the role and meaning of heirlooms in the context of exchange (Weiner 1992; Weiss 1996; Straight 2002). Heirlooms have been categorized as inalienable objects, drawing on the distinction first made by Marcel Mauss (1967 [1923/1924]). He contrasted between goods that can be received and owned without incurring the obligation for reciprocation (alienable) and gifts that represent the enduring need for reciprocity (inalienable). Mauss proposed that inalienable objects were perceived to absorb the *essence* (the *mana*) of the giver as it was transmitted between hands or across generations (Straight 2002, 9). Heirlooms as inalienable objects epitomise "the paradox of keeping-while-giving" (Weiner 1992) that was outlined in Annette Weiner's study of Polynesia. Weiner (1992, 6) observed that these possessions are:

"imbued with the intrinsic and ineffable identities of their owners which are not easy to give away. Ideally, these inalienable possessions are kept by their owners from one generation to the next within the closed context of family, descent group, or dynasty. The loss of such an inalienable possession diminishes the self and by extension, the group to which the person belongs."

The status of inter-generational objects has been refined further by Janet Hoskins (1993; 1998) in her studies of the Kodi of Sumba. She distinguishes between heirlooms as public history objects and biographical objects that are private possessions involved in the construction of personhood. Hoskins follows Appadurai (1986), Kopytoff (1986) and Mauss (1967 [923/1924]) in defining biographical objects as things which become endowed with the personal characteristics of their owners. In summary, then, archaeologists and anthropologists have theorized both heirlooms and biographical objects as serving a mnemonic function. However, heirlooms are viewed as public objects which help to construct collective ancestral memory, while biographical objects are personal possessions that prompt autobiographical memory.

What is the connection between these two categories of memory object? How do biographical objects become heirlooms? Are they perceived to have different values in public and private domains? How are they exchanged across cultural boundaries and between generations? When and why are heirlooms finally discarded to enter the archaeological record? This paper addresses these questions in the context of two contrasting medieval spheres, the household and the parish church. Medieval archaeology is particularly well placed to investigate heirlooms, given the relatively tight resolution in the dating of artefacts and complementary sources of documentary evidence.

Materiality and personhood: The making of heirlooms

My approach to heirlooms differs from previous perspectives in two key respects. First, I argue that the value of heirlooms is not only accrued through processes of exchange (Appadurai 1986; Kopytoff 1986). The *materiality* of heirlooms as sensuous objects may be equally significant in constructing their value. The importance of substance has been neglected in the discussions outlined above; for example, Hoskins (1998; 195) stressed that "it is not the physical characteristics of objects that make them biographical, but the meanings imputed to them as significant personal possessions." The concept of materiality combines both the physical quality of the object – its *thingness* – and the social value that is bestowed upon it (Meskell 2004, 13–17). Tim Ingold (2007) has called for more explicit attention to the *physical properties* of the materials used in making objects, rather than focusing on their intrinsic qualities of materiality.

The physical *patina* of old things enhances their value in some social contexts (McCracken 1990), and the meaning of objects can be transformed through destructive processes which alter their material properties, such as breakage, burial or burning (Pollard 2004; Jones 2007). Archaeologists have recently considered the materiality of heirlooms through the study of patterns of wear, fragmentation and reuse, employing use-wear analysis to chronicle the *ageing* of heirlooms through processes of exchange, curation and extended use (Woodward 2002; Overholtzer and Stoner 2011). I argue that medieval heirlooms were objects selected for special treatment partly because of the *physical materials* of which they were composed. These materials often possessed unusual value, whether utilitarian, cosmological, or frequently combining both characteristics (Lillios 1999, 242). The agency of medieval heirlooms was not restricted to memory or affect; heirlooms acquired *spiritual* power that made them the equivalent of amulets or relics, sacred objects with quasi-magical properties of healing and protection.

The second way in which my approach to heirlooms differs from previous perspectives is that it focuses on the material and social practices that transform the value of everyday objects into heirlooms that possess biographical, temporal and spiritual agency (Weiss 1996). The idiosyncratic value of heirlooms can be better understood with reference to Alfred Gell's theory that objects have the capacity to stimulate emotional responses (Gell 1998). Heirlooms prompt feelings of family affect, inter-generational memory and a sense of the passage of time between generations. But how do heirlooms acquire their distinctive agency as memory objects? It has been argued that objects accrue biographical value through direct association with life-transforming events such as life-crisis rituals (Hoskins 1998, 3). This connection is particularly relevant to rituals of personhood that construct gender. In the medieval context, for example, heirlooms are most frequently associated with life-course rituals such as marriage, childbirth and baptism (Gilchrist 2012). But this biographical association does not fully explain how the meanings of objects are transformed. What practices animated a particular object – *how* did people come to believe in its agency or affect (Morphy 2009, 6)?

Heirlooms in the medieval household: Biography and utility

The word heirloom derives from the Middle English *heirlome*, tools or implements which are transmitted to heirs (OED). Although the word has a medieval origin, archaeologists have rarely contemplated the possible presence of heirlooms from excavated medieval contexts. Medieval objects such as tableware and dress accessories were produced in large quantities and cheaply purchased, encouraging a disposable consumer culture, especially in medieval towns. The closely dated deposits from the London waterfront indicate that objects were generally discarded within a single generation of their manufacture (Egan 1998, 12). The more limited range of material culture available to the medieval peasantry may have extended the use-life of objects in rural contexts, but this premise has yet to be tested. Indeed, exceptional conditions of preservation reveal convincing evidence that certain types of object were sometimes retained for several generations in both rural and urban households (Gilchrist 2012). Documentary sources such as wills and inventories tell the stories of dynastic heirlooms transmitted between generations of elite medieval families (van Houts 1999). Here, in contrast, the emphasis is placed on ordinary people and their personal possessions, working outwards from the archaeological record to identify potential candidates for heirloom objects. My case studies are from later medieval and Tudor Britain, ranging from the twelfth to the sixteenth centuries. I will focus on archaeological examples that derive from well-dated and secure contexts, heirlooms that cannot be dismissed as *residual* objects that have migrated through archaeological stratigraphy as a result of the disturbance or reworking of archaeological deposits (Lucas 2008).

On what basis did medieval people select things to be kept and handed down to their heirs, rather than consigned to the rubbish heap? A wide range of materials was represented in the medieval household, typically including objects made from textiles, wood, basketry, pottery, leather, horn, bone, lead and tin alloys, iron, and more rarely, bronze, glass and parchment. A variety of factors influenced the choice to *curate* an object: the biography of the thing may have been inherently bound to a special person, place or event, or the artefact or the material of which it was made may have been deemed particularly efficacious for practical or cosmological use. In practice, *inter-generational objects* are likely to combine several of these qualities. The complexity of possible motives is illustrated by a single fragment of rare glass excavated from the Oxfordshire village of Seacourt. A sherd of blue glass with traces of gilt geometric design was recovered from the stone floor of a peasant house dated to the late thirteenth or early fourteenth century (Biddle 1961/1962, 96–104). The glass was manufactured in the eastern Mediterranean and has been identified as a possible scent bottle from Corinth (in the Peloponnese), dated typologically to the twelfth century, and unique in an English context. The sherd is 100 years older than its depositional context: why was it retained in an English village croft? Was it an *objet trouvé* or a biographical object? The glass may have held an aesthetic appeal as an unusual and colourful substance that was also considered useful: medieval people used reflective materials such as quartz as amulets for healing or protection. If the distant origins of the glass were broadly understood, it may have been regarded as *exotic* (Hinton 2010, 92). A biographical component may also be conjectured; for instance, the sherd may represent a personal keepsake of a life-changing journey of pilgrimage or crusade. Heirlooms were cherished for their combination of utility with biography, as reflected in the medieval origins of the word: tools or implements transmitted to heirs.

This point is demonstrated by a group of objects from an unusual *household*: the Tudor warship the *Mary Rose*, which sank on 19 July 1545, costing the lives of around 380 of its 415 crew. Among the remarkable objects preserved on board the *Mary Rose* was a chest belonging to the ship's barber-surgeon, identified by the range of medical equipment which it contained. Among the specialist instruments were nine pottery jugs, seven of which were complete stoneware jugs that retained their cork bungs and traces of the medicines they had contained (Castle *et al.* 2005, 220). The jugs are salt-glazed stoneware from Raeren in the Rhineland; their distinctive form began production around 1475 and continued up to around 1525. The jugs on the *Mary Rose* were therefore at least 20 years old when the ship was wrecked and possibly up to 70 years old (Gaimster 1997a; 1997b). Stoneware is an impermeable fabric that was chosen for pharmaceutical use because it did not absorb or taint the preparations it stored. The *Mary Rose* jugs may have been retained simply for their functional utility; however, these specialist containers are likely to have passed between professional or family generations of medical practitioners. Even such utilitarian objects might attract biographical agency: the tools of a skilled physician may be regarded as storing professional knowledge that will benefit the next generation. Heirlooms may serve as depositories of both family sentiment and cultural or professional skills (after Parkin 1999).

Two potential heirloom objects from the city of York are more obviously *biographical*: the bone artefacts were recovered from medieval houses in Coppergate. The first is an antler tine "carved in the form of a pointed phallus" (MacGregor *et al.* 1999, 1941) and excavated from a thirteenth-century deposit, but likely manufactured around 1000 AD. The antler tine was pierced for suspension to be worn as an amulet. The second object from Coppergate is a sword pommel carved from whale bone. It was recovered from a twelfth-century context, but its five-lobed form suggests it was carved two or three centuries earlier, in the ninth or tenth century (ibid., 1945). These objects are significant both for the materials of which they are composed and the rites of personhood with which they are likely to have been connected. They take on additional significance when viewed in the social context of Coppergate, a neighbourhood of Anglo-Scandinavian merchants and artisans who evidently valued their Viking heritage. The most celebrated find excavated from the site was a helmet, made in the mid-eighth century, but deposited in the fill of a shallow well in the late ninth or tenth century, together with a weaving sword. The helmet is likely to have been owned originally by a Northumbrian aristocrat; it may have first arrived at Coppergate as the booty of war, but it was subsequently retained by a merchant household for around 100 years, or three generations (Loveluck 2011, 61).

The *utility* of some materials combined cosmological and practical value. Medieval people believed that some substances harnessed the *occult* power of nature and possessed special properties understood to be manifest in the natural world, contained in certain plants, animals and mineral materials (Page 2004, 18; Kieckhefer 2000). Within the framework of *natural magic*, animal materials such as antler tine and whalebone were perceived as occult: their animal substance was believed to transmit the beneficial traits of the beast to its wearer. The power of the stag was traditionally harnessed for masculine amulets linked to fertility or hunting (MacGregor 1985). Whales were regarded as 'extraordinary and fearful beasts' (Gardiner 1997, 174), and the bone from beached cetaceans was prized for the carving of sacred objects such as caskets and reliquaries (ibid.); a weapon carved from whalebone would have conferred protection or skill on the warrior who wielded it.

It may be suggested that the objects from medieval Coppergate were active in practices of embodiment that created personhood. The sword hilt and the phallic amulet may have marked male rites of passage, such as a first hunt or the beginning of military training. They were retained as heirloom objects for at least two centuries and would have acquired a patina that evoked the warrior skills of past generations. Swords are powerful symbols of male personhood in many cultural contexts, and there is confirmation from elsewhere in medieval Britain that these objects were retained as heirlooms. Excavations in the Scottish burgh of Perth have identified two candidates for heirloom swords: the first was recovered by antiquarian investigations in 1848 (Fig. 12.1), but the second has a better documented archaeological provenance (Fig. 12.2). It can be dated stylistically to the ninth or tenth century but was excavated from a site in Perth High Street and dated *c.* 1150–1200 AD (Hall *et al.* 2005, 277). Like the Coppergate example, it was retained for approximately two hundred years before its disposal.

The biographical objects associated with female rites of passage are more likely to have been organic materials such as textiles that seldom survive in archaeological deposits. We have documentary evidence of women passing items of textiles to their daughters as dowry at marriage, such as bed sheets and coverlets, often conveyed in a

Figure 12.1. A complete sword excavated in 1849 from Watergate, Perth. © Perth Museum and Art Gallery, Perth and Kinross Council, Scotland.

Figure 12.2. Sword excavated from Perth High Street, dated stylistically to the ninth or tenth century and excavated from a context dated c. 1150–1200 A. © Perth Museum and Art Gallery, Perth and Kinross Council, Scotland.

dowry chest (Hanawalt 1993, 213). Medieval wills mention bequests of family heirlooms only very rarely (Richardson 2003); from this negative evidence, we can infer that heirlooms were gifted to the next generation during the owner's lifetime. Ethnographic literature confirms that marriage is the most common point for the transmission of heirlooms by parents, marking entry to a new stage of the life course for both giver and receiver (Lillios 1999, 242; Weiss 1996). Marriage chests were important in medieval homes for the secure storage of precious objects, including heirlooms, and the chests themselves were sometimes curated as heirloom objects (Gilchrist 2012, 241). The act of packing and securing a chest can be likened to compiling family memory; indeed, memory practice is conceptualized cross-culturally as an act of storage and containment (Fentress and Wickham 1992, 15).

The remains of a medieval chest were recently excavated from an intriguing context in the city of Cambridge: the chest is likely to have been made in the twelfth century, and it remained in use for two centuries before it was disposed of in a rubbish pit. The materiality of this heirloom item is noteworthy in two respects. The first is that it was roughly made from pine imported from Scandinavia: it is likely to have been crafted by an amateur as an individual piece, conceivably a dowry chest. The second is the manner of its disposal: it was deliberately smashed up and the boards used to line the bottom of a clay pit in the fourteenth century (Cessford and Dickens, in preparation). This may represent a quotidian act, but conversely we may be glimpsing the destruction of heirlooms as a deliberate strategy of *forgetting* ancestral ties or actively restructuring ancestral memory (Jones 2007, 39).

Certain materials may have been valued because they evoked places of family origin, such as the Scandinavian pine used for the Cambridge chest or the whalebone from which the Coppergate sword hilt was carved. For the Anglo-Scandinavian men of York, whalebone would have carried associations with the Viking homeland and the seafaring tradition. The value of these objects or materials was intensified by their crossing of geographical borders (Straight 2002): they embodied family myths of origin and journeys of migration, and their discard or destruction was crucial to the process of forging new social identities.

Shifting spheres: Heirlooms in the medieval parish church

Anthropologists have observed that inalienable objects "are kept [...] within the closed context of the family" (Weiner 1992, 6). It is perhaps surprising, then, that some of the most significant biographical objects were removed from the medieval household and transferred to the public context of the parish church. Medieval wills reveal that it was common to bequeath certain personal possessions to the church on the death of the owner. A 'gendered vocabulary of giving' (French 2008, 41) operated, in which men bequeathed books and liturgical items to their parish church, while women gifted more personal and domestic objects, including sheets, tablecloths, clothing and jewellery. These items of personal apparel were typically used to dress the images of saints. For example, the statue of the Virgin at Pilton (Somerset) was adorned with seven rosaries (*paternosters*) given by local women, including two of amber and five of jet, as well as two kerchiefs, three brooches, six pilgrims' signs and a velvet cloak on which 14 finger-rings were sewn (ibid., 43). The materials of the rosaries were significant, since jet and amber were amongst the most valued of occult materials. When rubbed, both substances develop a static charge and emit a smell. Jet was ingested, burnt or worn on the body to release anaesthetic and healing properties and apotropaic power: it was credited with the capacity to chase away the demons of hell and to baffle spells and malignant magic (Evans 1922). Rosaries were also given to parish churches for public use, as indicated in an advice manual dated to the fifteenth century, *The Commonplace Book of Robert Reynes of Acle*. The author advises the reader to make the best use of his time in church: 'take your beads in your hand' and say a prayer to the Virgin Mary 'that she will be your shield when you pass'. The final instruction confirms that communal

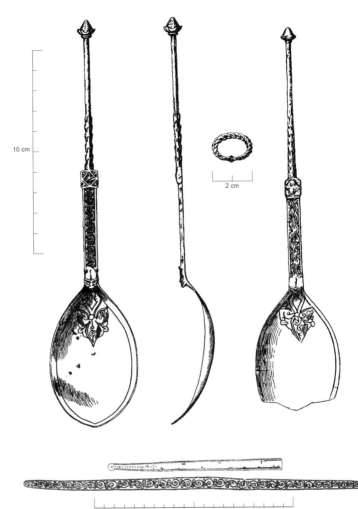

Figure 12.3. Heirloom objects buried in two separate deposits in the church and chapel of the nunnery at Iona (Inner Hebrides), including silver spoons and two gold fillets (after Curle 1924, Proceedings of the Society of Antiquaries of Scotland 58).

prayer beads were made available in the church: 'And when you leave the church, Leave the beads where you found them' (Shinners 1997, 369).

Archaeology sometimes reveals ritual practices that were never recorded in medieval documents. For example, church excavations provide evidence that there was an alternative mechanism for transferring heirloom and biographical objects to the religious sphere. I have identified a small number of cases where such objects were buried in churches as *special deposits* (Gilchrist 2012, 234–236). For example, at the Scottish nunnery of Iona, a group of four silver spoons and a gold fillet from a headdress were found wrapped in linen and placed beneath a stone at the base of the chancel arch of the church. Stylistically, the spoons are dated *c.* 1150 and the hair-fillet is from the thirteenth century (Fig. 12.3). The date of the deposit is unknown, but the nunnery was founded in 1203, half a century after the spoons were crafted. A second deposit was buried in the chapel of St Ronan in the precinct of the same nunnery, comprising a gold finger-ring and another gold fillet, the latter being tightly folded up within the circumference of the ring and kept in position with a fragment of wire (Curle 1924). The spoons were clearly heirlooms, but all of the objects are significant in another respect: they are things inextricably linked to the performance of Christian life-course rituals. The gold ring is a wedding ring which was consecrated by the priest during the sacrament of marriage. The gold fillets are likely to originate from headdresses, such as those worn by brides on their wedding day. Silver spoons were given as wedding gifts to prosperous couples and were also popular as baptismal gifts given to infants by godparents (Hanawalt 1993, 76).

Why did medieval people remove heirlooms and biographical objects from the private, domestic sphere of the family? The key can be found in the active role of these objects in medieval life-course rituals; both people *and* objects are transformed by the ritual process. Rites of personhood such as baptism and marriage were also sacraments of the church: objects used in any sacrament became *consecrated* materials that were governed by strict rules of disposal. For example, the consecrated materials of the mass, the Eucharistic bread and wine, were carefully disposed of to prevent their misuse for secular magic (Thomas 1973, 38). Similar imperatives surrounded the disposal of disused fonts and the chrisom cloths used for baptism. It was essential to remove from circulation any objects used in life-course rituals that were also sacraments of the church. This principle seems to have extended to personal objects of devotion such as rosaries, which were blessed by the priest for use in private prayer. While not consecrated objects *per se*, rosaries served a powerful apotropaic function. Beads which were blessed by the priest or came into contact with religious statues were believed to fend off evil and to protect the wearer from harm (Winston-Allen 1997, 116).

The gifting of biographical objects to the church fulfilled the essential requirement to keep inalienable possessions out of exchange (Weiner 1992, 150). To dress a religious statue with family jewellery was a medieval strategy for 'keeping-while-giving' (Weiner 1992). Subsequent use of these objects reveals their transformation into *sacred objects*. The items of dress that adorned statues were returned periodically to the domestic sphere: the girdles, brooches, rings and necklaces that embellished religious statues were loaned out by parish churches to local women to wear as amulets in the birthing chamber (Fissell 2004, 54), and the headdresses that bedecked the effigies of females saints were borrowed by brides to wear on their wedding day (Jones 2002, 224).

Ritual gestures: The *sacralisation* of biographical objects

Heirlooms are not simply *memory objects*, which served to commemorate either ancestors or biographical events. Reflection on the theme of medieval heirlooms highlights the importance of materiality and the social processes that transformed biographical objects into heirlooms or sacred relics. Medieval people emphasised the materiality of things when selecting items for curation as heirlooms. The most evocative heirlooms combined biography with a *physical material* that was prized for its cosmological meaning or utilitarian use. The materiality of objects such as the Viking sword pommel from York, carved from whalebone, may evoke origins myths or ancestral memory of a homeland.

They may also possess a sensuous quality that is enhanced over time, developing a patina that contributes to their agency. But the materiality of medieval heirlooms also referenced the cosmological framework of natural magic: objects of antler, whalebone, jet and amber were occult materials which served as the equivalent of amulets. Constant touch and handling of these natural materials creates a patina of age that may enhance the perception of their efficacy.

Biographical objects were transformed by the medieval ritual process, both in the home and in the parish church. Swords and dowry chests drew their potency from use in rituals of embodiment that constructed gendered personhood, such as a young man's military training or a young woman's preparation for marriage. Objects were more formally *sacralised* by their engagement with life-course rituals that were also sacraments of the church. Objects such as rings and chrisom cloths became consecrated materials through ceremonies of baptism and marriage. People came to believe in the quasi-magical properties of a particular object because it had been consecrated by a priest or had been in close physical proximity to statues of the saints. A similar ritual process may be perceived in the domestic sphere, when objects associated with secular rites of personhood acquire spiritual value to the family, such as pottery vessels or items of apparel linked with marriage (Gilchrist 2012, 238–240). These biographical objects are likely to have been the focus of ritual gestures in the home, including their withdrawal from everyday use for special occasions, their display and cleaning, their gifting at rites of passage and their use as mnemonics in family story-telling (Small 1999). Such domestic rituals conferred a change in status on family objects that may be likened to the process of consecration.

The medieval *sacralisation* of heirlooms is broadly consistent with the special quality of inalienable objects that was first articulated by Marcel Mauss (1967 [1923/1924]). Mauss observed that these objects absorbed the *essence* of the giver when they changed hands. The biographical *essence* of an heirloom contributes to its materiality and enhances its utility. An object is more efficacious if it has been used successfully by past generations (Weiss 1996), whether it is a medicinal pot, a sword used in battle, or a rosary or girdle worn in childbirth. Biographical objects kept in the home for generations became ancestral heirlooms, while those gifted to the church achieved the status of public relics. Through intimate proximity to the statues of saints, these objects acquired a spiritual *essence* that could be transferred temporarily back to the domestic sphere, as amulets borrowed to protect women in childbirth. Medieval heirlooms were not only *memory objects*, they were also *sacred objects*; their agency embraced family skills, knowledge and myths of origin, or quasi-magical properties of healing and protection. The *inalienable* quality of these objects was animated by a process of *sacralisation* that involved ceremonial use, ritual gestures and exchanges between the medieval domestic and religious spheres.

Acknowledgements

I am grateful to Craig Cessford, David Gaimster, Mark Hall and Chris Loveluck for drawing possible examples of medieval heirlooms to my attention.

References

Appadurai, A. (1986) Introduction: Commodities and the politics of value. In A. Appadurai (ed.) *The social life of things: Commodities in cultural perspective*, 3–63. Cambridge, Cambridge University Press.

Biddle, M. (1961/1962) The deserted medieval village of Seacourt, Berkshire. *Oxoniensia* 26/27, 70–201.

Binford, L. R. (1973) Interassemblage variability: The Mousterian and the 'functional' argument. In C. Renfrew (ed.) *The explanation of culture change: Models in prehistory*, 227–253. London, Duckworth.

Castle, J.; Derham, B.; Montagu, J.; Wood, R. and Hather, J. (2005) The contents of the Barber-surgeon's cabin. In J. Gardiner and M. J. Allen (eds) *Before the mast: Life and death aboard the Mary Rose*. Archaeology of the Mary Rose, 4, 171–225. Portsmouth, The Mary Rose Trust.

Cessford, C. and Dickens, A. (in preparation) *From king's ditch to department store: Investigations of an 11th–20th century suburb and the town ditch of Cambridge*.

Curle, A. O. (1924) A note on four silver spoons and a fillet of gold found in the nunnery at Iona. *Proceedings of the Society of Antiquaries of Scotland* 58, 102–111.

Egan, G. (1998) *The medieval household: Daily living c. 1150–c. 1450*. London, Stationery Office.

Evans, J. (1922) *Magical jewels of the Middle Ages and Renaissance*. London, Constable.

Evans, J. and Millet, M. (1992) Residuality revisited. *Oxford Journal of Archaeology* 11 (2), 225–240.

Fentress, J. and Wickham, C. (1992) *Social memory*. Oxford, Blackwell.

Fissell, M. E. (2004) The politics of reproduction in the English Reformation. *Representations* 87, 43–81.

French, K. (2008) *The good women of the parish: Gender and religion after the Black Death*. Philadelphia, University of Pennsylvania Press.

Gaimster, D. (1997a) *German stoneware 1200–1900: Archaeology and cultural history*. London, The British Museum.

Gaimster, D. (1997b) Rhenish stonewares from shipwrecks: The study of ceramic function and lifespan. In M. Redknap (ed.) *Artefacts from wrecks: Dated assemblages from the Late Middle Ages to the Industrial Revolution*. Oxbow Monograph, 84, 121–128. Oxford, Oxbow.

Gardiner, M. (1997) The exploitation of sea-mammals in medieval England: Bones and their social context. *The Archaeological Journal* 154, 173–195.

Gell, A. (1998) *Art and agency: An anthropological theory*. Oxford, Clarendon Press.

Gilchrist, R. (2012) *Medieval life: Archaeology and the life course*. Woodbridge, Boydell and Brewer.

Hall, M.; Hall, D. and Cook, G. (2005) What's cooking? New radiocarbon dates from the earliest phases of Perth High Street excavations and the question of Perth's early medieval origins. *Proceedings of the Society of Antiquaries of Scotland* 135, 273–285.

Hanawalt, B. (1993) *Growing up in medieval London: The experience of childhood in history*. Oxford, Oxford University Press.

Hinton, D. A. (2010) Deserted medieval villages and the objects from them. In C. Dyer and R. Jones (eds) *Deserted villages revisited*, 85–108. Hertford, University of Hertfordshire Press.

Hoskins, J. (1993) *The play of time: Kodi perspectives on calendars, history, and exchange*. Berkeley, University of California Press.

Hoskins, J. (1998) *Biographical objects: How things tell the story of people's lives*. New York and London, Routledge.

Ingold, T. (2007) Materials against materiality. *Archaeological Dialogues* 14 (1), 1–16.

Jones, A. (2007) *Memory and material culture*. Cambridge, Cambridge University Press.

Jones, M. (2002) *The secret Middle Ages: Discovering the real medieval world*. Stroud, Sutton.

Joyce, R. A. (2003) Concrete memories: Fragments of the past in Classic Maya present (500–1000

AD). In R. M. Van Dyke and S. E. Alcock (eds) *Archaeologies of memory*, 104–125. Oxford, Blackwell.

Kieckhefer, H. (2000) *Magic in the Middle Ages*. Cambridge, Cambridge University Press.

Kopytoff, I. (1986) The cultural biography of things: Commoditization as process. In A. Appadurai (ed.) *The social life of things: Commodities in cultural perspective*, 64–91. Cambridge, Cambridge University Press.

Lillios, K. T. (1999) Objects of memory: The ethnography and archaeology of heirlooms. *Journal of Archaeological Method and Theory* 6 (3), 235–262.

Loveluck, C. (2011) Problems of the definition and conceptualisation of early medieval elites, AD 450–900: The dynamics of the archaeological evidence. In F. Bougard, H-W. Goetz and R. Le Jan (eds) *Théorie et pratiques des élites au Haut Moyen Âge*, 21–68. Turnhout, Brepols.

Lucas, G. (2008) Time and archaeological event. *Cambridge Archaeological Journal* 18 (1), 59–64.

MacGregor, A. (1985) *Bone, antler, ivory and horn: The technology of skeletal materials since the Roman period*. London, Croom Helm.

MacGregor, A.; Mainman, A. J. and Rogers, N. S. H. (1999) *Bone, antler, ivory and horn from Anglo-Scandinavian and medieval York*. The Archaeology of York, The Small Finds 17/12. York, Published for the York Archaeological Trust by the Council for British Archaeology.

Mauss, M. (1967 [1923/1924]) *The gift: Forms and functions of exchange in archaic societies*. New York, W. W. Norton, first published in French, 1923/1924. Essai sur le don. Forme et raison de l'échange dans les sociétés archaïques. *L'Année Sociologique*, NS, (1), 30–186.

McCracken, C. (1990) *Culture and consumption*. Bloomington, University of Indiana Press.

Meskell, L. (2004) *Object worlds in ancient Egypt: Material biographies past and present*. Oxford and New York, Berg.

Morphy, H. (2009) Art as a mode of action: Some problems with Gell's art and agency. *Journal of Material Culture* 14 (1), 5–27.

Overholtzer, L. and Stoner, W. D. (2011) Merging the social and the material: Life histories of ancient mementoes from Central Mexico. *Social Archaeology* 11 (2), 171–193.

Page, S. (2004) *Magic in medieval manuscripts*. London, The British Museum.

Parkin, D. J. (1999) Mementoes as transitional objects in human displacement. *Journal of Material Culture* 4 (3), 303–320.

Pollard, J. (2004) The art of decay and the transformation of substance. In C. Renfrew, C. Gosden and E. DeMarrais (eds) *Substance, memory, display: Archaeology and art*. McDonald Institute Monographs, 47–62. Cambridge, McDonald Institute for Archaeological Research, University of Cambridge.

Richardson, C. (2003) Household objects and domestic ties. In C. Beattie, A. Maslakovic and S. Rees Jones (eds) *The medieval household in Christian Europe c. 850–1550: Managing wealth, power and the body*, 433–447. Turnhout, Brepols.

Shinners, J. (ed.) (1997) *Medieval popular religion, 1000–1500: A reader*. Peterborough, Ontario, Broadview Press.

Skeates, R. (1995) Animate objects: A biography of prehistoric 'axe-amulets' in the central Mediterranean region. *Proceedings of the Prehistoric Society* 61, 279–301.

Small, L. M. (1999) Sacred space (tremenos) and heirlooms (sacra) serve a totemic function within the homes of elder Americans. *Journal of Religion, Disability and Health* 3 (1), 99–114.

Straight, B. (2002) From Samburu heirloom to New Age artefact: The cross-cultural consumption of Mporo marriage beads. *American Anthropologist* 104 (1), 7–21.

Thomas, K. (1973) *Religion and the decline of magic*. Harmondsworth, Penguin.

Thomas, D. H. (1976) A Diegueno shaman's wand: An object lesson illustrating the 'heirloom hypothesis'. *The Journal of California Anthropology* 3 (1), 128–132.

van Houts, E. (1999) *Memory and gender in medieval Europe, 900–1200*. Basingstoke, Macmillan.

Weiner, A. B. (1992) *Inalienable possessions: The paradox of keeping-while-giving*. Berkeley and Los Angeles, University of California Press.

Weiss, B. (1996) Dressing at death: Clothing, time, and memory in Buhaya, Tanzania. In H. Hendrickson (ed.) *Clothing and difference: Embodied identities in colonial and post-colonial Africa*, 133–154. Durham, Duke University Press.

Winston-Allen, A. (1997) *Stories of the rose: The making of the rosary in the Middle Ages*. Philadelphia, Pennsylvania State University Press.

Woodward, A. (2002) Beads and beakers: Heirlooms and relics in the British Early Bronze Age. *Antiquity* 76, 1040–1047.

Chapter 13

Epilogue: Cultural biographies and itineraries of things: Second thoughts

David Fontijn

This book presents a broad, almost kaleidoscopic range of case studies that illustrate how things can mean something to people and, in particular, how their meanings change. Transformations can take place when objects change ownership and *travel*, though shifts in meaning are just as likely to happen when objects stay where they are. Reviewing the broad field of material culture studies in anthropology, archaeology or art history, one sometimes has the impression that it is not particularly the meaning of things that is studied, but rather changes in meaning. One could easily get the idea that the most essential point to be made in interpretations of material culture is that its interpretation is in a constant state of flux.

Using the metaphor of an itinerary to describe the meanings of things, the editors of this volume adopt a terminology that is less one of meaning *shifts, steps, transformations* or *reversals*, but rather one that acknowledges stability or subtle changes. As Hahn and Weiss put it, along an itinerary there may be long periods of inertness and stasis. However, most previous research on changes in the meanings of objects has been discussed in terms of *object biographies* (Hoskins 2006). This concept was introduced as 'the cultural biography of things' by Igor Kopytoff in 1986. Although criticized from the outset (Bloch and Parry 1989), Kopytoff's ideas on the cultural biography of objects seem to have set the agenda for the next two decades of interpretive material culture studies in anthropology and archaeology alike (see, for example, Gosden and Marshall 1999, which devotes an entire issue in *World Archaeology* to this topic, or Hoskins' chapter on this theme in the recent 'Handbook of material culture' by Tilley *et al.* 2006). The present volume may be one of the first to distance itself explicitly from the biography concept (cf. Hahn and Weiss's introduction), but going through the chapters of this book, the idiom of *biographies* is still ubiquitous. A truly seminal paper, Kopytoff's ideas seem to have had a lasting effect on the way we discuss the interpretation of material culture. For that reason it might be fruitful to rethink some of the case studies of object itineraries in this book with Kopytoff's theory in mind, in order to isolate some key issues in the discussion of the meaning of objects.

What Kopytoff's cultural biography concept is about

Perhaps one of the reasons why Kopytoff's article became so influential is that he provided a new idiom[1] and metaphor for thinking about what is perhaps the most essential distinction in material culture, that between objects that are like persons and those that are things (cf. Hoskins 2006, 74). The former are inalienable or singular items (Kopytoff's term) and are gifts in exchange transactions. The latter are alienable and are called *commodities* in exchange transactions. Different authors usually have a preference for one of these terms and avoid others. I will not go into the explicit or implicit theoretical assumptions behind such choices (on this, see Graeber 2005), but only wish to note that the different authors in this volume also seem to have their own preferences.

Following on from his previous studies of slavery (the commoditization of people), Kopytoff introduced the concept of a *biography* to describe shifts in the meanings of objects, with the commodity (alienable things) state on the one hand and the *singular* (personalized, or inalienable *gift*) state on the other. As Appadurai (1986, 13) points out, referring to Kopytoff's work, it is about objects "moving in and out of the commodity state". For both Kopytoff and Appadurai, being a commodity is a state rather than an intrinsic quality, and Kopytoff's emphasis on process had great heuristic value (Gosden and Marshall 1999; Hoskins 1998). However, almost as a victim of its own success, the cultural biography concept lost something of its original specific nature., and is now often used to describe any kind of change to the meaning of objects. Kopytoff's focus, however, was on the production of commodities as a cultural and cognitive process. It was not actual or specific object histories he tried to capture; rather, he was interested in "idealized biographies that are considered to be desirable models in the society and the way real-life departures from the models are perceived" (Kopytoff 1986, 66). Gosden and Marshall (1999, 171–172) referred to either generalized biographies or highly specific biographies, whereas Kopytoff used the adjective *cultural* to emphasize that what matters is a shared view of what would be the right trajectory for a particular kind of object. To my mind, Kopytoff's original point that people share notions of what is the proper treatment and path of certain things is still a valuable one. The present book has several examples of this. Take the discussion about the earring between Mrs Depner and Mrs Miller in the sixth chapter of this volume. Mrs Miller had clear expectations of what this earring was (a precious gold valuable of round, simple form) and of what would be its appropriate future life when she gave it to Mrs Depner (to be worn by the latter's young son as a special personal valuable in just one ear, a gift that would necessitate the piercing of one ear). The latter, however, appeared to have a very different opinion on this. To her, the earring was not small, simple or round, and in her opinion it was made of a material that would not qualify as real gold (*Turkish gold*). Depner's view on its future use was certainly not one in which a young boy would be wearing it, but rather a path that would take it directly into the dustbin. It is just such a confrontation, or rather, to quote Depner, such a "battlefield of culturally shaped beliefs about things and material" that elucidates how we define ourselves by our ideas about the trajectories of using, wearing and discarding objects. This "can make salient what might otherwise remain obscure" (Kopytoff 1986, 67). It is not just comparison that reveals tacit, but essential shared ideas of what things mean to us

– we can also learn about them through diversions from familiar paths. We are shocked by pictures of the looting and destruction of the Iraqi Museum of Antiquities in 2003 because they forcefully remind us that such treatment is completely at odds with what we see as the appropriate life-path of such antiquities, namely to be on display in a museum as inalienable possessions marking the progress of civilization. It is particularly by deviations that we become aware that we do have some vision of the appropriate treatment of what we consider a specific category of things.

The right beginning, the right ending?

A more implicit point in Kopytoff's original paper was that such trajectories have a perceived beginning (an element also captured by Hahn and Weiss's concept of itinerary). In elemental terms, material does not really cease to exist. For example, the gold and silver that Oakley discusses in his chapter on hallmarking can be re-melted time and time again and be subdivided to form new objects, but they still retain their identity as substances (cf. Hahn and Soentgen 2010). On the other hand, Oakley's chapter shows how meticulous hallmarking procedures in medieval to twentieth-century England effectively served to create the *right* beginning for precious metals circulating in society. This involves a particular way of stamping, in a specific space, specific legislation etc. In all, an almost ritualized procedure is used to create the cultural context into which metal was transformed into a particular object. So, in the creation of objects as a cultural, singular category, there is a stage that is *perceived* as a beginning. Or rather, there is a shared view of what should be the normative *right* beginning.

The views people hold on what would be *the right ending* of a particular category of object tend to be less clear than those on its beginning. It is often when we are confronted with deviations from the usual endings that we come to realize that we do have normative views about what would be an appropriate end. Often, these are stated in a negative way. Strolling around flea markets, one sometimes comes across photograph albums with intimate family pictures of people we do not know. Looking at the photographs and dress, it is easy to have an idea of roughly when they were taken. If they date to the 1980s or 1990s one usually starts to realize that the commercial sale of what must have been cherished personal possessions of a family living in the 1990s must represent an abrupt and unforeseen twist of fate. By means of such an exception, we come to realize that we do have some norm concerning the appropriate trajectory of such photograph albums. What the appropriate ending for such cherished possessions should be in our society, however, is not always straightforward. The fascinating research by Depner in this volume makes that very clear. She focuses on the decisions old people have to make in order to reduce their belongings drastically when they move to their final retirement home. Instead of taking as much as possible with them, as young people would expect them to, some old people chose rather to take nothing with them and prefer to dump everything we would regard as being loaded with meaning, including wedding pictures.

In other cases, there are clear views about what is perceived as the right ending. In our own society, a particular category of material has come to be regarded as waste or rubbish, with clear shifts in what is classified as such in recent decades. The culturally desired ending of most waste is for it to be removed from society or recycled (e.g. green or glass waste). Such procedures are also backed up by laws and official regulations, but have strong social backgrounds (cf. our association between piles of rubbish on the streets and social decay). However, cross-culturally we also find remarkably similar attitudes in *ending* the lives of certain objects that reflect spontaneous rather than organized, regulated actions. In the case of regime change, iconoclasm against statues of rulers or personalized symbols of overthrown powers tends to use the gestures of killing and execution. Statues are de-capitated, strangled, brought down, heads of statues are displayed as trophies, with the intensity of action increasing if the statues are close to the ruler himself (cf. the way in which statues of Marx and Lenin in Eastern Europe were often made ridiculous after 1989, compared to the fierce violence committed against statues of Saddam Hussein in 2003; Aly 1992; Göttke 2010).

Still, for many object categories their itineraries are not perceived to be ending. In her chapter on Roman coins, Ciric notes that the ideal cultural biography for coins is to circulate and be recycled endlessly. This is also true of many other objects, particularly ostentatious constructions in the landscape like burial mounds or buildings like temples. They are built to endure, under the assumption that the ideals and/or iconography with which they are portrayed will be projected into the future. Whether the expectations concerning their future life-paths will also be met is uncertain at the time they are built. And apart from that, as Knappett argues in this volume, things or buildings can endure beyond any expectations, and how society around them will change in the longer term can never be foreseen. An impressive number of objects and constructions made or built by past societies reflect not just 'a there-then', but just as much 'a here-now', to use Knappett's terminology. The widespread medieval and early modern folklore that regards prehistoric burial mounds in Europe as places where witches or goblins live can never have been part of the desired life-path of burial mounds as seen by the prehistoric people who built them. However, as visible elements in a late medieval or early modern landscape, there is a remarkable similarity both in how they were perceived and in what was considered the right way to deal with them (cf. Roymans 1995).

It is essential to emphasize that at the start people cannot foresee if what they consider the desired life-path of an object will also be met because, particularly in archaeology, changes in the meanings of objects can only be studied with hindsight. In the case of Roman coins, their perceived *emic* ideal biography may be one of endless circulation. However, as Ciric notes, the archaeological record shows that numerous coins did end up in the ground. Abdelhamid's chapter, on amphoras from shipwrecks, is an intriguing case study illustrating amphoras that unintentionally ended up in the archaeological record, thus revealing to us something about one moment during their use-life rather than their treatment when being intentionally discarded. In Van Gijn and Wentink's chapter on the itineraries of flint in the Neolithic, it is apparent that extremely large unused and un-useable Scandinavian flint axes are only known from peat bogs, whereas smaller used axes figure in graves and – usually in fragments – also in settlements. With the benefit of hindsight, this strongly suggests that in Neolithic Holland deposition of extremely large flint axes in peat bogs was seen as the *right* end for such objects. An entire system of selective deposition can even be observed in the later Bronze Age

(Fontijn 2002). In the case of amber in Mycenaean Greece, Maran argues in his chapter that there is actually no uniform way in which amber was deposited, but it is clear that amber beads – often originally part of necklaces – were re-worked on objects and on the body of the deceased in different ways. Something like a broadly-shared view of the *right* ending seems not to have existed.

An inherent drive towards commoditization?

Anthropologists and archaeologists who have used the biography concept since Kopytoff may have given too much attention to the *agency* of the objects themselves (Hoskins 2006, 75; Steiner 2001, 210; see also Warnier, this volume), making the biography concept into something different from the way it was originally conceived. For the present discussion, however, it seems relevant to place Kopytoff's work in the right context. It features prominently in a book that is entirely devoted first and foremost to the study of *commodities*, and his contribution was particularly about the process of becoming a thing (commoditization) on the one hand, and on becoming an item with special significance (singularization, de-commoditization or personalization) on the other. The importance of studying these processes for both scientific and societal purposes cannot be underestimated. Recent studies by historians like Snyder (2010) show how the commoditization of people that went along with the mass genocides of Stalin's and Hitler's regimes even surfaces in the way modern historians describe these events, for example, by referring to rounded-up numbers of anonymous dead. Snyder's entire book 'Bloodlands: Europe between Hitler and Stalin' can be seen as a humane attempt to counter this by, for example, consistently referring to figures for victims as exactly as possible, thus underlining the individuality of each victim. Thus he writes sentences like following: "each of the 681,692 people shot in Stalin's Great Terror [...] had a different life story" (Snyder 2010, 408).

Notwithstanding the relevance of their processual emphasis, there is also a problematic side to Kopytoff's and Appadurai's approach. Essentially, this is their view that there is an inherent drive towards the greatest degree of commoditization that the exchange technology permits (Kopytoff 1986, 72, 87; Bloch and Parry 1989, 16). One may get the idea that a society's most inalienable possessions are always at risk of being hollowed out by commoditization, something which only becomes worse with the development of exchange technologies and/or massive cultural change (modern economies; Davenport 1986, 22; Kopytoff 1986, 88). This comes close to a neo-liberal view of how money regulates and determines society. Interestingly, Kopytoff seems to consider commoditization as something that is constrained by cultural classification (ibid., 87). This may be taken to suggest that commodities are not cultural in themselves. I suggest that this view, in bracketing off the alienable and the inalienable, or commodities and gifts, is unhelpful. Rather, commodities and the singular seem to refer to each other in both shape and form of practice. In this volume, for example, we find Schmidt's fascinating discussion of the wampum shell money of the coastal Algonquian Indians. Termed 'commodity coupons' by Appadurai (1986, 25), Schmidt shows that although single wampum shells were indeed used in commercial, calculative transactions when they were strung together to form ornaments, generic beads became unique ornaments, perceived as a visible manifestation of completeness. The spatial boundedness of strung beads, Schmidt argues, is an iconic sign of the ending of a relationship after an economic transaction. As ornaments, wampum shells figure in the construction of a particular kind of personhood by being incorporated into funeral dress, thus reflecting shared beliefs and social values. Thus, *commodities* are used to turn individuals into specific, valued categories of persons. I see Schmidt's argument as reflecting a fundamental point about how we should see commodities and singular, inalienable items or gifts: as intertwined concepts that refer and have to refer to each other. Even modern money, the ultimate commodity, refers to higher sphere orderings. Over time, money is stamped with references to the overall social or moral order (iconography of gods, authorities, or with lines like *May God be with us* on the Dutch Euro, or *In God We Trust* on the United States dollar). Apparently, even in the most advanced exchange economies, with the introduction of new money (e.g. the Euro in 2002), we still find it important to hallmark coins with references to God or some other higher sphere ordering. Apart from the fact that commodities visually refer to the singular (wampum as a personal valuable consists of wampum beads that individually function as commodities), commodities are also the idiom used to express cultural values. The idiom we use to express commodity or gift concepts in many languages stems from the same root (for example, *price* vs. *praise*) or is entirely the same (Bazelmans 1998, 65).

As in the case of wampum beads used to embody values, the idiom of commoditization is also used to express higher sphere values, even though this is felt as inadequate. It is claimed that *money cannot buy class*, but this is exactly what people *try* to do when they buy an Armani suit (cf. Hart 2005, 164–165). We consider a human life to be priceless, but in court we negotiate financial compensation to make up for a life lost by murder. Even though no one will consider such money an appropriate price for a life, it is in the idiom of commoditization that people try to settle such issues. It is particularly the tension and uneasiness between what are felt as irreconcilable issues in such transactions that may prompt emotional responses or conspicuous practices. This is something different, however, from seeing everything of cultural value as being under the threat of becoming a commodity. Rather than drawing lines between commodities and gifts, Bloch and Parry (1989, 23–24) argue that we should consider entire transactional systems, "with on the one hand transactions concerned with the reproduction of the long-term social or cosmic order; on the other, a 'sphere' of short-term transactions concerned with the arena of individual competition." They argue that it is critical for short- and long-term spheres to be articulated. Money earned in commercial transactions should in some way be converted to sustain the overall order. A case in point is Warnier's chapter in this volume on the contemporary Cameroonian kingdom. The bodily substances of the Pot-King are 'value beyond value' (Warnier, this volume). However, exchange value is seen as a product that flows from it and that is given to the people. For that reason, something of the money earned in commercial life should return to its spiritual source as a token of acknowledgment for the life-debt any individual owes to the king and his royal ancestors. Thus, gifts and commodities are intertwined concepts that refer to and should refer to each other. In Depner's earring example, she told how Mrs Miller finally suggested that the earring could be sold – so being transformed from a personal valuable into money – but only if Mrs Depner bought something she considered more appropriate for her son (an equivalent in terms of personal and emotional value). So, even though the earring is translated into money, the money is meant to be restricted to the sphere of precious, personal markers of identity and intended to become an inalienable possession for Mrs Depner and her child, thus fitting Mrs Miller's expectations.

A Maussian approach: Objects like persons, objects *making* persons

After Hahn and Weiss's chapter, it is Mario Schmidt's that effectively take us away from the research path paved by Kopytoff and Appadurai. Schmidt's chapter in particular can be read as a plea to return to the seminal work of Marcel Mauss as originally conceived, emphasizing that the essence of Mauss's essay on the gift is seeing object and subject, thing and person, as commensurable. The personalization and singularization of objects come to the fore in the way objects are treated. Gilchrist's example of statues of saints in medieval churches shows an example of this. To some extent such statues are treated as if they are alive, coming to the fore in their adornment with *paternosters* (rosaries). But also, the deliberate destruction of cherished valuables when old people move to their final home, described by Depner in her chapter, is due to the fact that these objects are seen as imbued with something of the original owner, thus preventing them from enjoying a future, de-personalized use. But a number of the chapters in this book can also be seen as a plea to link Mauss's work on the gift (Mauss 1990 [1923/1924]) to the last essay he wrote, on the category of the person (Mauss 1996 [1938]). It is not just that objects can be like persons: they can also be used in the process of making individuals into persons (a social category; Carrithers *et al*. 1996). We have seen an example of this in Schmidt's chapter, where he shows how wampum ornaments served to embody roles and statuses. However, a number of Maran's examples of the portrayal of certain Mycenaean deceased may also be understood in this way, as may Ciric's cases of specific medieval death styles in Serbia. In the Mycenaean case, bodies and funeral objects are created that speak of access to (exotic?) worlds that probably extended far beyond the horizon of the original owner. In the Serbian case, the mourners dressed the body in such a way that it evoked something of a distant past. Referring to the work of Helms (1993, 46–47), it might be ventured that the very far away and the very old are perceived in more or less similar terms.

Discussing such meaningful objects, an interesting distinction can be made between valuables that signal communal identities and those that were used in the construction of personal identities (cf. Fontijn 2002, 26–27). Gilchrist's statues can be seen as an example of the former, Ciric's necklaces of the latter. In the case of the medieval rosaries described in Gilchrist's chapter, some seem first to have served as personal valuables but were later brought to the churches to adorn a saint's statue. Here, we see an interesting example of personal valuables being transformed into valuables related to communal identities. The bodily and material containers of life substances of the Cameroonian king described by Warnier, then, can be seen as a special case of valuables related to communal identities. Standing for a value that is highly significant to society, it stands for something that cannot be exchanged at all, but should be kept. This comes close to a category of ultimately inalienable possessions that are described in Godelier's book "The enigma of the gift" (Godelier 1999 [1996]). Godelier shows that, in the sphere related to the long-term reproduction of society (to use Bloch and Parry's terms), there are certain sacred objects that are seen to embody the key values of the society in question. As such, they stand for other valuables that are exchanged, but they themselves should not circulate but be kept.

Materiality

So objects can be used in the process of making persons, but, as so many anthropological studies show, symbolic references or name-giving can function in a similar way. Children and adults can change names when they pass what is considered to be an important stage in the life-cycle. So what, then, one might ask, is so special about material culture in the construction of personhood? At the risk of oversimplifying, material culture is more than a mental construct and is something different from a symbol. It is material, something that makes an impression because it can be seen, touched or smelled. It is something capable of evoking emotions by its visual and material qualities alone (Gell 1998). In a discussion of West African Vodun *art*, we find the apt statement "listen more to things than to words that are said" (Birago Diop, cited in Preston Blier 1995, 205). This material turn is evident in several contributions to this volume. González-Ruibal shows that the peculiar selection of items in the Mao hut is not some reflection of Mao identity; rather, the hut itself is an idealized experience of what it is considered to be Mao. We find a similar point in Maran's contribution on the use of amber in Mycenaean Greece. It is not just their non-local provenance that made these exotics special, but probably just as much their visual qualities as substances. Gilchrist emphasizes how important are physical properties like exotic materials or patina for turning a medieval object into a true heirloom. By the same token, it was not bare metal coins that medieval people collected from Roman ruins, but coins with pictures on them, heads of people that provoked imagination. Was it this iconography, referring to something that to the members of medieval communities was a remote, mythical past, that made them evocative objects? Medieval people must have had thoughts and stories about who the people depicted on Roman coins were and ideas about why these ancient items were relevant to stories they had regarding their own history and ancestry. Here was an iconography that was not their own, and for that reason it may pose an interpretive challenge (Sørensen 1987, 94). A case in point for the significance of materiality is Depner's study of the discarding of cherished possessions by old people when they move into their final home. They have all those memories and live with them, but it is precisely when things they have not seen or thought about in decades surface that memories are evoked: Marcel Proust's *mémoire involontaire* (Assman 2006, 2). Depner (this volume) aptly speaks of the object's 'uncomfortable presence'. It is their material presence that prompts action. Objects that are of significance to the inhabitants of the Cameroonian kingdom must be parcelled and wrapped up in order to keep them from the gaze of ordinary people (Warnier's chapter). The cherished possessions that old people cannot take with them are to be denied a future life, but this painful process often takes place out of sight of their former owners. Knappett, discussing Minoan sealings, argues that the visual presence of an imprint makes an absence apparent. I suggest that such engagements with materiality are still lacking in many archaeological accounts. The evocative nature of objects in burial, sacrificial or iconographic contexts is still very much understood solely in terms of their symbolic, referential nature. Hahn and Weiss also briefly refer to the astonishingly *rich* deposition of material in so-called early Celtic tombs in Southern Germany like Hochdorf (Biel 1985). It can be argued, however, that the entire idea of an early Celtic religion, supposedly symbolized by objects deposited in a tomb, is too simple. New research into such princely graves now shows that it was rather a particular treatment of material that mattered: the dismantling, breaking or folding of valuables seems to have been important (Van der Vaart 2011; Fontijn and Van der Vaart forthcoming).

Knowledge: Emic and etic

This finally brings me to the knowledge that went with objects that changed hands, or objects that came from what we know was a distant past. What sort of knowledge went with the amber that circulated over such vast distances? Did Mycenaean people know where the origins of this material were located? As archaeologists, we can argue that this material probably came from Wessex in southern England, but did the idea of a huge island so far away have any reality for Mycenaean people? And more importantly, did it matter to them? We can ask the same question with regard to the medieval re-use of Roman coins: although knowledge of Roman history was to some extent stored in transcripts in medieval abbeys, it is very doubtful that the people who buried their dead in the Serbian graves had specific knowledge of it. Would they have had any idea how long ago the emperor Augustus lived? Would they have distinguished between powerful and less powerful emperors depicted on coins, or were these regarded as anonymous icons of a mythical past? Rather, it seems that to them ancient Rome was a cultural concept materialized in ruins and artefacts they encountered in everyday life that figured in local folklore and stories (cf. Versluys, forthcoming). With González-Ruibal we are in a position to understand all the artefacts inside the Mao hut as a sort of *wild museography* and to see this collection as an ideal or even skewed image of Mao society. On the other hand, González-Ruibal (this volume) also argues that "the things that are selected are those that resonate with the present concerns of the Mao". They are *gwama swal shwombo*, the things of the house of the ancestral spirits. As scientists, we may disqualify such views as *false*, representing a past that never existed in such a way. Such views, however, do produce true material effects (see also the discussion in Barrett 1994, 77–81). It is particularly the confrontation between the emic and etic views of an object's itineraries that reveals this and ought to be studied.

Conclusion: Biographies or itineraries of objects?

This book is one of the first explicitly to steer away from describing changes in the meanings of objects in terms of object biographies. At the same time, we have seen that elements of the cultural biography terminology are still used in several contributions and that there are sometimes good reasons why this should be so. Generally speaking, this is also what we find when we consider other artefact and material culture studies in anthropology, archaeology or art history. There are instances where a theoretically charged concept like *cultural biography* seems to be used as theoretical veneer, covering an approach that is hardly thought through at all. Sometimes one has the idea that the concept is being used as a catch-all term for *everything that happens to an artefact*. Talking about *the cultural biography of a landscape*, as is fashionable in Dutch archaeology, also brings us further from the concept as originally defined by Kopytoff. One of the important aspects of the present volume is that the editors offer a new discussion of the cultural biography concept and present object itineraries as an alternative. With the above discussion in mind, it seems useful to compare the two.

Biographies and itineraries are both metaphors and carry inherent qualifications. Biographies colour the perception of objects with the quality of human life, itineraries with the quality of routes and paths. As I have argued, one of the good aspects of Kopytoff's theory was that his cultural biographies are about what is culturally perceived as a desired life-path. As such, his theory stands for an emic perception that is worth studying in itself. As noted above, it is certainly as useful to consider what is seen as the right start of such a biography as it is to think about the right ending. But the metaphor also brings in issues that do not always seem to matter and can even steer our research in the wrong direction. There can be views about a right ending, but that does not mean that this ending is perceived as the object's *death*. Bronze Age barrows in continental Western Europe only seem to have been used for a certain period of time as burial locations, but when people ceased to use them as such, it is inconceivable to see this as their *death*. Thus, while it may be fruitful to study (explicitly or implicitly held) shared perceptions of desired life-paths, it is not always useful to refer to them as *cultural biographies*.

Itineraries, on the other hand, are more neutral. They seem better suited to describing everything that happens to an individual artefact in an etic way. As social scientists, it may be crucial for us to go beyond emic, shared perceptions of desired life-paths. Views about what is culturally desirably do not exist outside of the agents, but come about and are effectively reified in each individual engagement of a human with an object. From an etic perspective, it also becomes important to question what an object actually is. The coppers that were used in the ceremonies of Northwest Coast Native Americans in the eighteenth and nineteenth centuries were often seen as sacred goods coming from higher realms. Metal analyses of the copper, however, show that many of them were manufactured out of European bronze, probably derived from ship sheathing (Jopling 1989). Native American sources are silent on this, but an important part of the *itinerary* of copper must have been this earlier circulation, re-melting and shaping to become highly sacred items for these Native Americans. How was European copper *conceptually* transformed? It is precisely the confrontation between the events we can reconstruct in our research and the indigenous perceptions of them that leads to exciting research. To unravel both is particularly important for archaeology, where we usually only have information on the moment the object was removed from society forever and where we have to work with the benefit of hindsight. We can reconstruct the ends of the itineraries of many artefacts, but these ends need not necessarily have been emically regarded as their desired ends (cf. the view in the Roman period that coins were to circulate endlessly and the archaeological observation that so many coins *did* end up in the ground during that period). Thus, both the study of *desired* use trajectories as perceived by social groups (to use a more neutral term than the biography metaphor) and the individual itinerary of each object or even material (e.g. the history of the metal before it was re-melted and re-shaped to become a ceremonial copper of the Northwest Coast natives) is what is needed.

Although there are advantages in speaking of itineraries of objects, it is important to see the conceptual limitations as well. Emphasizing itineraries is very much an object-centred approach. It is people, however, who do something with them, who push them forward on their route or leave them. In doing so, people act with alternative routes in their minds and with cultural or moral qualifications of those routes, and they are the ones who build routes for a future role or use of the object. The discussions that Mrs Depner has with Mrs Miller on the future use of the earring show that this is not a straightforward process. There is a tension between different understandings of the same object and its future use that prompts specific action. In this process, Mrs Depner and Mrs Miller both re-define their relation to an object, *and to each other*. Although the former does not write about it, discussion about the itinerary of the earring must have formed, qualified and transformed a social relationship.

Itinerary or biography: apparently we need metaphors when investigating material culture (Tilley 1999). One of the reasons why the cultural biography concept may have become so popular, especially in archaeology, must be because it exemplifies an interpretative or hermeneutic stance. In the functionalist approaches of continental archaeology of the 1980s and 1990s, talking about object biographies was perhaps more rhetorical than analytical. But a good metaphor tends to be remembered longer and suggests new ways of thinking. In a way, imbuing *things* with the metaphor of life may even have contradicted Kopytoff's emphasis on commoditization. However, as a fruitful metaphor that went on an entirely unforeseen itinerary, it came to suggest a view of material culture where things and persons are actually much closer together than the prison house of previous terminology allowed. One of the merits of the present volume is that is shows how close things and persons can get, though it is Kopytoff's metaphor that first gave us the words to talk about this.

Acknowledgments

Thanks are due to the editors for inviting me to write this epilogue. In particular I am obliged to Prof. Hans Peter Hahn for his help and encouragement and comments on earlier drafts. I also wish to thank Prof. Joseph Maran, Dr Philippe Stockhammer and Prof. Thomas Meyer (all of Heidelberg University), as well as Prof. Chris Gosden (University of Oxford), for inspirational discussions. I am also grateful to Dr Ir. H. Fontijn (Schipluiden) for a discussion of the work of Snyder. At the Faculty of Archaeology in Leiden, I benefitted much from talks with Prof. Raymond Corbey, Dr Alex Geurds and Sasja van der Vaart (MA). In particular, I wish to thank Dr Miguel-John Versluys.

Note

1   As Hans Peter Hahn pointed out to me, Kopytoff was not the first to speak of a *biography of things*. Sergej Tretjakow already published an article with this title in 1929, which was translated into German in the 1980s (new publication 2007). Unfortunately, it seems to have gone unnoticed by western social scientists.

References

Aly, G. (ed.) (1992) *Demontage … revolutionärer oder restaurativer Bildersturm?* Texte and Bilder. Berlin, Karin Kramer.

Appadurai, A. (1986) Introduction: Commodities and the politics of value. In A. Appadurai (ed.) *The social life of things: Commodities in cultural perspective*, 3–63. Cambridge, Cambridge University Press.

Assmann, J. (2006) *Religion and cultural memory: Ten studies*. Stanford, Stanford University Press.

Barrett, J. C. (1994) *Fragments from antiquity: An archaeology of social life in Britain, 2900–1200 BC*. Oxford, Blackwell.

Bazelmans, J. (1998) Geschenken en waren in premodern Europa. Enkele gedachten over de waarde van kostbaarheden uit schatvondsten. *Leidschrift* 13 (3), 59–78.

Biel, J. (1985) *Der Keltenfürst von Hochdorf*. Stuttgart, Konrad Theiss.

Bloch, M. and Parry, J. (1989) Introduction: Money and the morality of exchange. In J. Parry and M. Bloch (eds) *Money and the morality of exchange*, 1–31. Cambridge, Cambridge University Press.

Carrithers, M., Collins, S. and Lukes, S. (eds) (1996) *The category of the person: Anthropology, philosophy, history*. Cambridge, Cambridge University Press.

Davenport, W. H. (1986) Two kinds of value in the Eastern Solomon Islands. In A. Appadurai (ed.) *The social life of things: Commodities in cultural perspective*, 95–109. Cambridge, Cambridge University Press.

Fontijn, D. R. (2002) Sacrificial landscapes: Cultural biographies of persons, objects and 'natural' places in the Bronze Age of the southern Netherlands, *c.* 2300–600 BC. *Analecta Praehistorica Leidensia* 33/34, 1–392.

Fontijn, D. R. and Van der Vaart, S. A. (forthcoming) Dismantled, transformed and deposited: Prehistoric metalwork from the centre of mound 7. In D. R. Fontijn, R. Jansen and S. A. Van der Vaart (eds) *The seventh mound: An Early Iron Age 'princely grave' in the prehistoric funerary landscape of Oss-Zevenbergen*. Leiden, Sidestone Press.

Gell, A. (1998) *Art and agency: A new anthropological theory*. Oxford, Oxford University Press.

Godelier, M. (1999 [1996]) *The enigma of the gift*. Cambridge and Oxford, Polity Press, [First published in French: (1996) *L'Énigme du don*. Paris, Librairie Arthème Fayard].

Gosden, C. and Marshall, Y. (1999) The cultural biography of objects. *World Archaeology* 31 (2), 169–178.

Göttke, F. (2010) *Toppled*. Rotterdam, Post Editions.

Graeber, D. (2005) Value: Anthropological theories of value. In J. G. Carrier (ed.) *A handbook of economic anthropology*, 439–454. Cheltenham and Northampton, Edward Elgar Publishing.

Hahn, H. P. and Soentgen, J. (2010) Acknowledging substances: Looking at the hidden side of the material world. *Philosophy and Technology* 24 (1), 19–33.

Hart, K. (2005) Money: One anthropologist's view. In J. G. Carrier (ed.) *A handbook of economic anthropology*, 160–175. Cheltenham and Northampton, Edward Elgar Publishing.

Helms, M. W. (1993) *Craft and the kingly ideal: Art, trade, and power*. Austin, University of Texas Press.

Hoskins, J. (1998) *Biographical objects: How things tell the stories of people's lives*. New York and London, Routledge.

Hoskins, J. (2006) Agency, biography and objects. In C. Tilley, W. Keane, S. Küchler, M. Rowlands and P. Spyer (eds) *Handbook of material culture*, 74–84. London, Sage.

Jopling, C. F. (1989) The coppers of the Northwest Coast Indians: Their origin, development and possible antecedents. *Transactions of the American Philosophical Society* 79 (Part 1), i–xii; 1–164.

Kopytoff, I. (1986) The cultural biography of things: Commoditization as process. In A. Appadurai (ed.) *The social life of things: Commodities in cultural perspective*, 64–91. Cambridge, Cambridge University Press.

Mauss, M. (1990 [1923/1924]) *The gift: The form and reason for exchange in archaic societies*. London, Routledge, first published in French, 1923/1924. Essai sur le don. Forme et raison de l'échange dans les sociétés archaïques. *L'Année Sociologique*, NS, (1), 30–186.

Mauss, M. (1996 [1938]) A category of the human mind: The notion of the person; the notion of self. In M. Carrithers, S. Collins and S. Lukes (eds) *The category of the person: Anthropology, philosophy, history*, 1–25. Cambridge, Cambridge University Press, first published in French, 1938, Une catégorie de l'esprit humain. La notion de personne, celle de 'moi'. Un plan de travail. *Journal of the Royal Anthropological Institute* 68, 263–281.

Preston Blier, S. (1995) *African vodun: Art, psychology and power*. Chicago and London, University of Chicago Press.

Roymans, N. (1995) The cultural biography of urnfields and the long-term history of a mythical landscape. *Archaeological Dialogues* 2 (1), 2–24.

Snyder, T. (2010) *Bloodlands: Europe between Hitler and Stalin*. London, The Bodley Head.

Sørensen, M. L. S. (1987) Material order and cultural classification: The role of bronze objects in the transition from Bronze Age to Iron Age in Scandinavia. In I. Hodder (ed.) *The archaeology of contextual meanings*. New Directions in Archaeology, 90–101. Cambridge, Cambridge University Press.

Steiner, C. B. (2001) Rights of passage: On the liminal identity of art in the border zone. In F. Myers (ed.) *The empire of things: Regimes of value and material culture*, 207–231. Santa Fé, New Mexico, School of American Research Press.

Tilley, C. (1999) *Metaphor and material culture*. Oxford, Blackwell Publishers.

Tilley C.; Keane, W.; Küchler, S.; Rowlands, M. and Spyer, P. (eds) (2006) *Handbook of material culture*. London, Sage.

Tretjakow S. (2007 [1929]) Biographie des Dings. *Arbeitsblätter für die Sachbuchforschung* 12, S. 4–8. 02.06.2012, http://edoc.hu-berlin.de/series/sachbuchforschung/12/PDF/12.pdf

Van der Vaart, S. A. (2011) *Hail to the chieftain*. Unpublished MPhil thesis, University of Leiden.

Versluys, M. J. (forthcoming) Roman visual material culture as globalizing koine. In M. Pitts and M. J. Versluys (eds) *Globalisation and the Roman world: Perspectives and opportunities*. Cambridge, Cambridge University Press.

Index

———